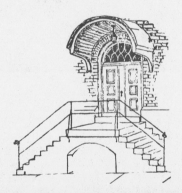

William Gilmore Simms
and the American Frontier

William Gilmore Simms and the American Frontier

Edited by JOHN CALDWELL GUILDS
and CAROLINE COLLINS

THE UNIVERSITY OF GEORGIA PRESS
Athens & London

© 1997 by the University of Georgia Press
Athens, Georgia 30602
All rights reserved
Designed by Walton Harris
Set in 10/13 Janson by G & S Typesetters, Inc.
Printed and bound by Braun-Brumfield, Inc.
The paper in this book meets the guidelines for
permanence and durability of the Committee
on Production Guidelines for Book Longevity
of the Council on Library Resources.

Printed in the United States of America
01   00   99   98   97   C   5   4   3   2   1

LIBRARY OF CONGRESS CATALOGING IN PUBLICATION DATA

William Gilmore Simms and the American frontier /
edited by John Caldwell Guilds and Caroline Collins.
     p.   cm.
Includes bibliographical references.
ISBN 0-8203-1887-6 (alk. paper)
1. Simms, William Gilmore, 1806–1870—Criticism and interpretation.
2. Historical fiction, American—History and criticism.   3. National
characteristics, American, in literature.   4. Frontier and pioneer life in
literature.   5. Southern States—In literature.   6. Southwest, Old—In
literature.   I. Guilds, John Caldwell, 1924–   . II. Collins, Caroline.
PS2853.W554   1997
813'.3—dc20
96-24254

BRITISH LIBRARY CATALOGING IN PUBLICATION DATA AVAILABLE

FRONTISPIECE: *Engraved portrait of William Gilmore Simms
(based on a sketch by Henry Brintnell Bounetheau;
courtesy of Mary Simms Oliphant Furman)*

*The Simms Society dedicates this volume
to the memory of Jay B. Hubbell*

Contents

Introduction

The twentieth century is slowly according to William Gilmore Simms some of the recognition as a major American writer that had been granted him prior to the Civil War. Since Simms was America's first advocate of *regionalism* in the creation of *national* literature, it is appropriate that his pivotal role as a kind of ancestral father to modern literature of the South is beginning to be acknowledged; as the first essay in this collection aptly observes, "Simms is to the South's literary birth what Faulkner is to the region's literary renaissance." After many years of scholarly neglect, Simms, since 1988, has been the subject of at least ten scholarly books devoted exclusively to his life and his works—a collection of critical essays, a full-length study of his fiction, a biography, an edition of his poetry, an anthology of his short stories, a book of his philosophical and poetic theory, and new publications of several of his novels.

It has been our goal, with this volume, to make a significant contribution to the growing body of critical writing on Simms. The essays included in *William Gilmore Simms and the American Frontier* emphasize Simms's multifaceted, often graphic portrayal of America's westward migration, examining his depictions of the frontier through traditional approaches as well as newer, more theoretical perspectives. As a whole, these essays represent a tribute to Simms's achievement and versatility: many of them will appeal to literary critics, and we hope that there will be much to interest historians and folklorists as well.

The volume begins with historical essays concerning the frontier of the Old Southwest. David Moltke-Hansen, in his comprehensive essay "Between Plantation and Frontier: The South of William Gilmore Simms," stresses the pivotal role of Simms in the conceptualization of the Southern identity in the early nineteenth century. Elliott West's "The American Frontier: Romance and Reality" establishes the historical perspective for an appreciation of Simms's fictional treatment of the Old Southwest.

The essays by literary scholars in this volume address Simms's poetry, short fiction, novels, literary criticism, and social criticism. Some examine Simms's realism. John Caldwell Guilds discusses Simms's innovative use of first-person narration in *Richard Hurdis*, and Rayburn S. Moore concentrates on Simms's first "regular" novel, *Guy Rivers*, as a pioneering graphic treatment of frontier violence and lawlessness. Jan Bakker reaffirms Simms as America's first realistic writer and makes a strong case for *Woodcraft* being America's first realistic novel. Caroline Collins identifies Simms's deft manipulation of romantic conventions as an essential part of his realism in *Guy Rivers* and *Richard Hurdis*.

Other essays analyze Simms's works in terms of the literary theory of Mikhail Bakhtin, a resource that Simms scholars have only recently begun to explore. Thomas L. McHaney notes both the social forces behind the polyphonic play of frontier voices and the elements of the carnivalesque in *Border Beagles*. Nancy Grantham investigates the dialogism in the collisions of cultures depicted in *The Yemassee*, *Vasconselos*, and *The Cassique of Kiawah*. And in an approach reminiscent of Bakhtin, David Newton examines the ways that the language of *Guy Rivers* becomes an imaginative site where struggles for power take place.

A number of scholars focus on Simms's use of frontier humor and the oral tradition. Mary Ann Wimsatt examines parallels between "The Arkansas Traveler" and Simms's *Southward Ho!* Molly Boyd probes the limitations of current definitions of frontier humor, exploring Simms's similarities to Southwestern humorists in *The Wigwam and the Cabin*. Edwin Arnold looks at Simms's response as a critic to the works of Henry Clay Lewis (Madison Tensas). Gerard Donovan addresses the influence of Irish folklore and its oral tradition on "How Sharp Snaffles Got His Capital and Wife" and "Bald-Head Bill Bauldy."

Several essays consider the ways in which Simms's writings respond to the changing face of the frontier. Miriam Shillingsburg analyzes how the Civil War changed Simms's portrayal of the frontier in *The Cub of the Panther*; and James E. Kibler, in "Stewardship and *Patria* in Simms's Frontier Poetry," explores the two versions of "The Traveller's Rest" for their revelations about the poet's changing attitude toward the wilderness.

The final two essays pursue Simms's relationship to other writers. Dianne C. Luce suggests that his treatments of the legend of John Murrell may have influenced passages of Faulkner. Sabine Schmidt, who notes Simms's experimentation with the *Novelle*, explores literary parallels between Simms and Friedrich Gerstäcker, the nineteenth-century German author who wrote of the American frontier and translated *The Wigwam and the Cabin*.

These essays originated in the Simms symposium held at the University of Arkansas in 1993. They have been revised and reconceptualized to support the theme of William Gilmore Simms and the American frontier. We are indebted to the University of Arkansas Press for permission to use portions of the afterword to *Richard Hurdis: A Tale of Alabama*, ed. John Caldwell Guilds (Fayetteville, 1995), 356–72, in "The 'Untrodden Path': *Richard Hurdis* and Simms's Foray into Literary Realism." The editors and the Simms Society as a whole are indebted to many scholars for their roles in chairing sessions, introducing speakers, and leading discussions during the symposium: Robert Cochran, Charles Adams, Keneth Kinnamon, and Willard A. Gatewood (who helped in other ways far beyond professional collegiality, as well), all of the University of Arkansas; John Idol, Clemson University; Pearl Amelia McHaney, Georgia State University; David B. Kesterson, University of North Texas; and Paula F. Dean, University of Texas-Pan American. Special thanks are owed to the Center for Arkansas and Regional Studies at the University of Arkansas for its sponsorship of the symposium, which served as the genesis of this volume. The secretarial staff of the Department of English at the University of Arkansas and the graduate students in the spring 1993 Simms seminar (English 6343) cheerfully performed a variety of tasks to the benefit of the conference and its participants, and we are much in their debt. We are grateful, too, to Melinda Word and the Writing Center at the University of Arkansas for assistance with computers and word processing. The editors also wish to thank their own spouses, Gertrud Pickar and Floyd Collins, who contributed in ways that were indispensable. Finally, we are especially grateful to Malcolm Call and to the University of Georgia Press for its commitment to publish this volume.

The Historical Context

DAVID MOLTKE-HANSEN

Between Plantation and Frontier: The South of William Gilmore Simms

Perhaps children brought up reading Lewis Carroll's *Alice in Wonderland* naturally see the world upside down. Or, it may be that, as solipsists, we cannot help dating backward from ourselves. There are also more historical reasons, however, why in our thinking the American South was old before it was new. Tocqueville in part is responsible. His (and others') writings about the end of the ancien régime in France made it easy for the next generations to treat the American Civil War and the abolition of slavery as the cataclysmic end of an old order. Aiding and abetting the historian, too, was the inclination of many after the war either to romanticize or to demonize life in the good (or bad) old days before 1861.[1] Just as compelling was the urge to look forward, not back, so from the historical to a new South. In addition, the American infatuation with origins has impelled historians to discover again and again the South in embryo in the Roanoke and Jamestown colonies or, more broadly, in the cultural traits—for instance, honor and Celtic impetuosity—or critical interests—among them, the slavery and staple crop agriculture—of dominant settler populations in parts of the region.[2]

Yet such arguments ignore the fact that no groups identified themselves as Southern in geographic, political, economic, social, or cultural terms until over two-and-a-quarter centuries *after* the Roanoke settlement and less than half a century *before* the Civil War.[3] And just as Rome was not ancient to its founders, the American South was not old to its framers, even if they often argued that certain of their institutions—slavery, for instance—and certain of their beliefs—among them, republicanism—were inheritances sanctioned by history. Elements of their regime might have been old, but their identity as Southerners was still relatively new on the eve of secession.

Indeed, though he died a Southerner in the Deep South state of his birth, William Gilmore Simms, preeminent man of letters of the Old South, was not born a Southerner. Widespread talk of the states to the south of Pennsylvania forming a political and economic block only began in earnest about the time that Simms entered his adolescence, in 1819, the year that the debate flared over the admission of Missouri to the Union as a slave state. Common talk of the South as a social and cultural region and of Southerners as a distinct subspecies of Americans came still later. Simms helped frame and direct that discussion through his writings, especially the three series of Southern romances that he began in the mid-1830s. In the process, he did as much as any single Southern writer or editor before the Civil War to make the South what it has since been: a commodity as well as a place, a creation as well as a birthright, and a global fascination as well as a domestic preoccupation.

Simms did so by focusing in much of his fiction and many of his essays and addresses on the South's historical development. Only one other Southern fictionist has written as variously and systematically on the subject: William Faulkner. The shape, horizons, and processes of Simms's fictional South deserve analysis as more than prologue to Faulkner's, however. While Faulkner wrote from the perspective of a hundred years of regionalism, Simms wrote near the very beginning of the conceptualization and assertion of Southern identity. Simms is to the South's literary birth what Faulkner is to the region's literary renaissance: a central figure.

And central to the fictional Souths of both William Gilmore Simms and William Faulkner is the relationship of the plantation to the frontier or backwoods. Neither author may ever explicitly have said what both implicitly understood: the South is a concept that united but did not resolve the tensions between these, and other, divergent realms of experience and identity.[4] For Faulkner, this understanding was compounded by memory: the remnants of wilderness that he knew in the Mississippi Delta were emblematic of the much wider wilderness traversed by Simms. In trying to understand William Gilmore Simms's relationships to and uses of the American frontier, most late-twentieth-century students cannot help but read him in the light of these intervening memories. One ought, however, also to remember that Simms helped frame as well as explore these developing linkages. After all, his South was progenitor of Faulkner's literarily as well as literally.

As the juxtaposition of Simms and Faulkner suggests, regional identity formation took place only gradually. For convenience, one can correlate different stages in this process with different generations, defined not by the time it takes babies to become parents, but by the relationships of age cohorts to critical events.[5]

By this definition, the first generation either to conceptualize the South as a political and economic unit or to characterize Southernness did so in its adulthood in the years after the end of the War of 1812. The members of this generation were in most instances children of those who had fought in the American Revolution. Born between about 1765 and 1795, they became politically mature during the period of the first American party system. The younger among them were the American soldiers during the War of 1812 and also, as in the cases of Henry Clay and John C. Calhoun, the emerging leadership in the region. Other noted members included Stephen Austin, Davy Crockett, Andrew Jackson, and Augustus Baldwin Longstreet. It was during their youth that the Louisiana Purchase was made, trans-Appalachian settlement became a flood, cotton became a major staple crop, the African slave trade officially ended, and Northern states began abolishing slavery within their borders. It was also during this first generation's youth that the United States began the fitful and painful transition to a postcolonial society. In the process, American writers and spokespersons faced the necessity of fashioning new collective identities and the public rituals and print vehicles to carry them.

The next generation began to formulate and incorporate Southern identity in its school years and was also the first to grow up reading Sir Walter Scott and James Fenimore Cooper. This generation saw most of the last of the Founding Fathers die both just as it was entering adulthood and just after the first great sectional debates over Missouri and the protective tariff. The generation later launched the early regional magazines, published the first "Southern" textbooks, and filled the ranks of many of the state secession conventions as well as emblematic positions in Northern abolitionist circles. Jefferson Davis, George Washington Harris, Caroline Lee Hentz, Angelina Grimké, Harriet Jacobs, Robert E. Lee, Edgar Allan Poe, and William Gilmore Simms were some of its members.

The first generation to have members grow up with a Southern identity was born roughly between the end of the War of 1812 and Andrew Jackson's second inauguration as president in 1833. It was from this cohort of the first birthright Southerners that most of the Confederate military and political leadership (also, earlier, most of the soldiers for the Mexican War) came. Henry Timrod, poet laureate of the Confederacy, belonged to this generation. So did Pierre T. T. Beauregard, Braxton Bragg, Mary Boykin

Chesnut, J. D. B. DeBow, Paul Hamilton Hayne, and J. E. B. Stuart. Though a member of this generation as well, Frederick Douglass did not share the Southern identity of these individuals; he did, however, engage it in his work as abolitionist, journalist, and race leader.

Most of the rank and file of the Confederate military came from the next generation, the first to inherit a Southern identity or to challenge the legacy of that identity. Its youngest members were too young to serve during the war except in the home guard. Most of Simms's children belonged to this generation. So did George Washington Cable, Kate Chopin, Henry W. Grady, Joel Chandler Harris, Sidney Lanier, Mark Twain, and Augusta Jane Evans Wilson.

The next generation passed its childhood during the Civil War and Reconstruction. George Washington Carver, Charles Waddell Chesnutt, Thomas Dixon Jr., Walter Hines Page, Booker T. Washington, and Tom Watson were members. Faulkner's generation were the children or, often, the grandchildren of these children of the Civil War, but there was at least one cohort between them and their parents or grandparents, made up of those born while the parents and grandparents were growing up and including writers such as James Branch Cabell, W. E. B. DuBois, Paul Laurence Dunbar, Ellen Glasgow, James Weldon Johnson, and Elizabeth Madox Roberts.

Depending on how one counts, then, there were four or, perhaps, five generations of Southern identity, and debate over that identity, between Simms and Faulkner. Consequently, Faulkner belonged to the sixth or seventh generation to write about the South.

The South that Simms earlier helped define and historicize through his writings could not have been imagined sooner than it was. Indeed, the South's imaginative development was still under way a hundred years later, as Faulkner was writing.

Before there could be a South, older ways of defining broad areas later incorporated into the region first had to be superseded. Chesapeake and Carolina writers had to stop seeing themselves as members of a metropolitan, London-based culture, for instance, just as Floridians and Louisianians had to stop defining themselves by reference to Paris or Madrid. Moreover, the British imperial habit of thinking of the mainland American and island Caribbean staple crop colonies together as the "plantation colonies" had to be broken.

The American Revolution began this deconstruction, but it took time before alternative frames of reference could be effectively constructed in a postcolonial America. The authors and orators who led in this process of reconstruction initially used two points of reference. One was old—the individual colony or state. The other was recent—the Revolution and the political entity that had resulted, the United States of America.

In the thirty years after the Revolution, writers from the future South joined both in the exploration of state histories and in the writing of a new genre, American history. The works in this new genre tended to emphasize Americans' common ideological antecedents and interests, arguing that centrifugal, localist tendencies should not obscure the shared commitments that had carried the Revolution to victory.[6]

Ultimately, this ideological argument proved unsuccessful as a national bonding agent in the face of debates over foreign policy, the tariff, and slavery's place in the Union. So American historians, North and South, began looking for alternative pasts. At the same time, and in response to the same exigencies, politicians began organizing sectional alliances on specific issues.

This regionalization of political concerns was fitful. Over time there were Southern block votes in Congress on an increasing number of issues, but those points of agreement proved an exceedingly slender basis for any kind of regional political unity. The intraregional bonds and interests were not sufficiently strong. Other, interregional bonds actually increased in number over time, though they arguably did not gain proportionately in strength because of countervailing regional pressures.

In the face of these circumstances, such concepts as the *South, Southerners,* and *Southernness* were problematic. Some later historians have even dismissed them as the bemusements of a few intellectuals and politicians seeking leadership roles. From time to time, Simms has been reduced in this way.[7]

Such an argument ignores important trends, however. Consider the social processes or conditions transforming the emerging region. Historians of colonial America have repeatedly noted the divisions between Chesapeake, low-country, and backcountry populations.[8] Until the peoples of these diverse areas mingled, a Southern society could not emerge. But mingle they did. The process took time, in part because distances between population streams were great. Still, contacts eventually became connections. At various points from Charlottesville, Virginia, through Sumter, South Carolina, to Augusta, Georgia, Easterners met and even began to

marry Westerners by the third quarter of the eighteenth century, following
a few daring examples of Virginians and South Carolinians who had earlier
bumped up against one another in eastern North Carolina.[9]

The post-Revolutionary generation extended the mingling in several
ways. Cities like Richmond and Charleston drew ambitious up-country
men, who moved east and married there. In South Carolina, Langdon
Cheves and James Louis Petigru are two of the more noted examples. Several of Petigru's sisters followed him and also made low-country matches.
Other Westerners married Easterners but remained in the up-country.
John C. Calhoun, Wade Hampton II, James Henry Hammond, and Ben-
jamin Franklin Perry are some of the best-known South Carolina examples
from among Simms's friends and acquaintances. Most often, however, tidewater, low-country, up-country, and Cajun settlers met in new states in the
Old Southwest. Initially, settlements there were defined by their distinct
origins back east or in formerly French and Spanish areas. Increasingly,
however, up-country and tidewater, Carolina and Virginia communities
intermixed.

By 1850, four out of nine South Carolinians alive were living outside
their native state, mostly in other states of the lower South. The numbers,
though not the percentages, of emigrant North Carolinians and Virginians
were much higher. In becoming Tennesseans, Alabamians, and Texans,
these Easterners were also becoming Southerners. The same developments
affected black as well as white populations.

Simms began formulating his understanding of the South's history during the years when the greatest part of this migration and mingling took
place. In the 1810s white migration from the Southeast to the Southwest
peaked. Starting in the late 1820s, Virginia and the Carolinas saw increasing black population outflows. Indeed, the Southeast in these years lost the
equivalent of all of its natural population increase to the Old Southwest
and neighboring states, despite experiencing the highest immigration of
the antebellum period. Not until well into the 1840s did the Southeastern
seaboard states grow again. By then the Southern frontier had shrunk
dramatically.[10]

It was over these same years, during which Simms nurtured his nascent
Southern romance series, that Southern social and cultural distinctiveness
began to appear as a leitmotif in a swelling number of travel accounts, fictional works, and private writings as well as in journalism and abolitionist
tracts.[11] The development is remarkable. In 1816, ten years after Simms's

birth and just after the War of 1812, the South existed as a distinct area on no maps except campaign theater maps from the Revolutionary War. It had no government and no formal institutions. Divided between Easterners and Westerners, Jeffersonians and Federalists, cotton and tobacco, plantations and backwoods, Scots-Irish and Africans, it had little apparent reason to be called into being. Yet, within twenty years, *the South* was a highly charged and widely used location designation and allegiance, and *Southern* had become an adjective with emotional as well as descriptive force far beyond its early functions as a political device.

The South-making processes about which Simms had just started writing were coming to a head on various fronts by 1836 and the election of Martin Van Buren to succeed Andrew Jackson in the White House. The Texas Revolution was under way, and James Simmons, Simms's old literary collaborator and adviser, would shortly be comptroller general of the new republic. He joined numerous other South Carolinians, such as Samuel Maverick, there. Soon, Simms's rival for cultural leadership in Charleston, James Louis Petigru, once a neighbor of Maverick and later a neighbor of Simmons, would be arguing futilely against the admission of Texas to the Union on the grounds that the Texans were too passionately Southern.[12]

In the same *drang nach westen* or march to the west, Southern states were conniving at the forced removal of the Creeks, Cherokees, and other eastern Indians to Texas and the neighboring Indian Territory. As a result, by 1835, the year when Simms's second and third Southern romances appeared, vast interior frontiers in the Southern Appalachians, in the Mississippi Delta, in Florida, and elsewhere were opening to invading hordes. Virginians, Carolinians, and Georgians flooded in behind the departing natives, though sometimes only after fierce fighting. Like Simms, James Simmons's older brother, William Hayne Simmons, would write about the Seminole War in his adopted Florida.

To the North and in England, other battles were heating up as well. Angelina Grimké, sister of Simms's fellow Charleston Unionist and friend Thomas Smith Grimké, saw her *Appeal to the Christian Women of the South* issued in 1836 by the American Anti-Slavery Society. In it she argued that "slavery is contrary to the declaration of independence, . . . the first charter of human rights given to Adam . . . [and] the example and precepts of our holy and merciful Redeemer, and of his apostles" (16). The next year, Simms attacked the antislavery sentiments of Britisher Harriet Martineau's newly published *Society in America* in a review essay, "Miss Martineau on Slavery," in the *Southern Literary Messenger*.

 The South literally was taking geographic, social, and polemical shape before Simms's eyes. Other factors than these developments were also forming Simms's perceptions of the processes involved, however. Simms's 1825 *Monody on the Death of Gen. Charles Cotesworth Pinckney* gave an early glimpse of his understanding of the place of the American Revolution, of American nationalism, and of the roles of social and political leaders in a republic. Scattered magazine sketches from the next several years suggest how Simms was beginning to formulate his approach to the fictional use of observations he made, and stories he heard, on repeated trips to Mississippi to visit his father and uncle.[13] Poems on recent French history, gathered together in an 1830 volume, *The Tri-Color; or The Three Days of Blood, in Paris*, show Simms continuing to reflect on the shaping influence of leading individuals as well as on the popular will as expressed in revolution, on the nature of a people or a nation as well as of progress, and on the role of art in capturing and distilling the meaning of historical experience. A year later, he was commenting in letters back to his Charleston, South Carolina, newspaper, the *City Gazette*, both about how the lure of the West undermined society and about how progress was inevitably and appropriately, if sadly, destroying Native American society in Georgia and the Old Southwest (*Letters* 1:29–38).

 From this point forward Simms was committed to a constellation of ideas that he would develop and modulate over time. In thinking about the South's past, he would almost always keep these key concepts, or their variants, in mind: liberty; progress or *mouvement*; civilization; the social principle; order; localism and nationalism; poetry and art; patriotism; leaders and leadership; revolution. The concepts themselves need not, but Simms's uses of them did, illustrate what historians have called a patriarchal cultural view. In this perspective, the male-headed, female-centered household was the model for the larger society and, so, the basis for ascription of social roles, distribution of responsibilities, and assertion of values.[14]

 In Simms's view, history was at one level the story of man's *mouvement* or progress toward full and proper realization and enjoyment of liberty. One measure of civilization, therefore, was the extent to which it provided liberty to those who were sufficiently advanced to use it properly. Another measure was the degree to which civilization fostered the social principle or a properly ordered society, and so promoted what in 1843 Simms would call "the sacred character of home . . . where the patriarchal and social virtues are yet most fondly cherished" (*Social Principle* 11, 21). Attachment to home and family became the basis for devotion to, and work for, one's local community as both a place and a society. This attachment in turn generalized itself to the nation as both a polity and a people.

Poetry and art, properly applied, helped one capture, communicate, and cherish the values, the meaning, and the experience or feeling of home, community, nation, and so of patriotism. The true, patriotic writer was thus a leader. Leadership required superiority of mind and character as well as devotion to the social principle, to civilization, to art, and to liberty. Leading minds and characters could—did—emerge at every level of society, but they needed to be trained as well. Consequently, leaders tended to rise first and farthest out of the higher ranks of society.

The greatest test of leadership was to build society while fighting off predators. Unfortunately, many men—in certain circumstances, most—are avaricious. They see gain, not domestic peace and fruitfulness, as the measure of happiness and success and act accordingly. The powerful can be particularly destructive. When they are, patriotic men need to step forward to lead the people, as the United States' Founding Fathers did in their revolution.

It was in the matrix created by the melding of these patriarchal understandings and commitments that Simms formed his conception of Southern history. Drawing for data on his wide reading in American colonial and Revolutionary history, on his western travels, and on family and local traditions, he developed his understanding in an ongoing series of novelistic studies of important episodes and aspects of the South's evolution. He launched his series in 1834–1835, self-consciously following the examples of Sir Walter Scott's historical romances of English and Scottish history and James Fenimore Cooper's Leatherstocking tales. Part of his rationale was that the United States was too large for the fictionist to treat, because it was too diverse for the fictionist to know, and the fictionist should write as much as possible out of personal knowledge.[15] Another part of his rationale was the South's distinctiveness from the North. A third part was really an extension of the second: the South was knit together internally by webs

of personal bonds, settlement patterns, economic behaviors, oral traditions, linguistic traits, and social assumptions.

 To explore the formation and spread of these features, Simms launched three distinct series of romances. The first, begun in 1834, he devoted to the South's expansion into Appalachia, into Kentucky, and along the Natchez Trace in his own lifetime. It had as its central concern the formation of society out of an "incoherent mixture of people" agitated by "strife, discontent, and contention" because of "the wild condition of the country—the absence of all civil authority, and almost of laws" (*Guy Rivers* 2:613). A central theme was the contest between the expectations, norms, and mores of the settled, hierarchical, plantation South and the physical, psychological, and social rudeness of the frontier. Implicit was the assumption that the South was developing out of the dialectical interactions of plantation and frontier, a point Georgia-born historian U. B. Phillips would take up three-quarters of a century later under the tutelage of Frederick Jackson Turner, distiller of the "frontier" thesis.[16]

 Following *Guy Rivers: A Tale of Georgia*, the first of his so-called border romances, Simms quickly saw through the press the initial titles in the other two series on which he would work over the next thirty-five years. Both romances appeared in 1835—*The Yemassee* in the colonial series and *The Partisan: A Tale of the Revolution* in the Revolutionary War series.

 The colonial series examined the characters and fortunes of the colonists and colonies planted by the Spanish, French, and English in the New World—especially the South—and the impact of these plantations on Native American peoples and cultures. Simms explained part of his sense of this subject in an 1842 address before students at the University of Alabama, published in 1843. As a boy of sixteen (the record suggests, rather, nineteen) he remembered being struck, while "Traversing the then dreary wastes of this south-western region . . . and . . . recalling the course of French, Spanish and British invasion[,] . . . that, of the efforts of these three powerful nations, to establish the banner of civilization within this wondrous province, two of them should so utterly have failed." He had concluded that English success and Spanish and French failure were fundamentally due to the motives and priorities that the representatives of these three empires had brought to bear in their colonization efforts. The English succeeded because they "sought for nothing but home." The French and Spanish failed because they "sought either for gold, for slaves, or for conquest" (*Social Principle* 8). His colonial romances illustrated his understanding of these different approaches to colonization and their results, in South Carolina, in Florida, in Louisiana, and elsewhere. Related works—for instance, a biography of Captain John Smith—extended these imaginative historical reconstructions.

The English impulse to settlement was at the heart, too, of their descendants' revolution. Simms made this belief central to his third series. "What mattered it to the Cavaliers of Carolina," he asked those same Alabama students in 1842,

> that the English government trampled upon the privileges of Massachusetts Bay—and why should the Puritans of New England care whether the Cavaliers of Carolina were or were not permitted the right of choosing their own . . . civil and military officers? There was no love lost between these separate communities. They had few affinities of taste or temper. Foes in the old country, they were not likely, very soon, to overcome their antipathies in the new. Yet they did overcome them, and with the sagacious instincts of the Anglo-Saxon nature, in the maintenance of those social securities . . . [,] they shook themselves free from the king of Great Britain for the same reason which first prompted them to seek refuge in the wilderness,—the comfort and the security of home. Not so much with the view to the assertion of an abstract principle . . . , but because of absolute present abuses and usurpations . . . as enumerated in the Declaration [of Independence]. (*Social Principle* 11–13)

In sum, according to Simms, though the French and the Spanish launched European civilization in the South, English cavaliers laid the basis of the future society in the region. Their descendants in turn successfully led the defense of that society against the encroachments of the British government and then extended their dominions and Western civilization into the wilds of the region's interior. Throughout this history liberty contested with both tyranny and license to define the social relations of free men; the urge for new land competed with the urge to build on and cultivate one's home ground; and the traditions of the Cavalier, modified by the conditions of the frontier, shaped a distinct culture with the aid of the labor of African slaves and the infusions of various European-descended peoples—Germans, Scots, and Irish among them. The resulting society was not aristocratic; in the New World old habits of deference and presumption had to give way to the rough equality of the frontier. Only gradually, fitfully was society establishing the order and hierarchy necessary for true civilization—a condition that was more of a promise than a realization of Southern history to date.[17]

The ethnocentrism of this argument is the obverse of its ethnological orientation. It assumes not only that there is a historically revealed hierarchy of ethnic and racial groups and values, but that culture, with genetics, is the fundamental determinant in human actions and interactions. It assumes, too, that culture is both transferrable and malleable. It further assumes that identity and allegiance are culturally derived—that Southern distinctiveness is a reflection of Southerners' particular antecedents. In its essentials, though stripped of its ethnic and racial rankings, this is the argument of such recent historians as Lewis Simpson, Richard Beale Davis, Raimondo Luraghi, Bertram Wyatt-Brown, David Hackett Fischer, and Grady McWhiney, despite the disagreements among these scholars on what the origins and defining characteristics of Southern culture (or cultures) are.

Simms's ethnological argument, including its ethnic and racial rankings, was generally accepted by Thomas Dew, Beverley Tucker, Edmund Ruffin, and most other writers from the planter and professional classes among Simms's near contemporaries in the South. It was a variant of that expressed by George Bancroft, another near contemporary, when expounding on the American people and character.[18] Indeed, so universal and self-evident did the ethnological argument seem that most historians felt compelled to find or invent cultural genealogies to explain political and other divergences of their own day. If one made the assumption that politics were a reflection of ethnicity (that is, of distinguishing genetic and cultural commonalities), one had no choice. The premise dictated the form and nature, if not the specific contents, of one's argument and conclusions.

Simms's ethnological approach to Southern history and George Bancroft's comparable approach to American history were both launched before the public in 1834, the year that the first volume of Bancroft's *History of the United States* as well as Simms's first Southern romance appeared. By emphasizing the putative European roots of differences among Americans and by at the same time emphasizing these European Americans' common cultural antecedents, Bancroft and Simms were joining in the effort to shift attention from recent ideological incompatibilities among Americans, and so offering alternatives to the failed historical justifications for the American Union developed by the Revolutionary generation.

The strategy was to encompass American differences within a framework of familial unity and historical progress. The formula was borrowed. German and British romantics were the lenders. In the American context, however, the use of the formula was modern in 1834. While European writers had begun framing historical accounts ethnologically a good deal earlier, Americans tended to be nearly a generation late in the absorption and application of many romantic influences and paradigms.[19]

Eventually, the Simms-Bancroft strategy also failed to satisfy a new generation. As sectional and other tensions became worse, the younger generation became impatient with the argument about common Anglo-Saxon ancestry split between Puritans and Cavaliers and insisted instead on focusing on the politics, sociology, and dynamics of sectional, class, and other interests.[20] Yet Simms and Bancroft kept on in the veins that they had opened earlier, writing out their visions. Increasingly, as a result, their newest volumes were greeted with the respect due the works of elders rather than the excitement generated by their earlier, less mature, and often less well realized works.[21]

Other factors were at play as well. Simms was most influential when he was programmatically allied in the Young America movement with others who shared some of his approaches to national (thus regional) literature and culture. During the decade from the late 1830s, fellow Young Americans trumpeted his vision and worth from New York, then emerging as the nation's literary capital. The dissolution of the group in 1848 in effect signalled the opening of the door to a successor generation and literary program, although former Young America members continued to promote Simms in their periodicals.[22]

Despite the fact that Simms was not quite 40 percent through his systematic fictional explorations of the South's antecedents and dynamics in 1848, then, he and his friends-in-arms were no longer the literary vanguard. Consequently, his historical vision began to assume the qualities of a historical artifact to younger readers even before it was fully rendered.[23] The pattern is familiar. Each succeeding generation feels it necessary to undercut and, so, seize in order to wrangle over the authority of its teachers. In scholarship, the process is called advancement, though whether it is advancement of knowledge and understanding or of scholars is sometimes unclear. In Southern studies, the process has helped fuel a variety of successive and competing interpretations of the region's origins, development, and nature.[24]

Of course, at the same time as one generation succeeds another, circumstances change as well. The South on which Simms focused was the region of his youth and early maturity. Already in 1842, when addressing those students at the University of Alabama, he recognized that the Southern frontier was giving way to, was being succeeded by, a more civilized, settled regime. That he continued to write about and explore the history behind his formative experiences even though that personal history did not fit the experiences or expectations of the rising generation was another factor in his gradual literary eclipse.

Scholars have paid more attention to yet another factor: the increase in sectional hostilities. By the time of his 1856 lecture tour in the North, arranged by George Bancroft, William Cullen Bryant, and others, Simms had growing reason to conclude that the "politico-social relations of the two great sections" were "in absolute and direct antagonism."[25]

The point may have been overemphasized in some of the scholarship. A factor considered neither by Simms nor by most later critics should also be remembered: the expropriation of the frontier, as both setting for and theme of fiction, from the Southern by the western. Paralleling this development and also neglected until recently was a popular shift of taste in literary genres.[26]

Initially Simms very successfully adapted Sir Walter Scott's Scottish Border Romance formula to Southern subjects. In the process, he did more than any other writer to create the *Southern* as a literary subgenre. As he reasoned (though not in these terms), the "genrefication," and thus the commodification, of the South was necessary if the region was to claim literary distinction and value.[27]

Simms very self-consciously joined history and romance, epic themes and realism, low comedy and high passion to make vivid the South's development and society. In this ambition, he had been anticipated by John Pendleton Kennedy and, on other American if not Southern subjects, by James Fenimore Cooper. Like his elders in the Knickerbocker circle, his successors often found his mixture unnatural or unseemly, designed to offend rather than please every taste by juxtaposing and melding conventions and aspiring to readerships meant to be kept apart.[28] The postbellum Southern was a very different vehicle in form as well as substance, whether found in Page's Old Virginia, in the company of Miss Minerva's William Green Hill, in Brer Rabbit's briar patch, or in Lady Baltimore's Charleston. Not until Faulkner did the Southern again challenge by conflating conventions as boldly as in Simms's hands to make the present historical.[29] In between, the historical novel and the romance both declined in favor. Newer understandings of history undercut the romantic, ethnological assumptions informing Simms's vision. Then, too, the Civil War and the apparent end of Simms's world had radically reconfigured Southern history.

When, in 1869, just months before Simms's death, Confederate veterans met in New Orleans to create the Southern Historical Society, they were focused on their own Confederate past, not on the region's remote origins and development. Braxton Bragg, Jubal Early, Zebulon Vance, and other founders were not concerned with their antecedents in this effort as much as with the maintenance of their war-based camaraderie and the establishment of their legacy. They did not want the fact of their loss to obscure the value of their bond, the bravery of their effort, or the nobility of their cause.[30]

The war did something else to the history that occupied Simms. It transformed that history from an unfolding to a closed story. As a result, for those interested in getting or looking ahead, it was no longer the guidebook Simms thought it. For those concerned to retain or assert identity and pride in the face of Confederate loss, on the other hand, this history became, instead of a progressive narrative about regional development from the frontier to civilization, a golden memory.

The memory served a variety of functions. When traveling back in their minds to life before the war, certain people were fortifying themselves with former plenty against current poverty. Some were also telling their children that the present was not normative, that they could hope and should work for better circumstances. In the process, too, many frequently were affirming an ideal social order that defined relations between the races, classes, and sexes in ways that did not necessarily correspond to antebellum realities but that nevertheless gave the Old South formidable power in its postbellum afterlife.

Other memories served other functions. The Lost Cause became a rallying cry and organizational vehicle in white Southerners' efforts to deal with Yankee troops, Republican politicians, and such emerging forces of change as the textile industry. Old soldiers' funerals, veterans meetings, and other ritual occasions went beyond the fellowship of shared experience to solidify the bonds and discipline of common leadership and to build and fortify responses to various political and social issues of the day. With the passage of time, the Lost Cause also became a vehicle for both socializing and educating the young. Youth learned obedience to commands, deference to elders, pride, the need for corporate action, the glory of valor, and the value of community identity.[31]

If, despite the protests of the Populists, growing segregation, textile strikes, and other signs of deep divisions, the South seemed solid, almost monolithic, to outsiders and many insiders alike by the 1890s, there was good reason. History was being used to forge identities and allegiances more successfully than anywhere before in America, at least since the days of the Mathers in New England. As Hawthorne had written of the power of this social glue among generations of Puritans, so Faulkner would write of its holding power among generations of Southerners.[32]

Simms's Southerners were not bonded by their history in the same way. Yet Simms's efforts to imagine a past to explain his region's present and project its future were validated by the South's postbellum historical turn. The South became a historical community about the time that Southerners stopped reading Simms. The further irony is that postbellum historical self-understandings in the region were much less rich and dynamic at the same time that they were much more personal and immediate than the Southern history synthesized by Simms out of earlier, colonial histories of parts of the region and out of the dialectic of the frontier and plantation societies of his own youth and young manhood.

In reading Faulkner, one needs to remember that he was able to combine, because he had inherited, both the postbellum and Simms's legacy. Simms did not have this dual history. A semi-orphan in a new country and even newer region, he had to construct his past much more radically. The construction did not allow the ironic self-reflexiveness of twentieth-century reconstructions, whether by fictionists such as William Faulkner and Eudora Welty or by historians such as C. Vann Woodward.[33]

NOTES

1. See, for instance, Paul Buck, Francis Pendleton Gaines, Paul Gaston 48–53, Lucinda Hardwick MacKethan, Wayne Mixon, and Louis D. Rubin Jr. et al.

2. See, for instance, David Hackett Fischer, Eugene Genovese (1961 and 1969), Mark D. Kaplanoff, Raimondo Luraghi, Grady McWhiney, Anne Norton, R. Nicholas Olsberg, John Solomon Otto, William R. Taylor, Kirk Wood, and Bertram Wyatt-Brown.

3. See, for instance, John R. Alden, Avery O. Craven 1–20, and Charles S. Sydnor 1–32.

4. Joseph V. Ridgely and John McCardell (1986) are among those students of Simms who have paid particular attention to these tensions. See also David Moltke-Hansen (1986) and John Mayfield. The theme is central to W. J. Cash, Faulkner's contemporary, as well as to U. B. Phillips (1909).

5. See David Moltke-Hansen (1986, 22–40 and note 52, 385–86; also 1992) and, for many of the writers mentioned below, Robert Bain et al. For other "generational" perspectives, see M. E. Bradford and Daniel Joseph Singal.

6. See Harry B. Henderson 16–42, and Arthur H. Shaffer (1975 and 1986).

7. See Drew Gilpin Faust (1988) 4–5, and Kenneth M. Stampp 246–69. Cf. Louis D. Rubin Jr. (1989) and Edward Pessen.

8. See, for instance, Carl Bridenbaugh and Clarence Ver Steeg.

9. This story has not been told but lies buried in local and family histories, in studies of parts of the migrant streams, and in social histories of various states of the region.

10. See Joan Cashin, James E. Davis, Donald B. Dodd and Wynelle S. Dodd, Peter D. McClelland and Richard J. Zeckhauser, Ulrich Bonnell Phillips (1906), Tommy W. Rogers, and Ralph A. Wooster.

11. See, for instance, Robert Bain et al., Howard Russell Floan, Francis Pendleton Gaines, Richard J. Gray, Fred C. Hobson (1983), Jay B. Hubbell, Eugene Schwaab, and William R. Taylor.

12. See William H. Pease and Jane H. Pease.

13. See James E. Kibler and, also, David Moltke-Hansen ("Ordered Progress") 128–34.

14. See, for example, Bertram Wyatt-Brown (1982 and 1985), Kenneth S. Greenberg, John A. Reesman, Michael Zuckerman, Steven M. Stowe, Michael P. Johnson, Drew Gilpin Faust (1982), John Mayfield, and Michael Rogin. John Mayfield first called attention to this argument from patriarchal models by Simms in a private communication to the author.

15. See John Caldwell Guilds (1957), also C. Hugh Holman (1972), Sergio Perosa 31–46, Mary Ann Wimsatt, and John Mayfield.

16. See Everett Dick, Clement Eaton 98–124, Ulrich Bonnell Phillips (1909), and Frederick Jackson Turner (1920 and 1932).

17. Parts of this section appeared earlier in David Moltke-Hansen (1992) 2–4.

18. See Drew Gilpin Faust (1977), Harry B. Henderson 16–42, David Levin 74–92, John McCardell (1979) 144–76, Rollin G. Osterweis, and William R. Taylor.

19. See David Moltke-Hansen (1992), Sergio Perosa 31–46, Arthur Shaffer (1975 and 1986), and Hayden White.

20. See David Moltke-Hansen (1992).

21. See Keen Butterworth and James E. Kibler, as well as William Henry Trescot for the reception of Simms.

22. This point is made by Jonathan Young, a graduate student in history at the University of North Carolina at Chapel Hill, in an unpublished paper written in 1992. See also Perry Miller.

23. See note 21.

24. See David Moltke-Hansen, "The Southern Difference Question Revisited."

25. See Miriam J. Shillingsburg 198.

26. See, for instance, James D. Hart, Sergio Perosa 47–70, and Kathleen Mary Tillotson.

27. See Dickson D. Bruce 212–32, Rollin G. Osterweis, William Gilmore Simms (1962), esp. 7–29, and William R. Taylor.

28. See Keen Butterworth and James E. Kibler as well as Jay B. Hubbell.

29. See Richard J. Gray, Fred C. Hobson (1983, 1991), Jay B. Hubbell, Lucinda Hardwick MacKethan, Wayne Mixon, Lewis P. Simpson (1975) 65–100, and Thomas Daniel Young.

30. See Susan Speare Durant 39–59 and Gaines Foster 50–54.

31. See Charles Reagan Wilson.

32. See Michael Davitt Bell, Lewis P. Simpson (1973), Mary Ann Wimsatt, and C. Vann Woodward.

33. See Louis D. Rubin Jr. (1975 and 1989), and Lewis P. Simpson (1973).

WORKS CITED

Alden, John R. *The First South*. Baton Rouge: Louisiana State University Press, 1961.

Bain, Robert, et al. *Southern Writers: A Biographical Dictionary*. Baton Rouge: Louisiana State University Press, 1979.

Bancroft, George. *A History of the United States, from the Discovery of the American Continent. . . .* 10 vols. Boston: Little, Brown, 1834–1875.

Bell, Michael Davitt. *Hawthorne and the Historical Romance of New England*. Princeton: Princeton University Press, 1971.

Bradford, M. E. *Generations of the Faithful Heart: On the Literature of the South*. La Salle: Sherwood Sugden, 1983.

Bridenbaugh, Carl. *Myths and Realities*. Baton Rouge: Louisiana State University Press, 1952.

Bruce, Dickson D., Jr. *Violence and Culture in the Antebellum South*. Austin: University of Texas Press, 1979.

Butterworth, Keen, and James E. Kibler. *William Gilmore Simms: A Reference Guide.* Boston: G. K. Hall, 1980.

Calhoun, Frances Boyd. *Miss Minerva and William Green Hill.* Chicago: Reilly and Britton, 1909.

Carroll, Lewis. *Alice's Adventures in Wonderland.* Boston: Lee and Shepard, 1888.

Cash, W. J. *The Mind of the South.* New York: Knopf, 1941.

Cashin, Joan E. *A Family Venture: Men and Women on the Southern Frontier.* New York: Oxford University Press, 1991.

Craven, Avery O. *The Growth of Southern Nationalism, 1848–1861.* Baton Rouge: Louisiana State University Press, 1953.

Davis, James E. *Frontier America, 1800–1840: A Comparative Demographic Analysis of the Settlement Process.* Glendale: Arthur H. Clark, 1977.

Davis, Richard Beale. *Intellectual Life in the Colonial South, 1585–1763.* 3 vols. Knoxville: University of Tennessee Press, 1977.

Dick, Everett. *The Dixie Frontier: A Social History of the Southern Frontier from the First Transmontane Beginnings to the Civil War.* New York: Knopf, 1948.

Dodd, Donald B., and Wynelle S. Dodd. *Historical Statistics of the South, 1790–1970.* University: University of Alabama Press, 1973.

Durant, Susan Speare. "The Gently Furled Banner: The Development of the Myth of the Lost Cause, 1865–1900." Diss. University of North Carolina at Chapel Hill, 1972.

Eaton, Clement. *The Growth of Southern Civilization, 1790–1860.* New York: Harper's, 1961.

Faust, Drew Gilpin. *The Creation of Confederate Nationalism: Ideology and Identity in the Civil War South.* Baton Rouge: Louisiana State University Press, 1988.

———. *James Henry Hammond and the Old South: A Design for Mastery.* Baton Rouge: Louisiana State University Press, 1982.

———. *A Sacred Circle: The Dilemma of the Intellectual in the Old South, 1840–1860.* Baltimore: Johns Hopkins University Press, 1977.

Fischer, David Hackett. *Albion's Seed: Four British Folkways in America.* New York: Oxford University Press, 1989.

Floan, Howard Russell. *The South in Northern Eyes, 1831–1861.* Austin: University of Texas Press, 1958.

Foster, Gaines M. *Ghosts of the Confederacy: Defeat, the Lost Cause and the Emergence of the New South, 1865–1913.* New York: Oxford University Press, 1987.

Gaines, Francis Pendleton. *The Southern Plantation: A Study in the Development and Accuracy of a Tradition.* New York: Columbia University Press, 1924.

Gaston, Paul. *The New South Creed: A Study in Southern Mythmaking.* New York: Knopf, 1970.

Genovese, Eugene D. *The Political Economy of Slavery: Studies in the Economy and Society of the Slave South.* New York: Vintage, 1961.

——. *The World the Slaveholders Made: Two Essays in Interpretation.* New York: Random House, 1969.

Gray, Richard J. *The Literature of Memory: Modern Writers of the American South.* London: Edward Arnold, 1977.

——. *Writing the South: Ideas of an American Region.* Cambridge: Cambridge University Press, 1986.

Greenberg, Kenneth S. *Masters and Statesmen: The Political Culture of American Slavery.* Baltimore: Johns Hopkins University Press, 1985.

Grimké, Angelina. *Appeal to the Christian Women of the South.* New York: American Anti-Slavery Society, 1836.

Guilds, John Caldwell. "Simms's Views on National and Sectional Literature." *North Carolina Historical Review* 34 (1957): 393–405.

——, ed. *"Long Years of Neglect": The Work and Reputation of William Gilmore Simms.* Fayetteville: University of Arkansas Press, 1988.

Hart, James D. *The Popular Book: History of America's Literary Taste.* New York: Oxford University Press, 1970.

Henderson, Harry B. *Versions of the Past.* New York: Oxford University Press, 1974.

Hobson, Fred C. *The Southern Writer in the Postmodern World.* Athens: University of Georgia Press, 1991.

——. *Tell About the South: The Southern Rage to Explain.* Baton Rouge: Louisiana State University Press, 1983.

Holman, C. Hugh. "The Influence of Scott and Cooper on Simms." *The Roots of Southern Writing.* Athens: University of Georgia Press, 1972. 50–60.

Hubbell, Jay B. *The South in American Literature, 1607–1900.* Durham: Duke University Press, 1954.

Johnson, Michael P. "Planters and Patriarchy: Charleston, 1800–1860." *Journal of Southern History* 46 (1980): 45–72.

Kaplanoff, Mark D. "Making the South Solid: Politics and the Structure of Society in South Carolina, 1790–1815." Diss. Cambridge University, 1979.

Kibler, James E. "The First Simms Letters: 'Letters from the West' (1826)." *Southern Literary Journal* 19, no. 2 (1987): 81–91.

Levin, David. *History as Romantic Art: Bancroft, Prescott, Motley, and Parkman.* New York: AMS, 1967.

Luraghi, Raimondo. *The Rise and Fall of the Plantation South.* New York: New Viewpoints, 1978.

McCardell, John. *The Idea of a Southern Nation: Southern Nationalists and Southern Nationalism, 1830–1860.* New York: Norton, 1979.

McClelland, Peter D., and Richard J. Zeckhauser. *Demographic Dimensions of the New Republic: American Interregional Migration, Vital Statistics, and Manumissions, 1800–1860.* Cambridge: Cambridge University Press, 1982.

MacKethan, Lucinda Hardwick. *The Dream of Arcady: Place and Time in Southern Literature.* Baton Rouge: Louisiana State University Press, 1980.

McWhiney, Grady. *Cracker Culture: Celtic Ways in the Old South.* University: University of Alabama Press, 1988.

Martineau, Harriet. *Society in America.* 3 vols. London: Saunders and Otley, 1837.

Mayfield, John. "'The Soul of a Man!': William Gilmore Simms and the Myths of Southern Manhood." *Journal of the Early Republic* 15 (1995): 477–500.

Miller, Perry. *The Raven and the Whale: The War of Words and Wits in the Era of Poe and Melville.* New York: Harcourt, 1956.

Mixon, Wayne. *Southern Writers and the New South Movement.* Chapel Hill: University of North Carolina Press, 1980.

Moltke-Hansen, David. "Conceiving Southern History." *Humanities in the South* 76 (fall 1992): 1–7.

———. "The Expansion of Intellectual Life: A Prospectus." *Intellectual Life in Antebellum Charleston.* Ed. Michael O'Brien and David Moltke-Hansen. Knoxville: University of Tennessee Press, 1986. 3–44.

———. "Ordered Progress: The Historical Philosophy of William Gilmore Simms." *"Long Years of Neglect": The Work and Reputation of William Gilmore Simms.* Ed. John Caldwell Guilds. Fayetteville: University of Arkansas Press, 1988. 126–47.

———. "The Southern Difference Question Revisited." Unpublished essay in possession of the author.

Norton, Anne. *Alternative Americas: A Reading of Antebellum Political Culture.* Chicago: University of Chicago Press, 1986.

O'Brien, Michael, and David Moltke-Hansen, eds. *Intellectual Life in Antebellum Charleston.* Knoxville: University of Tennessee Press, 1986.

Olsberg, R. Nicholas. "Desolate Places: The South Carolina Chivalry at the Time of the Civil War." Collection of the South Carolina Historical Society.

Osterweis, Rollin G. *Romanticism and Nationalism in the Old South.* New Haven: Yale University Press, 1949.

Otto, John Solomon. *The Southern Frontiers, 1607–1860: The Agricultural Evolution of the Colonial and Antebellum South.* New York: Greenwood, 1989.

Page, Thomas Nelson. *In Ole Virginia, or Marse Chan and Other Stories.* New York: Charles Scribner's Sons, 1887.

Pease, William H., and Jane H. Pease. *James Louis Petigru: Southern Conservative, Southern Dissenter.* Athens: University of Georgia Press, 1995.

Perosa, Sergio. *American Theories of the Novel: 1793–1903.* New York: New York University Press, 1983.

Pessen, Edward. "How Different from Each Other Were the Antebellum North and South." *American Historical Review* 85 (1980): 1119–49.

Phillips, Ulrich Bonnell. "The Origin and Growth of the Southern Black Belts." *American Historical Review* 11 (1906): 798–816.

———, ed. *Plantation and Frontier Documents: 1649–1863, Illustrative of Industrial History in the Colonial & Ante-Bellum South.* 2 vols. Cleveland: H. H. Clark, 1909.

Reesman, John A. "A School for Honor: South Carolina College and the Guard House Riot of 1856." *South Carolina Historical Magazine* 84 (1983): 195–213.

Rogers, Tommy W. "The Great Population Exodus from South Carolina, 1850–1860." *South Carolina Historical Magazine* 68 (1967): 14–21.

Rogin, Michael Paul. *Fathers and Children: Andrew Jackson and the Subjugation of the American Indian.* New York: Knopf, 1975.

Rubin, Louis D., Jr. *The Edge of the Swamp: A Study in the Literature and Society of the Old South.* Baton Rouge: Louisiana State University Press, 1989.

———. *William Elliott Shoots a Bear: Essays on the Southern Literary Imagination.* Baton Rouge: Louisiana State University Press, 1975.

Rubin, Louis D., Jr., et al., eds. *The History of Southern Literature.* Baton Rouge: Louisiana State University Press, 1985.

Schwaab, Eugene Lincoln, comp. *Travels in the Old South, Selected from Periodicals of the Times.* 2 vols. Lexington: University Press of Kentucky, 1973.

Shaffer, Arthur H. "David Ramsay and the Limits of Revolutionary Nationalism." *Intellectual Life in Antebellum Charleston.* Ed. Michael O'Brien and David Moltke-Hansen. Knoxville: University of Tennessee Press, 1986. 47–84.

———. *The Politics of History: Writing the History of the American Revolution, 1783–1815.* Chicago: Precedent, 1975.

Shillingsburg, Miriam J. "Simms's Failed Lecture Tour of 1856: The Mind of the North." *"Long Years of Neglect": The Work and Reputation of William Gilmore Simms.* Ed. John Caldwell Guilds. Fayetteville: University of Arkansas Press, 1988. 183–201.

Simms, William Gilmore. *Guy Rivers: A Tale of Georgia.* 2 vols. New York: Harper and Brothers, 1834.

———. *The Letters of William Gilmore Simms.* 5 vols. Ed. Mary C. Simms Oliphant, Alfred Taylor Odell, and T. C. Duncan Eaves. Columbia: University of South Carolina Press, 1952–1956. (A sixth volume, *The Letters of William Gilmore Simms: Supplement [1834–1870],* ed. Oliphant and Eaves, was published by the University of South Carolina Press in 1982.)

———. *Monody on the Death of Gen. Charles Cotesworth Pinckney.* Charleston: Gray and Ellis, 1825.

———. *The Partisan: A Tale of the Revolution.* 2 vols. New York: Harper and Brothers, 1835.

———. *The Social Principle.* Tuscaloosa: Erosophic Society of the University of Alabama, 1843.

———. *The Tri-Color, or The Three Days of Blood, in Paris with Some Other Pieces.* London: Wigfall and Davis, 1830.

———. *Views and Reviews in American Literature, History, and Fiction. First Series.* Ed. C. Hugh Holman. Cambridge: Harvard University Press, 1962.

———. *The Yemassee: A Romance of Carolina.* 2 vols. New York: Harper and Brothers, 1835.

Simpson, Lewis P. *The Dispossessed Garden.* Athens: University of Georgia Press, 1975.

———. *The Man of Letters in New England and the South: Essays on the History of the Literary Vocation in America.* Baton Rouge: Louisiana State University Press, 1973.

Singal, Daniel Joseph. *The War Within: From Victorian to Modernist Thought in the South, 1919–1945.* Chapel Hill: University of North Carolina Press, 1982.

Stampp, Kenneth M. *The Imperiled Union: Essays on the Background of the Civil War.* New York: Oxford University Press, 1980.

Stowe, Steven M. *Intimacy and Power in the Old South: Ritual in the Lives of the Planters.* Baltimore: Johns Hopkins University Press, 1987.

Sydnor, Charles S. *The Development of Southern Sectionalism, 1819–1848.* Baton Rouge: Louisiana State University Press, 1948.

Taylor, William R. *Cavalier and Yankee: The Old South and American National Character.* New York: G. Braziller, 1961.

Tillotson, Kathleen Mary. *Novels of the Eighteen-Forties.* Oxford: Clarendon, 1954.

Tocqueville, Alexis de. *L'ancien régime et la revolution.* 3d ed. Paris: Michel Levy Fréres, 1857.

Trescot, William Henry. " . . . Oration Before the South Carolina Historical Society." *Russell's Magazine* 5 (July 4, 1859): 289–307.

Turner, Frederick Jackson. *The Frontier in American History.* New York: Holt, 1920.

———. *The Significance of Sections in American History.* New York: Holt, 1932.

Ver Steeg, Clarence L. *Origins of a Southern Mosaic: Studies of Early Carolina and Georgia.* Athens: University of Georgia Press, 1975.

White, Hayden. *Metahistory: The Historical Imagination in Nineteenth-Century Europe.* Baltimore: Johns Hopkins University Press, 1973.

Wilson, Charles Reagan. *Baptized in Blood: The Religion of the Lost Cause, 1865–1920.* Athens: University of Georgia Press, 1980.

Wimsatt, Mary Ann. *The Major Fiction of William Gilmore Simms: Cultural Traditions and Literary Form.* Baton Rouge: Louisiana State University Press, 1989.

Wister, Owen. *Lady Baltimore.* New York: Macmillan, 1906.

Wood, Kirk. "The Union of the States: A Study of Radical Whig-Republican Ideology and Its Influence upon the Nation and the South, 1776–1861." Diss. University of South Carolina, 1978.

Woodward, C. Vann. *The Burden of Southern History*. Baton Rouge: Louisiana State University Press, 1960.

Wooster, Ralph A. *The People in Power: Courthouse and Statehouse in the Lower South, 1850–1860*. Knoxville: University of Tennessee Press, 1969.

Wyatt-Brown, Bertram. *Southern Honor: Ethics and Behavior in the Old South*. New York: Oxford University Press, 1982.

———. *Yankee Saints and Southern Sinners*. Baton Rouge: Louisiana State University Press, 1985.

Young, Thomas Daniel. *Selected Essays, 1965–1985*. Baton Rouge: Louisiana State University Press, 1990.

Zuckerman, Michael. "Penmanship Exercises for Saucy Sons: Some Thoughts on the Colonial Southern Family." *South Carolina Historical Magazine* 84 (1983): 152–66.

The American Frontier:
Romance and Reality

W hat is the modern romance itself?" William Gilmore Simms asked in his preface to *The Yemassee*. "The reply is instant," he answered: "Modern romance is the substitute which the people of today offer for the ancient epic" (3). Simms was referring to "epic" in its literary sense, a marvelous story full of "adventures among the wild and wonderful," with exotic settings and peoples and plenty of primal emotions. While reading Simms's Border Romances, however, it is important to remember that *epic* can be used in another sense, this one historical. By this second definition, an epic is a statement of collective identity. Through it, a people retell their history in a particular way and for a special purpose. In its historical sense, an epic is a story that a people tell about themselves to proclaim that they are distinct and different from all other people. With it, they explain where they have come from, who they are, and how they have gotten that way.

In writing *The Yemassee, Guy Rivers,* and other works, Simms was drawing upon the closest thing that European Americans have had to a national epic—the story of the American frontier. The settings of Simms's novels have been quite different, ranging from the Carolina backcountry of the early eighteenth century to the gulf coastal frontiers more than a century later. In all of them, however, he was drawing material from a common historical experience that became the raw stuff of national myth. During the four centuries after the first English settlements along the Atlantic coast, a wave of westward expansion rolled over the continent to the Pacific, washing over indigenous peoples and other European rivals. That expansion differed in its particular expressions; western Connecticut's story in 1700 was unlike Mississippi's in 1810 and Montana's in 1870. But there were enough common elements to create a sense of a "frontier experience." All the Border Romances unfold within that experience. Each is set at that stage of a region's history when European settlement has moved into it and has begun to change things.

As such, Simms's novels were part of the making of that national historical epic, the story of the moving frontier and the creation of a distinctive
American people.[1] This deceptively simple narrative has had astonishing
staying power and persistence, paradoxically, because it has continually
changed; its details, nuances, and emphases are constantly made over to
reflect evolving beliefs, attitudes, values, fears, and intolerances. Politicians,
from Jackson and Lincoln through Theodore Roosevelt to Kennedy, Johnson, and Reagan, have appealed for votes with its images. Its themes run
through our "high" literature, while pulp western fiction sells at an astonishing pace. Fans of Louis L'Amour buy eighteen thousand copies of his
books every day. Advertisers have long exploited the frontier's appeal. After
the movies *Dances with Wolves* and *Unforgiven*, westerns are now two-for-
four in the competition for the Academy Award for best film. After two
centuries and thousands of variations, the story of a westering people and
their trials and transformations continues to hold the attention and allegiance of a large portion of the public, and there is nothing to suggest it
will lose its appeal anytime soon. Its grip seems as firm as a John Wayne
handshake.

And yet because that frontier story—as epic, as national myth and sacred narrative—is so compelling, it has tended to obscure the actuality of
the frontier, its basic nature, and its significance for the history of North
America. Studying Border Romances is a fine enterprise, but the significance of mythic tales like those of Simms can be fully grasped only when
balanced against what was in fact occurring as Euro-Americans pushed into
the interior of North America. *Realism*, like *epic*, also takes a different meaning among historians than among literary scholars. As a literary realist,
Simms touched on topics and had his characters speak in dialogue truer to
the details of daily life than in the more stylized novels of the time. But to
a historian, Simms's broader presentation of events, however realistic some
of the particulars might be, is fundamentally romantic. It expresses a view
of national development indistinguishable from the romantic vision of an
American character emerging from the triumphs and tragic testing of the
frontier.

So while it is valuable to give a much closer study to Simms, one of the
most important of the frontier's mythmakers, it is also worthwhile to take
a look at a few aspects of the historical frontier beyond the Appalachians,
contrasting them occasionally with the frontier of romance, and so suggest

some of the importance and complexity of that history that has become such a prominent part of American dreaming.

That is a tall order. To keep things reasonably under control, I use as my focus a single, fairly well-known moment involving the most famous frontiersman of the era, a man familiar to the frontier of both romance and reality. The figure was Daniel Boone, and the episode was his first encounter with Indians during his first trip into Kentucky.

This moment was first described in print in the book that introduced Boone to the public: John Filson's *The Adventures of Colonel Daniel Boon*, first published in 1784 as an appendix to *The Discovery, Settlement and Present State of Kentuke*.[2] According to Filson's narrative, Boone, his brother-in-law John Stewart, and four others set out in May of 1769 "to wander through the wilderness of America in quest of the country of Kentucky." After a difficult journey through the mountains, they topped a ridge and "beheld the beautiful level" of that promised land. For six months they scouted and hunted this magnificent country. Then, on December 22, after Boone and Stewart had passed the day on "a pleasing ramble," a party of Indians ambushed and seized them. "The time of our sorrow was now arrived," says Filson's Boone. The savages took all their possessions and held them in rough bondage, but after a week Boone and Stewart were able to slip away and continue their wanderings and adventures.

Boone's encounter with the Indians was a crucial moment in the making of an American icon. It is a centerpiece in each of his many biographies. Luckily, it is also an episode documented by sources other than Filson, including later descriptions by Boone, and when this other evidence is pieced together, the actual event seems to have differed from Filson's account in significant and interesting ways.

Here is what actually seems to have happened on that December afternoon in 1769.[3] Boone and Stewart had been hunting when they were surprised and disarmed. The Indians, collectively and individually nameless in Filson's account, were Shawnees from Chillicothe in Ohio. Their leader introduced himself by his white names—Captain Will and Will Emery. (He may have used what we know from other sources was one of his favorite phrases, "Howdydo! Howdydo!"). Will Emery spoke tolerable English, and after questioning the two intruders he confiscated their furs and horses. In Filson's account, Boone says the Indians "treated us with common savage usage," but Daniel later told relatives that Emery behaved "in the most friendly manner" and, rather than holding them prisoner, he gave them two pairs of moccasins apiece, some doe skin for patching those moccasins, some powder and lead to help them hunt on the way home, and a small French gun. He ended with a little speech: "Now, brothers, go home and stay there. Don't come here any more, for this is the Indians' hunting ground, and all the animals, skins, and furs are ours. And if you are so foolish as to venture here again, you may be sure the wasps and yellow-jackets will sting you severely." Boone and Stewart's response, however, was to track down the Shawnees and steal back their horses, only to be hunted down and surprised again. This time the Indians marched with the men back toward the Ohio, probably meaning to keep their eye on them until they could get back across the river, but the two crept away while the Shawnees were asleep, first to hide in a canebrake and then to go on to full freedom and to separate paths: Stewart to a lonely death a few months later, Boone to a long life that would take him to the top of our mythic heap.

Nobody can read these two accounts of the same event without asking some questions about them. Three seem to me especially intriguing. First, there is the question of motive. The Boone of Filson's story is driven by a vague compulsion to seek the unknown, to "wander through the wilderness in quest of Kentucky," an Appalachian version of a more recent romantic hero, Captain James T. Kirk. As for Filson's Indians, they are just *there*, more or less part of the fauna, like bears and catamounts, and presumably they jump on the pioneers because that's what Indians do. All this is perfectly in line with the mythic frontier. It is also part of a deeper belief about what the frontier was and was not. On the frontier, according to our tradition, people act not so much out of social purposes but from pure individual and natural instinct. We seem to believe that if a man walked westward fast enough and far enough, he could cross over a line, as if entering one of Walt Disney's magic kingdoms, and leave behind all society and institutions. He could make the ultimate break, become exempt from social restraints, expectations, and motivations. If a man could make it past that magical line, in other words, he could walk away from history.

But both Boone and the Indians were acting from reasons that had a great deal to do with the world beyond Kentucky. Everyone in the story was an eager participant in a complex economic system that stretched over a hundred and thirty meridians, from Eastern Europe to the Great Plains. The mainstay of that system was an exchange of goods between Native Americans and whites. That trading was going on here will surprise nobody; traders like Granger in *The Yemassee* have been stock characters in all descriptions of the frontier, romantic and otherwise. But historians only recently have begun to appreciate the many influences and implications of trade on people and events, and the result is a more interesting and complicated story.

Boone may have been driven partly by curiosity, but his main purpose in coming to Kentucky was to look for new territory in which to pursue his business—hunting for profit. Between midsummer and December his party of voracious hunters had accumulated several hundred deerskins, scraping and drying them and pressing them into packs. (They also were gathering large quantities of a North American variety of ginseng, which brought an impressive price back east as an aphrodisiac.)

The Indians' actions are more puzzling; they treat Boone and his friends with a blend of sternness and a kind of backslapping fellowship. But if their response seems contradictory, that is because by 1769 trade had left native peoples an ambivalent heritage, and Boone, as an English hunter, represented to them a mix of blessings and threats.

It is helpful to think of trade as a great wave of influence that rippled into the continent far ahead of white settlement.[4] As Filson's book was being published in the 1780s, Indians on the upper Missouri River, in present North Dakota, were enjoying a variety of European goods, including peppermint candy and corduroy trousers.[5] Trade could bring the various cultures into close and extensive contact. In 1724 a French expedition returned from central Kansas to Paris with a delegation of Osage Indians, who performed dances at the opera and demonstrated their hunting skills by riding bareback and killing large numbers of Louis XV's peacocks. Carried home to Kansas, they reported that they had a grand time, but that the perfumed women of the court smelled like alligators.[6] All this was ten years before Boone was born in Pennsylvania and forty-five years before and a thousand miles west of his encounter with the savages in that untouched Eden of Kentucky.

Indians responded eagerly to such contact because, from the first, trade offered enormous advantages and raised their standard of living. In novels like *The Yemassee* Simms touches on some of the material appeal of English trade goods, but as in most fictional accounts of this period, there is little sense of the complex interactions triggered by trade. Indians gained all sorts of things that allowed them to practice their own chosen way of life more comfortably and with less labor. It also brought changes in the economic and familial roles of husbands, wives, and children and revised the very structure of tribes and bands. But soon enough it became clear that trade also brought with it two especially pernicious influences.

First, it introduced European imperial rivalries into native politics, and with that it intensified conflict among Indian groups, scrambled power relationships, and set tribes into a series of movements that historians will probably never sort out. Boone's Shawnee captors could have told us something about that. They had been on quite an odyssey.[7] In the mid–seventeenth century, more than a hundred years earlier, the Iroquois had swept southwestward out of New York to expand their trade and power, driving the Shawnees out of Ohio. Some fled southward to live with the Creeks in Alabama. Others moved down the Ohio River and into the lower Mississippi Valley—Marquette saw some in Arkansas—then gradually filtered eastward through the gulf coastal region, to Georgia, up the Atlantic coast eventually into Maryland and Pennsylvania, then westward, back to Ohio. Theirs was only one of many such cases of diaspora and regathering. We are fond of thinking of pioneers like Boone as restless and ever-moving and Indians as always in place, but the Shawnees Boone met were likely far better traveled and more worldly than he. Certainly they knew more about the frontier's disruptive consequences.

Secondly, these Indians competed so vigorously because trade was changing profoundly the relationship between people and things and, through that, between people and the world around them.[8] Indians, after all, were becoming increasingly reliant on goods they could not make for themselves, and that obviously left them in a weak bargaining position. The long-range consequences of this were disastrous. A good illustration was offered by the experience of the Yemassee and their war of 1715, the setting and subject of Simms's novel of 1835.

Historians are in general agreement that the Yemassee launched their war in South Carolina because they were deeply in debt to white traders and feared that they would be enslaved as payment for their debts.[9] The Yemassees' debt was estimated at about one hundred thousand deerskins, or around ten thousand pounds sterling, a sum that probably equalled two or three years of their total trade in skins and furs. But *why* were they so deep in the hole? The problem, apparently, was that the Yemassee had less and less access to the two things they had to have to pay off that debt: slaves and deer. For decades they had raided weaker neighbors and sold captives to the English, who used them for the brutal work of an expanding agricultural economy. But by 1715 the Yemassee had stolen almost all the local bodies available to sell to the English. As for the deer, the Indians probably were overhunting, particularly as the slave trade declined, but just as important were the effects of thousands of new white farmers who were moving in with cattle and pigs to destroy the deer's habitat. Besides that, new rice plantations were flooding tens of thousands of acres the animals had previously browsed.

The Yemassee were stuck in a familiar depressing cycle. It went like this: Indians became increasingly reliant on certain goods available only from a white society. White traders would exchange those goods only for certain local products, notably animals. At the same time, that same white society was changing the world into one that allowed fewer and fewer of those products—those animals—to exist. This was not a happy situation, and it left Indians in an ambiguous, conflicted, tenuous relationship with an expanding white society. It is in this context that we ought to look back on Captain Will's reception of Boone and his friends. Surely the Shawnee hunters saw those intruders for what they were—part of a society that was providing what they desperately wanted, as well as hunting competitors and the vanguard of long-range calamitous changes. No wonder, then, that they greeted Boone with a mixture of "Howdydo!" and "Get the hell out."

The Yemassees' problem should also encourage us to ask a second question about Boone's encounter. When he looked around him, what did he see (besides Captain Will)? What was the natural setting of Kentucky, and what can it teach us? Once more, Simms's novels touch lightly on a few of the ecological changes that came with Anglo-American pioneers—the clearing hacked out of the forest by a frontier family, for instance. But for the most part the land is seen as a primeval fastness, largely unaffected by either white or native peoples.

Nowadays, by contrast, historians emphasize that the Europeans' arrival was, among other things, a biotic, botanical, zoological, and chemical invasion. Like the trade frontier, this one rolled rapidly into the interior, far ahead of white settlers, and began immediately to produce changes of almost unimaginable complexity.[10]

Much of this process was hopelessly misinterpreted by pioneers because their perceptions were badly warped, fuddled by extraordinarily powerful and persistent fantasies. Immediately before his capture, according to Filson, Boone had passed through a great forest where "nature was . . . a series of wonders, and a fund of delight," and on the very day of his brush with

the Shawnees he had marvelled at "myriads of trees . . . a variety of flowers and fruits, beautifully colored, elegantly shaped, and charmingly fla-
vored."[11] Boone was expressing the ancient dream of Eden, an essential
element in the frontier of romance. The more familiar term, then and now,
was *wilderness*. If you pushed westward fast enough and far enough, past
that line and out of history, that was what you would find: wilderness, a
realm of astonishing beauty, a land bursting with natural bounty, virgin
country undefiled and unstroked by the hand of man.

But in fact, these white newcomers were not, as we still like to think,
discovering an American wilderness; they were rather *creating* one as they
came. I mean that in two senses. First, they brought with them many contact diseases that decimated native peoples who did not have the immuni-
ties that whites had inherited. Peter Wood recently estimated that between
1695 and 1790 the number of Indians between the Appalachians and the
Mississippi dropped by nearly 70 percent, from about 166,000 to 53,000.
(During the same time, natives in South Carolina, Yemassee country, declined from around 10,000 to 300.)[12] This bloodthirsty biological frontier
swept ahead of the European Americans, emptying the interior of people,
so when whites did arrive, the illusion of a wilderness, a land relatively free
of human influence, was possible.

Secondly, whites created a wilderness by projecting on this newly emp-
tied region, this biological war zone, their desire for a place of innocence
and beauty. That is what Filson's Boone wanted, and that is what he found.
After describing his "ramble" through that great forest of plenty, he
summed it up: "We esteemed it a second paradise." He saw a land free
of the corruptions of ordered society. There animals lived untainted even
by knowledge of humanity's predatory nature. Boone told of "extensive
plains," and on them great herds of buffaloes that were "fearless, because
ignorant, of the violence of man" (51).

That, of course, was preposterous. For hundreds of years native peoples
had been hunting all sorts of game in Kentucky. What, after all, did Boone
think his Indian captors were doing there? Sightseeing? Natives also had
been manipulating the environment in sophisticated ways. Those "extensive plains" got their open look from Indians burning them over and clearing the forest understory to allow more and better browsing and grazing
for game and, through that, to stimulate animal populations and direct
their patterns of movement. Far from virgin, this land was quite familiar
with the touch of the hands of humans.

These changes were dwarfed, however, by what came with Europeans. Among the "variety of fruits and flowers" seen by Boone were many Old World plants that had beaten him there, including Kentucky bluegrass, an English-Eurasian mix that probably first arrived as seeds in the straw the French used to pack trade goods, and peach trees, which had spread from Spain through Florida into trans-Appalachia, where they grew in great wild snarls. Plants hitchhiked on people's clothes and animals' coats and in the guts of cattle, who then laid down the seeds, conveniently fertilized, in the new land. Those fresh arrivals, including dandelions and crabgrass, competed with the old floral order, just as cattle quickly moved in to graze those "extensive plains" created by Indians for their game. Even more influential were the thousands of half-wild pigs set loose to forage in the woods, a veritable porcine assault force seizing turf previously used by deer and other game.

People, too, competed for animal resources. They took control of the salt licks vital to deer, bison, and other ungulates, and for their first roads they preempted travel routes and paths long used by buffaloes and other game, who were the real trailblazers of the region. They were also, of course, killing the game outright for food and trade. Even the most heroic myths underestimate the extent of pioneer hunting. Once more Boone is a good case in point. Over his lifetime he slaughtered thousands of deer, bison, elk, and bear. In the 1790s, when he was in his sixties, he once killed 155 bears in three weeks, eleven one day before breakfast.

On that particular trip Boone was with his wife, Rebecca, which brings up another point. These ecological transformations were accomplished by pioneer families—not, that is, by heroic males pressing on their own into the great unknown to pave the way for women and children. The mythic tradition is like that in Filson's story, with Boone and Stewart as hairy-chested solitaires against the wild. And so they were on that occasion. But when Boone was ready for the *real* conquest, he brought the wife and kids.

These families were astonishingly prolific, as illustrated by the case of one obscure emigrant, William Gregory. Born in Virginia and married in North Carolina, Gregory moved with his family to Kentucky in 1806, then to Indiana five years later, and finally to Iowa about 1843. His migratory route was roughly that of tens of thousands of others. Along the way his wife bore children in 1796, 1798, 1800, 1802, 1804, 1806, 1808, 1810, 1812, and 1814. Then she died. Gregory quickly remarried, and before his second wife died she produced babies in 1815, 1817, 1819, 1821, 1825,

1827, 1829, 1831 (with stillborn twins in 1823). Another wife took up where she left off. When Gregory died in 1858 at the age of eighty-two, his oldest child was sixty-two, his youngest seven. On the southern frontier of 1800, nearly 60 percent of the population was under the age of sixteen.[13] The Boones, as usual, were good examples. Daniel was one of ten children, Rebecca one of eleven. They produced ten of their own, and adopted six more.

The Boones were more than affectionate; they were practical. Families were extraordinarily efficient machines of production, transformation, and protection. They were the yeast cells of westward expansion. Most of the process of frontier conquest, the good and the bad of it, was done by men, women, and children acting as a unit, and consequently, few chose to live outside a household. Unattached adults were like unstable chemical elements, moving through the world in search of a bond. Bachelors quickly found wives, and widows soon remarried. The leading demographer of this period concludes that less than 1 percent of adult pioneers were single and planned to stay that way. On the frontier of fact, then, that prototype of the western hero, the supremely self-reliant long hunter,[14] the character based on Filson's Boone and expressed as Cooper's Leatherstocking and scores of others—that character was not just unusual. He was a freak.

Families were the mechanism by which the trans-Appalachian world was transformed. As with trade, what we see here is an initial shock of new influences, which quickly set off sequences of changes that went tumbling off in every direction, transformations of soil and plants and animals, mostly beyond the intent and certainly beyond the understanding and control of those who started them, all of this meshing with and diverting the course of earlier changes initiated by Indians who were, of course, also participating in the newer developments, by overhunting deer, for instance, in order to acquire trade goods, including guns with which they could both hunt animals and try to push out the whites who had got all these changes going in the first place.[15] In short, things got complicated.

That complication should prompt us to ask the third question about Boone's meeting, this time a more general one. The most intriguing questions of the historical account arise from its details: the French gun; Captain Will's name; the language, tone, and cadence of his peculiar speech about yellow jackets. Those details are the most striking departure from Filson's version. Filson's Indians are utterly unrecognizable as anything but creatures of the forest, almost as if they are a separate life form, whereas in the historical account their relationship to Boone is far more complex, a mix of antagonists and fraternity brothers. What is going on here? As ought to be evident after the discussion so far, the Shawnees' behavior, looks, and speech all were evidence of intricate developments that had been under way for more than a century. Boone was entering a world in which native and white cultures and lives already were inextricably wound into a knot beyond anyone's untangling.

If we could go back to that time and place, we would notice this first in material culture. The frontier of romance has always recognized that whites wore the Indians' buckskins and moccasins, but Indians also dressed in linsey-woolsey shirts, calico dresses, silk handkerchiefs, and felt hats. For that special occasion, natives of the Ohio country liked heavy silver earrings and black ostrich plumes for their hair. Early white farmers often lived in wigwam-like houses; some Indians lived in log cabins, cooked in brass kettles, ate on pewter plates, and slept in feather beds. So also in economic life. Shawnees raised cattle; Choctaws and Seminoles were the frontier's premier horse breeders and traders. We are used to thinking of Indians falling in love with white trade goods, but we should also remember that white settlers were forever gawking and grabbing at what they found in the Indians' trunk of marvels. Pioneers grew native crops—corn, beans, squash, pumpkins—by the native technique of intercropping. In fact, in the ways they supported themselves, families like the Boones were hunters and gatherers, slashers and burners basically no different from the peoples whose lands they were taking. Economic and material exchange inevitably led to an intertwined social life. At the Indian trading village of Auglaize in Ohio, for instance, French and English traders, Miami chiefs, and at least one Indian woman all attended meetings of a fraternal club they had formed called "The Friars of St. Andrews."[16]

This exchange was most intricate, and most troubling, among families, in particular in cases of the hundreds of so-called white Indians, Euro-Americans who moved back and forth among various cultures, usually after being captured and adopted into native society.[17] This group included many prominent figures, including the Iroquois leader Old White Chief, and Simon Girty, probably the most hated figure of the era. Boone, of course, was captured again by Shawnees during the Revolutionary War, adopted by chief Blackfish, and renamed Sheltowee, or Big Turtle—not to be confused with Little Turtle, the most respected military leader among the Miamis, whose wife, captured as a child, was named Peggy Ford. Their

son was William Wells, who was taken from a prominent Kentucky family
at the age of thirteen.

In all this, the most intriguing questions are, as always, the most difficult to answer. As native and white cultures grew toward common life-
ways, did they come as well to think alike? As the frontier's various peoples
stole each other's children and butchered and learned from one another,
did they also find themselves looking out on the world and seeing the same
things?

There are some provocative hints. Take, for instance, frontier religion.
White pioneers developed a distinctive religion that stressed a stark duality
of good and evil, the sudden grace of salvation, and a powerful God who, at
the End Time, would cleanse a world rotten with corruption. Their faith
inspired an astounding emotionalism, most famously in the camp meetings
early in the nineteenth century, in which hundreds sometimes fell into fits
of convulsive twitching and writhing. However else this religious style
might be explained, it at least reflected lives of unrelenting stress, the good-
and-evil perspective from a cabin surrounded by a host of dangers, and
above all the overwhelming presence of natural forces and power beyond
their understanding.

During the same years there arose among the Indians several new religions that borrowed heavily from Christianity, the most famous that of the
Shawnee prophet, born Lalawethika, brother of the military and political
leader Tecumseh. From a vision of his own death and resurrection, Lalawethika proclaimed a new gospel, given him by the Master of Life. This
new teaching expressed both hostility toward whites and a respect for their
seductive culture, which in his vision took the form of a gigantic, hideous
crab that had crawled out of the Atlantic, specifically from Boston, and was
marching into the continent. His disciples were to follow certain rigorous
moral teachings, to turn away from whites and their trade, and to perform
new rituals, one of which called for confession of sins while running strings
of beads slowly through their hands. If all this was done, the Master of Life
would restore harmony to the world and drive whites out of it. To an-
nounce his rebirth and new purpose, Lalawethika took a new name: Tenskwatawa, meaning the Open Door, or the One Who Opens the Door, probably inspired by Christ's words in (what else?) the Book of Revelation,
specifically chapter 3, verse 8: "Look, I have set before you an open door,
which no one is able to shut." [18]

What this looks like, from one angle, is a sprawling multicultural camp meeting, with Peter Cartwright and Tenskwatawa as twin revivalists in a common great awakening. As they dressed and hunted and fought alike, Indians and whites were growing *toward* each other in the ways they thought about God: the pioneers' view reflecting their forest world, the Shawnees' drawing on a Christian discipline and eschatology.

But, just to complicate things further, this common perception of the world could also be misleading. If whites and Indians came to think in similar ways, that definitely did *not* mean that their situations were the same. Indians and whites knew full well that they were headed toward different futures, and their religions reflected that, too. Backwoodsmen and Native Americans all were wrestling for control in a changing world, but while settlers were crying out to God for protection as those changes were being accomplished, the Open Door preached in desperation to reverse those same transformations. His was a theology of the last chance.

And Tenskwatawa, of course, had every reason to despair. Within a decade the frontier had rolled over and beyond his country, leaving a legacy that literary and historical romance cannot begin to suggest. A romance, Simms wrote in his preface to *The Yemassee*, is characterized by a "unity of plan, of purpose, and harmony of parts." The romantic frontier was a country with pieces distinct and in their places, and where lines and lessons were clearly drawn. But the historical frontier was a turbulent, bloody, fascinating mess: a cultural, biotic, social, economic, religious, viral, sartorial mess, and its lessons were of ambiguity, of conflict and confluence, of garbled identities, and of changes broader and deeper and more rapid than in practically any other period of our collective story. The frontier was a glorious confusion.

This is not to say that the frontier of romance is without consequence for the historian. Far from it. The mythic vision of the frontier was so seductive, its form and messages so appealing and so useful for so many needs of the expanding white society, that soon—amazingly soon—it became a shaping force in its own right. Even as the historical frontier was reaching its crest, the romantic telling of it was taking hold, bending reality in the minds not just of distant readers but of the actors in the story that still was unfolding. Myth became a participant. In this spirit we should let Boone have the last word. Many years after the encounter with the Shawnee, a visitor spent an evening listening to Boone read aloud from Filson's book. As he spun out this tale about his own wanderings in Eden, with its hairbreadth escapes from bold savages, the now-famous pioneer warmed to the moment, his face alight, and at the end put down the book and called out to the room: "All true! Every word true! Not a lie in it!"[19]

NOTES

1. The frontier and its part in the making of a national myth have inspired a large literature. For a representative sampling among the many works, see Henry Nash Smith, *Virgin Land*; Richard Slotkin, *Regeneration Through Violence*; R. W. B. Lewis, *The American Adam*; Arthur K. Moore, *The Frontier Mind*; and James R. Grossman, ed., *The Frontier*.

2. I have used a recent reprint: John Filson, *The Adventures of Colonel Daniel Boon [sic], Formerly a Hunter. . . .* The original appeared in John Filson, *The Discovery, Settlement, and Present State of Kentucke. . . .*

3. The following account is from John Mack Faragher's (79–82) recent biography of Boone, *Daniel Boone,* by far the best of many.

4. Historians and anthropologists recently have devoted considerable attention to the subtle and complex changes that the fur trade brought to Native American societies. Two outstanding examples are Arthur J. Ray, *Indians in the Fur Trade*; and Adrian Tanner, *Bringing Home Animals.* For an essay summarizing and discussing much of the new literature, see Jacqueline Peterson and John Anfinson, "The Indian and the Fur Trade."

5. W. Raymond Wood and Thomas D. Thiessen, eds., *Early Fur Trade*; and Abraham P. Nasatir, ed., *Before Lewis and Clark.*

6. Frank Norall, *Bourgmont.*

7. Some of the best synopses of movements of tribes in the Ohio Valley and Great Lakes area are found in Helen Hornbeck Tanner, ed., *Atlas.*

8. A pathbreaking study of this interrelationship among Europeans, Native Americans, and their environments is William Cronon, *Changes in the Land.*

9. Richard L. Haan, "The 'Trade Do's Not Flourish as Formerly.'"

10. The best survey of such changes remains Aldred W. Crosby, *Ecological Imperialism.*

11. Filson, *The Discovery, Settlement, and Present State of Kentucke . . .* , 52.

12. Peter H. Wood, "The Changing Population of the Colonial South." For an overview of the literature on Native American demographic decline, see Russell Thornton, *American Indian Holocaust and Survival.*

13. James E. Davis, *Frontier America,* 35, 75.

14. The expression "long hunter" comes out of Kentucky folklore and early Appalachian history. It refers to the first white hunters who crossed the Appalachian mountains from the piedmont and who were the first to scout and hunt in what is now Kentucky and Tennessee.

15. For basic studies of the trans-Appalachian frontier, all of which deal to some degree with the family and its significance, see Malcolm J. Rohrbough, *The Trans-Appalachian Frontier*; Reginald Horsman, *The Frontier in the Formative Years*; Terry G. Jordan and Matti Kaups, *The American Backwoods Frontier*; and Thomas D. Clark and John D. W. Guice, *Frontiers in Conflict*.

16. For a fascinating case study of this cultural mixing, see Helen Hornbeck Tanner, "The Glaize in 1792." The seminal work on this process and its implications is Richard White, *The Middle Ground*.

17. For an insightful discussion of this subject, see James Axtell, "The White Indians of Colonial America."

18. On Tenskwatawa and his religion, see R. David Edmunds, *The Shawnee Prophet*. For a discussion of such movements generally, not only among Native Americans but in other areas of European colonial expansion, see Vittorio Lanternari, *Religions of the Oppressed*.

19. Faragher, *Daniel Boone*, 7.

WORKS CITED

Axtell, James. "The White Indians of Colonial America." *The European and the Indian: Essays in the Ethnohistory of Colonial North America*. New York: Oxford University Press, 1981. 168–206.

Clark, Thomas D., and John D. W. Guice. *Frontiers in Conflict: The Old Southwest, 1795–1830*. Albuquerque: University of New Mexico Press, 1989.

Cronon, William. *Changes in the Land: Indians, Colonists, and the Ecology of New England*. New York: Hill and Wang, 1973.

Crosby, Aldred W. *Ecological Imperialism: The Biological Expansion of Europe, 900–1900*. New York: Cambridge University Press, 1986.

Davis, James E. *Frontier America, 1800–1840: A Comparative Demographic Analysis of the Settlement Process*. Glendale: H. H. Clark, 1977.

Edmunds, R. David. *The Shawnee Prophet*. Lincoln: University of Nebraska Press, 1983.

Faragher, John Mack. *Daniel Boone: The Life and Legend of an American Pioneer*. New York: Holt, 1992.

Filson, John. *The Discovery, Settlement, and Present State of Kentucke. . . .* Wilmington: James Adams, 1784. Rpt. as *The Adventures of Colonel Daniel Boon [sic], Formerly a Hunter. . . .* Xenia, Ohio: Old Chelicothe, 1967.

Grossman, James R., ed. *The Frontier in American Culture*. Berkeley: University of California Press. Chicago: University of Chicago Press, 1994.

Haan, Richard L. "The 'Trade Do's Not Flourish as Formerly': The Ecological Origins of the Yamassee War of 1715." *Ethnohistory* 28 (1981): 341–58.

Horsman, Reginald. *The Frontier in the Formative Years, 1783–1815*. New York: Holt, Rinehart and Winston, 1970.

Jordan, Terry G., and Matti Kaups. *The American Backwoods Frontier: An Ethnic and Ecological Interpretation*. Baltimore: Johns Hopkins University Press, 1989.

Lanternari, Vittorio. *Religions of the Oppressed*. New York: Knopf, 1963.

Lewis, R. W. B. *The American Adam: Innocence, Tragedy, and Tradition in the Nineteenth Century*. Chicago: University of Chicago Press, 1955.

Moore, Arthur K. *The Frontier Mind: A Cultural Analysis of the Kentucky Frontiersman*. Lexington: University Press of Kentucky, 1957.

Nasatir, Abraham P., ed. *Before Lewis and Clark: Documents Illustrating the History of the Missouri, 1785–1804*. St. Louis: St. Louis Historical Documents Foundation, 1952.

Norall, Frank. *Bourgmont, Explorer of the Missouri*. Edmonton: University of Alberta Press, 1988.

Peterson, Jacqueline, and John Anfinson. "The Indian and the Fur Trade: A Review of Recent Literature." *Scholars and the Indian Experience: Critical Reviews of Recent Writing in the Social Sciences*. Ed. R. R. Swagerty. Bloomington: University of Indiana Press, 1984. 223–57.

Ray, Arthur J. *Indians in the Fur Trade: Their Role as Hunters, Trappers and Middlemen in the Lands Southwest of Hudson Bay, 1660–1870*. Toronto: University of Toronto Press, 1974.

Rohrbough, Malcolm J. *The Trans-Appalachian Frontier: People, Societies, and Institutions, 1775–1850*. New York: Oxford University Press, 1978.

Simms, William Gilmore. *The Yemassee: A Romance of Carolina*. New and rev. ed. New York: Redfield, 1853.

Slotkin, Richard. *Regeneration Through Violence: The Mythology of the Frontier, 1600–1860*. Middletown: Wesleyan University Press, 1973.

Smith, Henry Nash. *Virgin Land: The American West as Symbol and Myth*. New York: Vintage, 1950.

Tanner, Adrian. *Bringing Home Animals: Religious Ideology and Mode of Production of the Mistassini Cree Hunters*. New York: St. Martin's, 1979.

Tanner, Helen Hornbeck. "The Glaize in 1792: A Composite Indian Community." *Ethnohistory* 25 (1978): 15–39.

——, ed. *Atlas of Great Lakes Indian History*. Norman: University of Oklahoma Press, 1987.

Thornton, Russell. *American Indian Holocaust and Survival: A Population History since 1492*. Norman: University of Oklahoma Press, 1987.

White, Richard. *The Middle Ground: Indians, Empires and Republics in the Great Lakes Region, 1650–1815*. Cambridge: Cambridge University Press, 1991.

Wood, Peter H. "The Changing Population of the Colonial South: An Overview by Race and Region, 1685–1790." *Powhatan's Mantle: Indians in the Colonial*

Southeast. Ed. Peter H. Wood, Gregory A. Waselkov, and M. Thomas Hatley. Lincoln: University of Nebraska Press, 1989. 35–103.

Wood, W. Raymond, and Thomas D. Thiessen, eds. *Early Fur Trade on the Northern Plains: Canadian Traders Among the Mandan and Hidatsa Indians, 1738–1818; The Narratives of John Macdonell, David Thompson, Francois-Antoine Laroque, and Charles McKenzie.* Norman: University of Oklahoma Press, 1985.

Simms and Literary Technique:
The Genre of the Frontier Novel

The "Untrodden Path": *Richard Hurdis* and Simms's Foray into Literary Realism

With *Richard Hurdis,* Simms was ahead of his time, anticipating realism and naturalism; he was again treading the "untrodden paths," creating a "new field" for himself.[1] Influenced by his knowledge of the John Murrell crime syndicate, Simms in *Richard Hurdis* made much more explicit use of the Murrell legend than in *Guy Rivers* in portraying the Mystic Brotherhood, a network of criminals that "harass[ed] the country from Georgia to Louisiana" (140).

Even the syndicate's leader in *Richard Hurdis,* Clement Foster, seems modeled upon the real-life Murrell. Foster, too, is a polished confidence man well educated and articulate enough to pose convincingly as a frontier evangelist trying to save the souls of riverboat gamblers and backwoods ruffians. And like Murrell, Foster rationalizes his crimes as actions against the wealthy committed on behalf of the poor, victimized and oppressed by an elitist privileged class. An emissary, in a well-rehearsed recital of propaganda for the Brotherhood, presents the Mystic Brotherhood as a benevolent Robin Hood–like society: "we are not common robbers, my brother; far from it. . . . Know from me that we are simply seekers of justice. . . . We are those who redress the wrongs and injuries of fortune, who protect the poor from the oppressor" (238–39).

Foster is pictured as a crafty, self-assured, at times witty and philosophical criminal whose leadership is unquestioned and whose authority is unchallenged by his selected followers. Yet in Simms's portrayal he is not devoid of compassion: in fact, Foster's character is ambivalent enough that, ironically, his presumably fake professions of idealism and altruism do not seem utterly the machinations of a charlatan, as Foster himself claims.

Simms was wont to portray outcasts and criminals more sympathetically than were most authors of this time, and his characterization of Clement

Foster illustrates the point. Without mitigating Foster's criminality, Simms presents Foster through the filtered vision of Richard Hurdis, who appears, almost against his better judgment, to be favorably disposed toward the racketeer. Almost from the beginning Hurdis seems to recognize that Foster is not the frontier's customary cold-blooded ruffian committed to greed and violence; Hurdis discerns in Foster "some lingering sentiments of humanity." Later, when Hurdis has ample opportunity to capture or kill the fleeing fugitive, he is reluctant to follow through. He is, however, spared the necessity of making a decision concerning Foster's fate by the outlaw's daring escape. Foster's departing good-humored shout to Hurdis demonstrates that strife and peril have affected neither his wit nor his will: "We shall meet some day in Arkansas, where I shall build a church in the absence of better business, and perhaps make you a convert. Farewell" (401–2).

Foster's heroics in eluding the clutches of the law create a kind of comic catharsis achieved nowhere else in Simms's fiction; this authorial capacity "to wonder and laugh at the complacent impudence" of the escaped outlaw is credible because it reflects the outlook of characters like Colonel Grafton as well as Hurdis. The position—that there are more important things to be done than to fret about one "clever scoundrel" who may one day "become an honest man"[2] and who in any event is moving out of the region to Arkansas—accurately reflects the attitude of the Alabama frontier of that day. Laissez-faire: leave well enough alone.

Clement Foster is not the only interesting outlaw in Simms's portrayal of the Mystic Brotherhood, and Simms is effective in bringing to life animated backwoods ruffians given to coarse manners and coarser language. Matthew Webber, Ben Pickett, and—to a lesser degree—Bully George are convincingly delineated; but Webber in particular merits consideration. Unlike the urbane and polished Foster, Webber is an uneducated underling of the lower class, whose smoldering resentment and envy of the elite rich are unmitigated by any veneer of sophistication. He is greedy and avaricious and, unlike Foster, he actually commits murderous deeds to fulfill a craving for money and status.

Webber is consumed with hatred for his superior, Colonel John Grafton, but not blind to the colonel's merits. In a particularly revealing commentary, Webber displays both his colorful vernacular and his pent-up anger: "Once, to tell you a *dog-truth*, I rather did like him myself. He was gentleman, to say the littlest for him; and, dang it! he made me feel it always when I stood before him. It was that very thing that made me come to dislike him" (164–65). Webber goes on to say that he "stood" Grafton's superior bearing "while I worked for him"—but once Webber "set up business" for himself, he "didn't care to have such a feeling." However it was not until Grafton "took it upon himself to give me advice . . . just as if he was my godfather" that Webber "kicked" and "broke loose" and "told him my mind" (165).

When Hurdis questions Webber's ability "to match with Colonel Grafton," Webber demonstrates his rage not only with words ("By my grinders . . . I would gripe him . . . [in] a death-hug") but also with his seemingly uncontrollable physical reaction: "The fellow's teeth gnashed as he spoke, and his mouth was distorted, and his eyes glared with an expression absolutely fiendish. . . . [D]ropping the end of the segar from his hand, he stuck forth his half-contracted fingers, as if in the effort to grasp his opponent's throat; and I almost fancied I beheld the wolf upon his leap. The nails of his fingers had not been cut for a month, and looked rather like the claws of a wild beast" (166).

Webber's animal-like arousal anticipates that of later naturalistic characters like Frank Norris's McTeague; but when Hurdis, appalled at the "hatred . . . festering in [Webber's] heart," immediately responds with a pointed query, "Why, if you hate him, do you not fight him?" the ruffian's predatory instinct is checked by a rational process that deters action even while sustaining rancor. Recognizing the reception such a challenge would evoke, he rejects Hurdis's suggestion: "Fight it out, indeed!—and how am I to make him fight? Send him a challenge? Ha! ha! ha! Why, he'd laugh at it, and so would you, young sir, if he showed you the challenge." Webber recognizes that it is the disparity of their positions that would evoke such humor: "What a joke for my neighbor democrats! Every rascal among them . . . would . . . laugh to split their sides to think of the impudence of that poor devil . . . in challenging . . . 'Squire Grafton, the great planter of Grafton Lodge!" His concluding line defines the underlying problem with effective simplicity: "You must think of some other fashion for righting poor men in this country" (166–67). Hurdis's suggestion that "[t]here is such a thing, you know, as taking the road of an enemy" brings scorn from the belligerent Webber: "Ha! . . . and . . . what do you think it would bring me to, here in Tuscaloosa county? I'll tell you in double quick time—the gallows. It wouldn't bring you to the gallows, or any man passing for a gentleman, but democrats can't bear to see democrats taking upon themselves the airs of gentlemen. They'd hang me, my good friend, if they didn't burn me beforehand" (168).

As if Simms were concerned that the reader might fail to note the social criticism at the heart of Webber's argument, or might discount it because of its source, Simms lets Hurdis ponder Webber's words and grant them a certain credence. Thus Hurdis, though shocked at Webber's concept of a societal system of justice so in favor of the landed gentry, nevertheless concedes that "[t]here was certainly some truth in what the fellow said."

Here, and throughout the Border Romances, Simms portrays a frontier justice that is governed by vigilante will more than by judiciary process, a situation he himself had personally observed. But he does more than depict the realities of the frontier: he allows his fictional figures to provide insight into the motivations, pointing out the inequities that so rancored the disenfranchised—and the manner in which these maligned, unfortunate, and sometimes vicious people sought to confront these injustices—and thereby records a significant era in American history.

In its original edition, *Richard Hurdis*—like *Guy Rivers* before it—was attacked (in Simms's own words) for having "too gloomy and savage a character" (10). Simms's response is a defense of realism in literature:

But the entire aspect of a sparsely-settled forest, or mountain country, is grave and saddening, even where society is stationary and consistent; and, where society is only in process of formation the saddening and the grave in its aspect are but too apt to take on even sterner features, and to grow into the gloomy and ferocious. It is quite enough, in answer to the objection, to say that the general portraiture is not only a truthful one, in the present case, but that the materials are really of historical character. The story is a genuine chronicle of the border region where the scene is laid, and of the period when the date is fixed. (10)

Simms concedes that "softer coloring" might have relieved "the intense and fierce aspects of the story" but, again in vindication of literary forthrightness, rejects such amelioration as inappropriate (10).

What Simms tries to do in *Richard Hurdis* is to portray the Alabama frontier of the 1820s and 1830s in its true colors, demonstrating its "wild and savage" nature as recorded in the "general history of the outlawry prevailing in the Mississippi valley." Twelve years earlier in a letter to a magazine editor he had proclaimed: "a true writer—an earnest man, full of subject . . . must lay it as bare as possible. He must roll up his sleeves to it, and not heed the blushes of the sophisticated damsel, who is shocked at the bare, brawny arms" (*Letters* 1:263). Can there be any doubt that Simms's approach to depicting the frontier was to "roll up his sleeves" and "lay it . . . bare"?

Simms's personal predilection was for genteel city and plantation life (witness his choice for Charleston—and later, Woodlands—over the Southwest); yet Simms perceived that the frontier held the key to America's development. And portrayal of the frontier in his fiction reflects that insight: ugly and violent, cruel and corrupt, the frontier tested the courage, the perseverance, the very hardihood of the pioneers; yet it provided them opportunity to begin life anew, to find hope and meaning as individuals, as contributing members of a society still in formation. The "Mississippi mad" emigrants from "one of the poorest parts of North Carolina" who were "bent to better their condition in the western valleys" are a case in point: "They were a simple and hardy people, looking poor, but proud; and though evidently neither enterprising nor adventurous, yet once abroad and in the tempest, sufficiently strong and bold to endure and to defy its buffeting. There was a venerable grandfather of the flock, one of the finest heads I ever looked upon, who mingled the smiling elasticity of youth, with the garrulity of age. He spoke as sanguinely of his future prospects in Mississippi, as if he were only now about to commence the world" (66). But to the young protagonist-narrator, Richard Hurdis, the "mere movement" of the "self-expatriated wanderer, with his motley caravan" winding its way through the forest and prairie wilderness, was "picturesque in the last degree"—a picturesqueness "not a whit diminished by the something of melancholy" (67). Such strains of romanticism recur in Simms even in otherwise realistic depictions of the frontier; that he possessed a romantic sense of delight in the beauty of nature is manifest in sensuous passages such as this:

> The afternoon . . . was one of the loveliest among the lovely days so frequent in the Alabama November. The glances of the oblique sun rested with a benignant smile, like that of some venerable and single-hearted sire, upon the groves of the forest. . . . The cold airs of coming winter had been just severe enough to put a flush-like glow into the cheeks of the leaf, and to envelop the green, here and there, with a coating of purple and yellow, which served it as some rich and becoming border, and made the brief remains of the gaudy summer seem doubly rich. (102)

In sharp contrast to the almost poetic quality of this tranquil description is the stark intensity of the graphic and fierce death struggle of Emmeline

Walker. While, as Thomas L. McHaney has noted, the young woman "dies of a broken heart, suffering shock, madness, and death over the murder of her betrothed, like so many daughters of sentimental fiction," the depiction of her state is exact and disturbing; in McHaney's understated assessment, "there is little sentimentality in the way Simms's handles it" (187). The passage detailing Walker's excruciating death (279–81) testifies to Simms's willingness to be explicit at a time when the use of unpleasant details was deemed inappropriate and offensive. In *Richard Hurdis*, as in *Guy Rivers*, "the ugliness, the lawlessness, the brutality of the early nineteenth-century American frontier were fully exposed. Long before William Dean Howells, Simms perceived the necessity of replacing belles-lettres's 'ideal grasshopper . . . the good old romantic card-board grasshopper' with a 'real grasshopper . . . simple, honest, and natural.'" Simms's frontier, like Howells's grasshopper, is ugly and real—not ideal and uplifting—and deserves recognition of its authenticity (cf. Guilds 58–59).

In one particular aspect *Richard Hurdis* stands out from its predecessor *Guy Rivers* and its sequel *Border Beagles*, for Simms's foray into literary realism extends here beyond the revelation of the "simple, honest, and natural" as advocated by Howells, beyond the "lay[ing] it . . . bare" he himself advocated and practiced. In *Hurdis* Simms approaches another dimension of literary realism: he makes trial with the idea of limiting point of view to that of a "single vessel of consciousness," a technique perfected some four decades later by Henry James. In *Hurdis* Simms experiments with narrative voice and point of view; he adopts a first-person protagonist-narrator who not only records his own thoughts, emotions, words, and actions, as would be expected, but also—by "filling up gaps in his own experience" through "the report of others," and by writing his story "after a lapse of time"— reports events in which he does not participate. Thus, in a sense Simms attempts to have it both ways: he seeks to achieve the sense of reality in the narrative by having the vision limited to the protagonist; and at the same time he seeks to present a well-rounded tale, usually dependent upon authorial omniscience.[3] The narrative stance Simms follows here allows Hurdis as narrator to address the reader directly and to take the reader into his confidence. Simms playfully attributes authorial concern to his protagonist-narrator, allowing him, for example, to state: "Let me unfold the doings of others, necessarily connected with my own, which are proper to be made known to the reader in this place, though only known to me long after their occurrence" (72). Commentary that reflects Simms's own views is also now cast as Richard Hurdis's own: "Enough, for the present, to know that he was even then meditating as dark a piece of villainy, as the domestic historian of the frontier was ever called to record."

In the "Advertisement" to the 1855 Redfield edition, Simms argues that "something is gained" in this "peculiarity in the arrangement of the story" and points to a "more energetic, direct and dramatic character," attributable in no small part to the narrator's personal involvement in the action of the novel and to a greater "rapidity of . . . action" resulting "from the exclusion of all circuitous narration" customarily associated with omniscience (11–12). Simms's efforts to restrict point of view to a single introspective protagonist-narrator caught the attention of Edgar Allan Poe, himself interested in narrative innovation. In an 1841 review of *Confession*, another of the novels in which Simms experimented with narrative stance, Poe claimed that Simms's "fine talent" should not be buried in "themes," as in *The Yemassee*, because his "genius does not lie in the outward so much as in the inner world," which Poe termed Simms's "proper field of exertion" (306). Poe's commentary—though it also supports his own theory of literature—points up a largely overlooked fact: Simms was not only a forerunner in his advocacy and practice of realism in language and in subject matter, he was also a precursor in exploring a technique later to be associated with literary realism.

Despite an absence of scholarly recognition of Simms as a literary experimentalist, his new ideas in the development of fiction as well as his pioneering efforts in putting these theories to test must be taken into account in any credible assessment of his overall achievement. And that achievement—of which his realistic delineation of the frontier is no small part—is of a magnitude now slowly being recognized: "Simms's fiction breathes with the vitality of the American frontier. The harsh, brutal frontier of Simms's experience and observation contrasts sharply with the idealized frontier of Cooper's imagination and reading. Realistic portrayal of the frontier is uniquely the power and the glory of Simms as an author" (350).[4]

NOTES

We are indebted to the University of Arkansas Press for permission for the use of portions of the afterword to *Richard Hurdis: A Tale of Alabama*, ed. John Caldwell Guilds, in this essay.

1. *Charleston Courier*, July 19, 1834. See Guilds 55.

2. When asked, "Shall I give him a shot, colonel?" Grafton replies: "No, no! let him go. He is a clever scoundrel and may one day become an honest man" (402). (Earlier Grafton had commented that Foster "seems not without good qualities" [381]). In another connection, illustrating the prevailing concept of frontier justice, Grafton expresses no desire "to bring [Eberly] to trial," despite knowledge of the youth's commission of crime (385).

3. See 146, 155, 290–91, 300, and 384 for additional evidence of Simms's struggle with narrative technique. The "authorial" insertions by the fictive narrator Hurdis are designed to elucidate the nature of the narrative itself. This allows Simms to maintain the fiction that Hurdis is writing of events in which he himself had firsthand knowledge—a feature designed to buttress the authenticity of the tale while allowing him as narrator to supplement his own personally experienced scenes with information garnered subsequently and hence to flesh out his tale for the reader. Only at times does Simms allow Hurdis to provide information to which he was not privy without explanation as to his acquisition of that information.

4. Guilds 350.

WORKS CITED

Guilds, John Caldwell. *Simms: A Literary Life.* Fayetteville: University of Arkansas Press, 1992.

McHaney, Thomas L. "William Gilmore Simms." *The Chief Glory of Every People: Essays on Classic American Writers.* Ed. Matthew J. Bruccoli. Carbondale: Southern Illinois University Press, 1973. 173–90.

Poe, Edgar Allan. Rev. of *Confession*, by William Gilmore Simms. *Graham's* 19 (1841): 306.

Simms, William Gilmore. *The Letters of William Gilmore Simms.* 5 vols. Ed. Mary C. Simms Oliphant, Alfred Taylor Odell, and T. C. Duncan Eaves. Columbia: University of South Carolina Press, 1952–1956. (A sixth volume, *The Letters of William Gilmore Simms: Supplement [1834–1870]*, ed. Oliphant and Eaves, was published by the University of South Carolina Press in 1982.)

———. *Richard Hurdis: A Tale of Alabama.* New and rev. ed. New York: Redfield, 1855.

———. *Richard Hurdis: A Tale of Alabama.* Ed. John Caldwell Guilds. Fayetteville: University of Arkansas Press, 1995.

RAYBURN S. MOORE

William Gilmore Simms's *Guy Rivers* and the Frontier

G*uy Rivers*, William Gilmore Simms's first "regular novel," as he calls it, was begun in 1832, the year following his return from his third trip to the Southwest, was finished—"bating corrections"—by December 1833, and published in the early summer of 1834.[1] Though Simms had not traveled in the North Georgia mountains at the time of composition, the book obviously owed much to his journeys elsewhere in Georgia—he knew the area from Augusta to Milledgeville to Macon to Columbus pretty well—and to his experience in the Southwest. The novel also owed much to his reading about the "upper part" of the state, then in the news because of the attempt to suppress and drive out the Cherokees and the concurrent discovery of gold in the Auraria region in the late 1820s and early 1830s.[2]

Both of these topics are touched on at the beginning of the novel. The very first sentence in chapter 1 notes the Cherokee matter: "Our scene lies in the upper part of the state of Georgia, a region at this time fruitful of dispute, as being within the Cherokee territories." Two paragraphs later the significance of gold to the scene is mentioned: "We are," the narrator observes, "upon the very threshold of the gold country, so famous for its prolific promise of the precious metal. . . . Nor, though only the frontier and threshold as it were to these swollen treasures, was the portion of country now under survey, though bleak, sterile, and uninviting, wanting in attractions of its own" (14).[3]

Nevertheless, despite the fact that these subjects serve generally as context for a story, as Simms points out in the "Advertisement" to the first edition, concerned with the "career of crime" and its causes, a focus substantially maintained in his revision twenty years later in 1855 in the Redfield edition (11), the frontier itself serves as a powerful influence on the lives of some of the characters and on the action of the novel.

The story line, for example, involves young Ralph Colleton, the nephew of a well-established South Carolina planter at odds with his uncle over the hand of Edith, his cousin. Leaving Carolina for Tennessee, Ralph is way-laid on the frontier in North Georgia by Guy Rivers, a former respectable lawyer now engrossed in crime in this new territory, and his colleague, Wat Munro, a local landlord, publican, and member of the Pony Club, a band of ruffians based upon the notorious group of the same name, widely known in the region for stealing horses and preying on innocent travelers. Consequently, most of the novel's action takes place in or near Chestatee, a village in the "gold country" in many respects resembling, according to the narrator, "some ten out of every dozen of the country towns . . . in all the interior settlements of the South and West" (60). Moreover, this largely lawless area is the "wildest . . . of the then little-settled state of Georgia" (56).

In this "debatable land," Ralph is shot and wounded during his con-frontation with Guy Rivers and is then rescued by Mark Forrester, a backwoodsman, whose name surely characterizes him aptly. Subsequently, Ralph is wrongly accused of murder and is saved from conviction by the intervention of Lucy Munro, the landlord's niece who is smitten with Ralph, and other settlers. In the final analysis, he is reunited with Edith, forgiven by his uncle, and all's well that ends well.

The frontier, then, is border country, sparsely settled and without the conventions of civilization. Guy Rivers, as Simms declares early and late, is a "border novel," a tale "of a frontier and wild people, and the events are precisely such as may occur among a people in a region of that character" (*Letters* 1:55).

Such country, to be sure, is wild in that nature has not yet been tamed by the settlers and law and order have not yet been firmly established. The people who have come to the area are there to seek new land and opportu-nity or to get away for one reason or another from an older society, and frequently they tend not to be overly nice about establishing or reestab-lishing certain forms and practices they had left behind.[4] In the case of Guy Rivers himself, for instance, there is downright antipathy to the old order and a determination to disavow and denigrate traditional standards of justice and democratic rule. Of course, some, as in the case of Jared Bunce, a typical Yankee peddler, are only too happy to ply their trade and line their pockets by the same guile and chicanery they practiced before leaving home in the first place. Bunce, it should be noted, remains in partnership with his brother in Connecticut until near the end of the novel. And, assuredly, Ralph, Edith, and William Colleton plan to return to Carolina to carry on the well-established plantation life to which they all belong. Though a frequent proponent of "paddling his own canoe," as he puts it, Bunce nevertheless decides to set up a "country store" among them.

But those who plan to stay in the border country, even for a short time, have little use for the constraints of the law and the frustration of tradition and convention. Peter Pippin, the pettifogging lawyer, for example, moves on to Mississippi and eventually is "elevated," the narrator notes ironically, through the agency of his "fine practice" and the notoriety of his "stump-speeches," to the state legislature.

Despite certain formulaic qualities in some of the scenes and characters, Simms manages, on occasion, to imbue his background and people with the stamp of reality. The area into which Ralph Colleton wanders in the beginning of the novel offers a good example of the natural world of the Chestatee area: "one of those regions of brown, broken, heathery waste, thinly mottled with tree and shrub, which seem usually to distinguish the first steppes on the approach to our mountain country. Though undulating, and rising occasionally into hill and crag, the tract was yet sufficiently monotonous; rather saddened than relieved by the gentle sunset, which seemed to gild in mockery the skeleton woods and forests, just recovering from the keen biting blasts of a severe and protracted winter" (18).

Into this "mournful barrenness" Ralph Colleton, his melancholy spirit appearing to be in "full unison" with his surroundings and "unable . . . to avoid the train of sad thought which such a scene was so eminently calculated to inspire," is barely aware of "the faint hum of a single woodchuck, . . . the only object which at intervals broke through the spell of silence which hung so heavily upon the scene" (18). Thus in less than a page the character and scene are related and linked.

Still, it must be admitted, stereotypes abound among those of the planter class and those of the criminal group as well. Ralph Colleton, for example, is a typical young Carolinian of good family who goes forth to make his fortune elsewhere in order to return to win Edith's hand and show his Uncle William that he can make his own way without help or support from his father's brother. He fails in this mission and is saved from backwoods justice by the intervention of Mark Forrester and the testimony of Lucy Munro, the niece of Guy Rivers's chief henchman, Wat Munro. Nevertheless, Ralph gets his girl and his uncle's approval and apparently what will be a long and happy life in Carolina. The frontier, seemingly, has had little influence on his character, though it has provided rich experience that would, under other circumstances, have helped him to grow up.

Some of the other characters are, if anything, even more typical than he is. Emily is sweet and innocent and true. William Colleton is the heavy-handed father on the one hand and on the other a guardian who is blinded by pride and success and cannot bridge the generation gap until the end. Lucy Munro may be more independent and not so well-bred as Edith, but she is a carbon copy of Edith's virtue on a lower social scale. The frontier, one may observe, has hardly changed these characters. Not so with Guy Rivers and Wat Munro. Rivers is a Byronic figure who has been, in his view, ill-treated by society and who goes into another country to recoup his fortune and plan his revenge. His lieutenant, Munro, follows his lead, but balks at times, especially when Lucy's fortunes are involved. Nevertheless, this lawless locale allows them to express freely the worst sides of their natures.

Moreover, the well-born characters speak a language very much like that of similar characters in the fiction of the period and described later by Mark Twain in his famous essay on Fenimore Cooper (1895) as "gilt-edged" and "hand-tooled." Consider, for example, part of the conversation between Ralph and Edith when the former tries to explain to his betrothed Lucy Munro's refusal to see Edith. Ralph announces: "Now, Edith, you who know me so well, tell me, can you think it possible that I have done, or said anything which has been calculated to make you suppose that I loved her— that I sought her. In short, do you think me capable of playing the scoundrel?" (482). Edith's response is equally high-toned: "Pshaw, Ralph, how can you afflict yourself with any such notions? I have no doubt of the perfect propriety of your conduct, and I will venture to say that Miss Munro entertains no reproaches" (482). Nor can Lucy Munro, despite her lower social rank, find a language much different when she finally agrees to join Ralph and Edith in their new home in Carolina in a sort of virtuous ménage à trois: "Do with me as you will, Edith, my sister," murmurs Lucy "lovingly" (486).

Earlier Lucy and Rivers himself had used the language of melodrama as he "was hauling her away" (263).

> With a husky horror in her voice, she cried out:—
> "You dare not! monster as you are, you dare not" then shrieking, at the full height of her voice—"Save me, uncle! save me! save me!"

"Save you! [Rivers exclaims] It is he that dooms you! He has given you up to any fate that I shall decree!"

"Liar! away! I defy you. You dare not, ruffian! Your foul threat is but meant to frighten me." (262)[5]

And Rivers uses a similar idiom when he mortally wounds himself in his last tryst with Ellen, another of those women whom he has "dishonored": "It is well, I am weak," he says. "Let me place my head upon your bosom. It is some time, Ellen, since it has been there. How wildly does it struggle! Pray, Ellen, that it beat not long. It has a sad office! now—lips—give me your lips, Ellen. You have forgiven me—all—everything?" (502).

This language, of course, is that of most contemporaneous fiction, as Mark Twain suggested in his criticism of Cooper, and it is therefore hardly strange that Simms employs it in a plot including well-born characters and a love story. It also serves as a contrast to the earthy dialect of backwoods folk, a matter touched on by Mary Ann Wimsatt and others, but as yet, as far as I can tell, to be dealt with fully in *Guy Rivers*.[6]

The speech of the frontier characters is erratic, however. Mark Forrester, for example, uses the backwoods lingo in some instances, but in his love scenes with Katharine Allen, his grammar and vocabulary are hardly different from Ralph Colleton's. Forrester's first talk with Colleton—whose wounds he is tending—deals with the "hubbub" in the village and is close to the vernacular:

> Well, squire, did you ever see a live Yankee? . . . He's a pedler you know, and that means a chap what can wheedle the eyes out of your head, the soul out of your body, the gold out of your pocket, and give you nothing but brass, and tin, and copper, in the place of 'em. Well, all the hubbub you hear is jest now about one of these same Yankee pedlers. The regilators have caught the varmint—one Jared Bunce, as he calls himself—and a more cunning, rascally, presumptious critter don't come out of all Connecticut. (69)

This diction may be readily contrasted to Mark's speech as he seeks to explain to Kate why he must leave for the Southwest without her: "It is this very thought, Kate, that I have made you miserable, when I should have striven only to make you happy. The thought, too, that I must leave you, to see you perhaps never again—these unman—these madden me, Katharine" (218).

Other language, on occasion, is saltier than Forrester's idiom, as in the case of Jared Bunce and an emigrating farmer headed for the "valley of the Mississippi" with his "old woman," his two sons, and a small "*force*" of six slaves and "three or four little negro children." When the farmer's wagon is stuck in a "slough," Bunce helps remove it and is thanked accordingly: "Well, by dogs, we've had a tough 'bout of it, boys; and, hark 'ye, stranger, gi' us your hand. I don't know what we should have done without you, for I never seed man handle a little poleaxe as you did that same affair of your'n" (315). And Bunce is quick to reply: "Well, now, I guess, friend, you an't far wide of your reckoning. I've been a matter of some fifteen or twenty years knocking about, off and on, in one way or another, with this same instrument, and pretty's the service now, I tell ye, that it's done me in that bit of time" (315).

Simms also demonstrates that he can handle Negro dialect, as the reader learns from Caesar, one of William Colleton's slaves, who seeks unsuccessfully to accompany Ralph on his journey to Tennessee: "And what we all for do here, when you leff? speck ebbery ting be dull, wuss nor ditch-water. No more fun—no more shuffle-foot. Old maussa no like de fiddle, and nebber hab party and jollication like udder people. Don't tink I can stay here, Mass Ra'ph, after you gone; 'spose, you no 'jection, I go 'long wid you? You leff me, I take to de swamp, sure as a gun" (55).

And the unidentified narrator himself can readily employ the idiom of the forest, as may be observed in the introduction of Mark Forrester to the wild region where Ralph Colleton lies wounded: "There was a whoop and a halloo, and then a catch of song, and then a shrill whistle, all strangely mingled together, finally settling down into a rude strain, which, coming from stentorian lungs, found a ready echo in every jutting rock and space of wood for a mile round" (57).

The frontier, then, in *Guy Rivers* is a mixture of elements, as is the novelistic form, and Simms frequently refers to the book as a novel in discussing the first edition in the early 1830s and also in describing the revision in the mid-1850s. The frontier is that land where primitive conditions prevail and where civilization has yet to take hold. The characters and the language illustrate this mixture of the savage and the civilized, and Georgia at the time of the novel is "little-settled" and wild, "doubly wild," according to the narrator, "as forming the debatable land between the savage and the civilized—partaking of the ferocity of the one and the skill, cunning, and cupidity of the other" (56). Still, this is new territory, and Simms is the first to deal with it in a novel. Longstreet, it is true, was publishing his sketches of Georgia scenes in Augusta and Milledgeville papers in 1832–1834, but these pieces were not collected until 1835, a year after the publication of *Guy Rivers*. Whatever the novel's faults, then, it is a pioneering attempt to introduce and deal with fresh American background and materials. As John Caldwell Guilds observes: "In *Guy Rivers* for the first time in our literature the ugliness, the lawlessness, the brutality of the early nineteenth-century American frontier were fully exposed. . . . Simms's frontier . . . is ugly and real—not ideal and uplifting, but it is deserving of belated recognition of its authenticity" (58–59).

NOTES

Some of the material in this essay was collected for the appearance of *Guy Rivers* in the proposed centennial edition of *The Writings of William Gilmore Simms*, a volume, among others, that failed to appear because of insufficient funds. I am grateful to John C. Guilds, the late John R. Welsh, and E. L. Inabinett, South Caroliniana Library, for gracious hospitality and constant cooperation then, and to Margaret B. Moore for generous help with word processing now.

1. See *The Letters of William Gilmore Simms* 1:55, 57, 59–61; 5:357. Subsequent references are to volume and page number and are included, where practicable, within the text. Simms's memory apparently fails him when he states in the "Dedicatory Epistle" to the revised edition that "the first volume . . . was written before I was of age" (10).

2. For Simms's travels to the Southwest, see Hampton N. Jarrell, W. Stanley Hoole, James E. Kibler Jr., "*The Album*" and "The First Simms Letters," and Miriam J. Shillingsburg. That Simms used experiences from his trip through Georgia in 1831 was subsequently maintained by a member of the family he had visited "thirty miles west" of Macon. "The wild stories then in circulation of daring adventure and the wild lawless life of the frontier had attracted [Simms's] attention," John Crowell observed in 1872, "and he determined to see for himself. It was upon this journey," Crowell concludes, "that he obtained materials for Guy Rivers." See Hoole 335–46. For Auraria and the Georgia gold rush, see E. Merton Coulter.

3. Since recent reprints are usually based upon Simms's revision of the novel, all citations to *Guy Rivers* are to the Redfield edition (New York, 1855), unless otherwise specified, but since the focus of this essay is upon Simms's treatment of the frontier in the early 1830s, they have been collated with the first edition. Page references are given in the body of the text. The new edition of *Guy Rivers* edited by John Caldwell Guilds (Fayetteville: University of Arkansas Press, 1993)

was not available when I prepared this essay, but I have consulted it in subsequent revision.

4. A passage in the second chapter of the first edition, considerably modified in revision, is to the point here: "He [Ralph Colleton] knew the danger and hopelessness of a second encounter with men sufficiently odious, in common report, to make him doubly cautious, after the adventure so nearly fatal. Exiled from society, after having acquired a large taste for many of its enjoyments, they found in the frontier impunity for those crimes and offences, for the punishment of which it had imposed ineffectual and defrauded penalties; and conscious of no responsibility to divine or human spirit, the result of their tact outlawry, had prompted them to retort upon men the stern severities of justice" (1:24–25). For the revised passage, see the Redfield edition (1855), 33.

5. Part of this passage was added in the revised edition in 1855. In this instance, twenty years had done little to change Simms's language.

6. Wimsatt's most recent treatment of the novel may be found in chapter 5 of *The Major Fiction of William Gilmore Simms* (120–27).

WORKS CITED

Coulter, E. Merton. *Auraria: The Story of a Georgia Gold-Mining Town.* Athens: University of Georgia Press, 1956.

Guilds, John Caldwell. *Simms: A Literary Life.* Fayetteville: University of Arkansas Press, 1992.

Hoole, W. Stanley. "A Note on Simms's Visits to the Southwest." *American Literature* 6 (1934): 334–36.

Jarrell, Hampton N. "Simms's Visits to the Southwest." *American Literature* 5 (1933): 29–35.

Kibler, James E. "*The Album* (1826): The Significance of the Recently Discovered Second Volume." *Studies in Bibliography* 39 (1986): 62–78.

———. "The First Simms Letters: 'Letters from the West' (1826)." *Southern Literary Journal* 19, no. 2 (1987): 81–91.

Shillingsburg, Miriam J. "The Senior Simmses—Mississippi Unshrouded." *University of Mississippi Studies in English* 10 (1992): 250–55.

Simms, William Gilmore. *Guy Rivers: A Tale of Georgia.* 2 vols. New York: Harper and Brothers, 1834.

———. *Guy Rivers: A Tale of Georgia.* New and rev. ed. New York: Redfield, 1855.

———. *Guy Rivers: A Tale of Georgia.* Ed. John Caldwell Guilds. Fayetteville: University of Arkansas Press, 1993.

———. *The Letters of William Gilmore Simms.* 5 vols. Ed. Mary C. Simms Oliphant, Alfred Taylor Odell, and T. C. Duncan Eaves. Columbia: University of South

Carolina Press, 1952–1956. (A sixth volume, *The Letters of William Gilmore Simms: Supplement [1834–1870]*, ed. Oliphant and Eaves, was published by the University of South Carolina Press in 1982.)

Twain, Mark. "Fenimore Cooper's Literary Offences." *Collected Tales, Sketches, Speeches, and Essays, 1891–1910*. New York: Library of America, 1992.

Wimsatt, Mary Ann. *The Major Fiction of William Gilmore Simms: Cultural Traditions and Literary Form*. Baton Rouge: Louisiana State University Press, 1989.

JAN BAKKER

Simms on the Literary Frontier; or, So Long Miss Ravenel and Hello Captain Porgy: *Woodcraft* Is the First "Realistic" Novel in America

We dare not speak of legs, or thighs, in the presence of many nice ladies. . . . We . . . have had to soften one of [Shakespeare's *Merry Wives of Windsor*] words into "female dog," "feminine dog," or something equally inoffensive and equally stupid; but while it would be perfectly moral to say "bitch," where the sense called for it, it would be proof of an immodest thought, in the mind of the speaker, who should say "female dog."
> —WILLIAM GILMORE SIMMS TO PHILIP C. PENDLETON,
>   August 12, 1841 (*Letters* 1)

Melo-dramatically considered real life is frequently a failure.
> —JOHN WILLIAM DEFOREST, *Miss Ravenel's Conversion*

I am trying to be as commonplace as I can be.
> —GERTRUDE STEIN, *The Autobiography of Alice B. Toklas*

Realistic characters and scenes in William Gilmore Simms's *Woodcraft* (1852–1854) are not incidental to a romance design. A preferential use of literary realism is Simms's sui generis intent throughout the novel. My thesis is supported by other studiedly realistic tales he wrote in the decades of the 1850s and 1860s, and by specific ideas on writing he expressed in letters and magazine articles throughout his literary life. Simms's pervasive use of realistic detail or elements in *Woodcraft*, his major novel, sets a remarkable and heretofore unacknowledged antebellum Southern precedent for the believable, the actual, the everyday, and the commonplace in American fiction as these basic elements of literary realism are later employed or, better, imitated by John William DeForest in his major postbellum Northern fiction, the critically and erroneously touted "first" consistently realistic novel in the American canon, *Miss Ravenel's Conversion from Secession to Loyalty* (1867).

Of William Gilmore Simms's many fictions, there is no doubt for me that his self-termed "domestic novel," *Woodcraft* (1852–1854), is his real masterpiece. To be sure, there is that annoying preference some people, such as Louis D. Rubin Jr., insist on having for *The Yemassee* (1835) as Simms's best long fiction. Such strange preference for this turgid romance of colonial Indian warfare in South Carolina has enabled unsympathetic readers and critics to relegate Simms to the status in the canon of a second-rate romancer somewhere below James Fenimore Cooper. So much for William Gilmore Simms, then.

For me, though, there is no question that in *Woodcraft* Simms finds his true narrative voice and it places him squarely on the frontier of American literary realism. For one thing, here he is at his relaxed and comic best in writing style and story direction. And, for that most significant other thing, realism in *Woodcraft* is not incidental to a romance design. Literary realism is William Gilmore Simms's sui generis intent throughout, although I must admit to having lumped *Woodcraft* among antebellum Southern romances in a previous study of American pastorals (68–82). My thesis is supported both by other consciously realistic tales he wrote during the 1850s and 1860s, and by ideas on writing he expressed in letters and in magazine articles during his entire career as a novelist.[1]

Simms's persistent, very conscious use of realistic detail or elements in *Woodcraft* sets a remarkable and heretofore unrecognized precedent in antebellum Southern fiction for the believable, the actual, the everyday, and the commonplace in the American novel as these qualities of literary realism later are used or imitated in John William DeForest's rather ineptly titled *Miss Ravenel's Conversion from Secession to Loyalty* (1867). Erroneously so far, critics have touted this, his major postbellum Northern fiction, as the "first" realistic novel in the American canon. The focus of my discussion here of the pervasive realism of *Woodcraft* is limited to what generally are considered the three essential elements of the realistic literary mode: character, action, and scene.

Look at Simms's unusual hero in *Woodcraft*: fat, gluttonous, bibulous, pig-eyed, garrulous Captain Porgy of Swamp Fox Francis Marion's Revolutionary War partisans. Great-bellied Porgy: gentlemanly in manner, heroic in deed, thoughtful in philosophy, an Old South Falstaff or Simms himself, who, I have read in William Peterfield Trent, sometimes actually identified himself with Porgy (109). He is Simms's most memorable character. Porgy is the greatest hero-protagonist of any, I will say, in the fiction of the antebellum South. This evaluation holds as well for the novel's heroine, Widow Eveleigh. The widow is Porgy's plump and middle-aged planter neighbor and savior in civilian life. She is a steel magnolia if ever there were one. So, if it holds true that a large part of the definition of literary realism involves an emphasis on character, I would have to say that *Woodcraft* surely fits the bill on the basis of these two "hero" characters alone.

Simms's emphasis is on Porgy's character. And as selfmockingly extravagant in his conversation as Porgy usually is, he is in the end a mere farmer, an unexceptional impoverished army veteran of the American Revolution, living in fiction in the era of another exceptional frontier—the founding of an independent and democratic United States. He is a very ordinary man, one as commonplace as the great generator of realism in United States fiction, William Dean Howells, could have advocated. There is nothing "Marvelous"—a tag Nathaniel Hawthorne gives the romance in his preface (1) to *The House of the Seven Gables* (1851)—about Porgy or his friends or his antagonists, or about the story of the restoration of his plantation. There is nothing marvelous or "wild and wonderful" or "epic"—tags Simms himself gives the romance in his preface (v–vi) to *The Yemassee*—in any of the characters, actions, and scenes in *Woodcraft*.

For the first time ever in American fiction, the action in a novel is all about a soldier's return home from the war, and the day-to-day restoration of his ruined property through lots of hard work, some bold action, and just good luck. There is nothing melodramatic or cataclysmic or high-flown in Simms's descriptions here, as there is, say, in Herman Melville's Ahab and his grand quest for Moby Dick and the resulting crashing death of the *Pequod* and her crew; or in the stagey life and death of Simms's own Faustian Guy Rivers or Voltmeier. *Woodcraft*'s final great hand-to-hand fight between the villains M'Kewn and Bostwick, for instance, is indicative of nothing more than the typical eyegouging, ear- or nose-tearing fistfights of the American frontier that Simms the hunter, fisherman, and traveler of the South's back roads knew as well as he knew the plantation-house parlor.

No: if anything, *Woodcraft* in its characters, actions, and scenes simply attains that element of truth, of adherence to the actual in life that Simms (like William Dean Howells) often commented is the end of fiction and its validation. In terms of the other kind of American fiction produced in the time of *Woodcraft*—such as Melville's *Moby Dick* (1851), Harriet Beecher Stowe's *Uncle Tom's Cabin* (1852), Caroline Lee Hentz's *Marcus Warland* (1852), Hawthorne's *The House of the Seven Gables*—(and with thanks to Gertrude Stein for the phrasing [225]), Simms's masterpiece is just as commonplace as it can be. It shows Southern life in the ordinary light of day, all "true to the motives, the impulses, the principles that shape the life of actual men and women," as Howells put it (92–104) in those germinal statements for realism in fiction he makes in *Criticism and Fiction* (1891).

Briefly, then, let us take a closer look at Porgy's character, and that of the Virginia planter on the Union side in the Civil War whom John William DeForest depicts in *Miss Ravenel's Conversion*. DeForest's picture of Colonel John Carter has been praised often for its worth both as a sharp literary characterization and as an astute criticism of the dissolute Southern planter type: "In his strong passions, his capacity for domestic sympathies, his strange conscience (as sensitive on some points as callous on others), his spendthrift habits, his inclination to swearing and drinking, his mixture in short of gentility and barbarism, he was a true child of his class and state" (164). How well this description fits Simms's Captain Porgy.

A gentleman by birth and often by performance, Porgy is a brave warrior. In battle Porgy is "A mountain in a passion, and in progress—a human avalanche" (*Woodcraft* 153). Porgy is a glutton. As such he is something of a vice character as well as a hero; he is something of a lowlife, and hence Simms's not overly complimentary portrait of the Southern planter type. "If one must think," Porgy pontificates, "its most agreeable exercise, to my experience, is over toast and tankard" (129). Convivial Porgy is deeply attached to his male wartime companions. To those who live with him at novel's end, after his futile courtship of two local widows, Porgy vows to devote the rest of his bachelor life to his restored plantation, Glen-Eberley. Dour Sergeant Millhouse says of Porgy's resolution, "The grapes is sour" (537). But Porgy as fictional character has found himself, at least—he is a nurturer of his ragtag followers, the truly dispossessed.

Porgy is equally, and more deeply, attached to his devoted slave, Tom. Yet Simms's Tom has a will of his own, too. He also is no stick figure of the dedicated slave out of antebellum romance. He objects very strongly, for example, when on several occasions a maudlin Porgy says he would rather shoot Tom than part with him through the wiles of the novel's major villain, M'Kewn (139, 209, 427). And survival-smart Tom will not hear of Porgy giving him his freedom (528). He is wise enough to see that in the slave society in which he lives, he is very well off with a whimsical, lazy master like Porgy.

Yet, strangely, for all his affinity for his black batman, Tom, Porgy does not recognize his old Mammy Sappho when she comes out of swamp hiding to greet him on his return to Glen-Eberley. The scene is rather chilling— well, callous—on Porgy's part. Sappho is the black woman who nursed him when he was a baby: "you mudder nuss," she touchingly reminds an at first noncomprehending Porgy (332). Dirty and terrified, and utterly believable in her starved debasement and pathetic ingratiation of forgetful Porgy, she has hidden for months on and off with other slaves in a nearby swamp to avoid being rounded up by Tory and British marauders for sale in the Caribbean. Whether Simms intended this or not, in Porgy's nonrecognition of his "mudder" Sappho there is a startling revelation, I think, of the essential expendability of slaves to their Southern masters. As often as not, in Allen Tate's words in *The Fathers* (1938), the blacks were seen by owners as "liquid capital" (54) as much as bosom friends.

So, Simms's criticism of the Southern planter class can be as pointed and as apposite in antebellum Porgy as DeForest's is in postbellum Carter. For another example, Porgy's plantation is ruined as much by his pre– Revolutionary War spendthrift ways as it is by later Tory or slave depredations while the master is away. Simms describes his planter hero as having been "a *fast* youth. He had never been taught the pains of acquisition. Left to himself—his own dangerous keeping—when a mere boy, he had too soon and fatally learned the pleasures of dissipation" (128). To his admiring young lieutenant, Lance Frampton, Porgy admits that "I've been a d----d fool in my time." Lance's ready agreement discomfits Porgy, and provides the reader both insight and another of the novel's delightfully humorous moments (136).

Then there is Simms's amazing heroine in *Woodcraft*, Widow Eveleigh. She is an independent Southern woman in the best tradition of the concept, as, say, Stark Young presents the type in *So Red the Rose* (1934) or Margaret Mitchell in *Gone With the Wind* (1936). Like DeForest's profligate, "double-faced as Janus" (143) Mrs. Larue in *Miss Ravenel's Conversion*, Widow Eveleigh has compromised herself by dealing with both sides during *her* war, and coming out on top. And like Larue, whose character is often praised for its realism, Eveleigh never is punished for her culpability. Simms admires her. She survives the war well, and manages to save the plantation of her rebel neighbor, Porgy. "She had friends at court, no matter who was sovereign for the season. Her husband had been a popular officer in his British majesty's army, and, when not on service, had been a favorite among his neighbors. The widow shared his popularity" (357). So, Mrs. Eveleigh has access to the British garrison town, Charleston, after hostilities have ended. Here she boldly faces down the British Colonel Moncrieff—who praises her to M'Kewn for having "a head of her own" (43)—over getting back her slaves and Porgy's that Moncrieff and M'Kewn have stolen for Caribbean sale.

What I like in this scene particularly is Eveleigh's handling of Moncrieff's pistols and swords when he leaves the room to confer with M'Kewn. "The widow possessed some rather curious tastes for a lady," Simms writes. "She rose, took up the pistols, and examined them without any of that shuddering feeling which most ladies would exhibit at the contemplation of such implements" (40). It is almost as if she wants to be caught thus armed in an intimidating stance should the colonel unexpectedly return. And, sure enough, he does, and recoils with unconcealed wonder as he catches sight of the widow waving a "Turkish scimitar . . . upward with a somewhat gladiatorial air" (47). To M'Kewn and his squatter henchman, Bostwick, Moncrieff says with chagrin after Eveleigh has departed: "We are handsomely bedeviled, i'faith, and by a woman. But such a woman! In truth, she *is* a woman, and worth half the men I know" (52).

Not only does she frankly refuse Porgy's marriage proposal, preferring his faithful, confidential friendship to the "fetters of matrimony" (531), Mrs. Eveleigh also asserts her independence to her devoted son, Arthur, when he has the temerity to object to Porgy's attentions to her. As Moncrieff says, "such a woman!" And she is characterized by Simms strongly and truly:

hear farther, Arthur Eveleigh.—While I acknowledge my responsibilities to you, as your mother, and the representative of your father, I still hold an independent relation to you in all matters which concern myself. On these, I will submit to no dictation. I shall be the mistress of my own thoughts, feelings, and sympathies, as far as it lies in my power to be so. I shall account to you in no respect, unless I am pleased and prefer to do so. . . . if it should seem to me wise, and right, and grateful to take another husband, it shall be my own will that I shall consult in the matter. . . . I must have affections and sympathies—I must have devotion and society—I must have love, Arthur, and must be beloved—at all events, I must be confided in. (435)

And then there is Simms's arch-villain in *Woodcraft*. M'Kewn also has collaborated with the British and plots to foreclose on Porgy's estate. There is nothing of the stock villain figure in romance about M'Kewn, though. There is nothing, for example, of the Faustian maniac Simms himself creates in his other backwoods bandit, Guy Rivers; or of the satanic seducer, Alfred Stevens, he offers readers in his retelling of the Kentucky Tragedy in *Charlemont* (1842) and *Beauchampe* (1856). M'Kewn is very believable as a trapped human being in Simms's scheme of literary realism in *Woodcraft*.

This is because, unlike any other villain I have encountered in my reading of antebellum Southern fiction, M'Kewn is scared from the start. Always on the razor's edge, he is scared of being exposed for his various frauds and thefts by his dirty-work cohort, Bostwick. When the squatter comes to confer with M'Kewn and Moncrieff over the return of the widow's and the captain's slaves, at Bostwick's entrance M'Kewn "looked disquieted" (44). And so he remains throughout the novel—"satisfied with himself and his successes, or striving to be so" (477)—disquieted whenever shaggy, malarial, swamp-rat Bostwick comes on the scene.

But even as vile as Bostwick appears to be on the surface with his crude associates and diversions, his starved appearance and illiterate dialect, Simms, always the realist in *Woodcraft* where humanity is concerned— Simms gives Bostwick a streak of appealing if pathetic humanness. This occurs in his love for his gentle, kind, beautiful daughter, Dory. It is for her that desperate Bostwick blackmails unhappy M'Kewn for five hundred guineas. This is a bid for Dory's advancement out of the squatter's cabin that leads to a miserable death for both men. "And you better bring 'em, M'Kewn," ill Bostwick says, "for you see, Dory must be a lady. I must make her rich as a queen; she must be able to carry as high a head as the widow Ev'leigh, and then she kin marry young Arthur. . . . and you shall be at the wedding, M'Kewn, though, by blisters, I should like to see you hanging up, with your feet upon nothing. . . . bring the guineas, and make haste about it. Lord! How my head aches and jumps. How my eyes burn! Bring the guineas; I'm a-longing to get shet of you, and to call in Dory, and make her a lady" (514).

What DeForest is praised for most in *Miss Ravenel's Conversion* is the realism of his battle action. DeForest gives his readers no romantic battle generalizations of flashing sabers, snapping plumes, snorting, foaming steeds, or shining human eyes and teeth such as presented by his fellow postbellum author, Confederate veteran, and Simms's friend, John Esten

Cooke, in his romance *Mohun* (1868; 24–25, 34, 75–76, 115, passim). Neither, of course, does Simms in *Woodcraft*. To be sure, the details of De-Forest's Louisiana battles are grim, bloody, burning. This is revealed in the following passage detailing the action of the day of John Carter's death—he is now General—when "a Minie-ball struck him in the left side, just below the ribs, with a *thud* which was audible ten feet from him in spite of the noise of the battle" (456). It is the sound of such battle wounds that is especially unique in DeForest's descriptions of war: "On went the regiments. . . . The dead were falling, the wounded were crawling in numbers to the rear; the leisurely hum of long-range bullets had changed into the sharp, multitudinous *whit-whit* of close firing; the stifled crash of balls hitting bones, and the soft *chuck* of flesh-wounds mingled with the outcries of the sufferers; the bluff in front was smoking, rattling, wailing with the incessant file-fire; but the front of the brigade remained unbroken" (455).

This is the real battle thing, all right. DeForest had experienced it. Stephen Crane, on the other hand, had never experienced combat. Yet he, too, is praised for the stark, bloody realism of his battle scenes in *The Red Badge of Courage* (1894). And why not also praise Simms, who had never seen combat either, for the realism of his two armed skirmishes in *Woodcraft*?[2] The first occurs with wonderful movement—the minutiae, for instance, of the riders' maneuvering of their horses as Porgy and Millhouse close in on the brigand, Jeff Brydiges, and then the latter's careful calculations in the handling of his pistol.

Simms had never been a cavalryman in battle, but he was a horseman and a hunter and he knew the business of riding and shooting. And there is other sound action detail in the following passage, from which I quote at some length in order to give as much of the stirring effects of the action's stark realism as I can: the hot-pursuit death of the robber, and the grim activity of the victor at the end when one-armed Millhouse strips Brydiges's corpse. Simms attains what I call some wonderful camera angles and action shots here, his author's lens moving back and forth, in pan shots and close-ups.

This remarkable action scene in *Woodcraft* takes place after Bostwick, Brydiges, and other renegades have failed in robbing Widow Eveleigh and Arthur. Captain Porgy and his men have come to the rescue:

> They were off, separated by an interval of fifty yards, perhaps, and coursing through the pine woods at a tearing gallop. A few minutes

hard riding gave them [Porgy and Millhouse] a fresh glimpse of the fugitive. He was making up for lost time, and going through the undergrowth, and among the thick-set trees. . . .

"He goes well, but it can't last!" muttered Porgy, as he applied his *persuaders* anew to the flanks of his own high-spirited courser. It was wonderful to see how well the animal sped with such a bulk upon his back. . . . The fugitive looked about him as he fled. . . .

The onset of Porgy was well calculated to prompt such feelings [of fear in Brydiges]. A mountain in a passion, and in progress—a human avalanche descending upon the plain-crashing, rending, overwhelming, as it goes—such in some small degree, was the image presented to the mind of the trembling enemy, seeing the headlong rush of our plethoric Captain!

. . . He now saw his other assailant, Sergeant Millhouse, who, less rapidly, but quite as certainly, was making toward him on the right. He felt very sure that the game was up with him. . . . But he was a drilled and practiced ruffian . . . and . . . was a man with whom the exigency only brought out the coolness, the determination and resource. He did not show his pistol, but he cocked it! He saw the course which Porgy rode, and he slightly inclined his horse to the right, in order that he should use his pistol-hand more freely. Porgy suspected his object and made a corresponding change in his own course. . . .

[Brydiges] kept his coolness, however, and his course; and as Porgy came on with a speed suddenly accelerated, and while he was measuring the distance which he should first overcome before rising in his stirrups to execute the fatal stroke, the outlaw pulled trigger under his left arm. The steed of Porgy swayed round at the flash, threw out his fore-feet wildly, then settled heavily down upon the earth, in the immediate agonies of death!

. . . Sergeant Millhouse . . . was on the *right* of the outlaw, who, ignorant of the left-handed, and single handed, condition of the remaining pursuer [Millhouse had lost his right arm in the war], fancied that some change in their relations was necessary to enable the other to use his sword. But he really saw no sword, and his object was simply to escape the pistol. But, against this, Millhouse was desperately resolved. He had hitherto kept his steed rather in hand. He now plied him with the terrible Spanish rowels which he wore . . . then, as the outlaw fumbled to extricate his remaining pistol from the left holster, he beheld, to his increased surprise, a gleaming saber suddenly plucked from an invisible scabbard, and wielded with a wonderful ease, in the left hand of his enemy! He bowed his body to the opposite side of the saddle, drove the spurs into his beast, bore down upon the curb to the left—almost swinging the horse about as he rode—all this in a single moment—but all too late! A swift, sharp flash, as of lightning, seemed to darken his sight, and the next moment the keen, heavy steel might have been heard to grinde [*sic:* but get the wound noise here] through the solid skull of the victim. Down he sunk, hanging to one stirrup, while the frightened horse . . . became tangled and held, until caught by Millhouse. . . .

"See what the rascal has about him, sergeant," said Porgy; and like a good trooper, perfectly aware of what cases usually required, Millhouse searched the clothes, and turned out the "silver lining" of the pockets of the dead man, with all the dexterity of a Parisian chiffonnier. He stripped him of everything of value; and, seeing that he wore a tolerable pair of English boots, he had them off in the twinkling of an eye;—though how the thing was done—*our* chiffonnier with one hand only—it is as difficult to describe as to conceive. (152–56)

Furthermore, in Simms's *Woodcraft* there is no soft idealization, any more than there is in DeForest's *Miss Ravenel's Conversion*, of that ultimate paradigm of the good life in the Old South, the plantation house. In its varying degrees of grandeur, the plantation house recurs in the fiction of Simms's Southern contemporaries as an image of comfort, security, and success— an image of status and power. Just consider the significance of the plantation's main house in John Pendleton Kennedy's *Swallow Barn* (1832), the antebellum fiction credited with starting the whole "big house" thing; in William Alexander Carruthers's *The Kentuckian in New York* (1834); in Caroline Howard Gilman's *Recollections of a Southern Matron* (1838); in Caroline Lee Hentz's *The Planter's Northern Bride* (1854); or in that softest of all antebellum Southern romances, *The Last of the Foresters* (1856), by Simms's young literary friend and a truly dedicated romancer, John Esten Cooke of Virginia.

The first image we get of Porgy's house at Glen-Eberley is in a scene of ruin resulting from Revolutionary War. Such a scene, in hindsight, is a disconcertingly realistic one to have come out of the South in that last decade before war and ruin came again. Remember, too, in terms of Simms's

unrelenting urge to realism and to some social criticism in *Woodcraft*, that
such ruin might have come to planter Porgy's emblematic estate anyway as
a result of his profligate ways. It is the practical and strong-willed survivor
and Southern lady, Widow Eveleigh, and the practical yeoman farmer
and Southern worker, Sergeant Millhouse—these commonplace, everyday, Howellsian folk—who help idle, ruminative, good-natured Porgy to
put his house in order again.

Unlike Simms, however, whose depiction of the ruined Southern plantation house is unimpassioned and unpolitical, John William DeForest's
depiction of a similar Southern ruin fifteen years later is noticeably vindic-
tive. For a typical Union officer like DeForest, the planter's mansion was
an ugly symbol of Southern oligarchy, aristocracy, pride, and oppression.
The plantation great house, hence, was a structure best destroyed. For
Simms, on the other hand, who had a big house of his own at his Woodlands Plantation near Charleston, the mansion was a symbol of social tran-
quility best restored, of frontier brutishness best diminished. *Woodcraft* is,
after all, a novel about the restoration of local Southern power when the
hero-soldier returns to his land. For the sake of my limited purposes in this
essay, I just want to show how Simms's persistent use of realistic detail in
his major novel sets another scene on Porgy's farm that is one more precedent for the believable, the actual, the everyday in United States fiction as
these elements are later employed by DeForest.

In *Miss Ravenel's Conversion*, DeForest describes a deserted sugar plantation and its ruined mansion on the Mississippi River some miles above New
Orleans, occupied by General Butler's Union forces. DeForest describes
the big house as a square "plain wooden mansion" similar to a New England saltbox house. The Louisiana house has a "spacious veranda" and,
along with the slave cabins to the rear, it rests on "props of brick-work,
leaving room underneath for the free circulation of air, dogs, pigs and
pickaninnies." DeForest reveals how

> the field-hands, who had hid in the swamps to avoid being carried to
> Texas [by the Confederates], came upon the house like locusts of de-
> struction, broke down its doors, shattered its windows, plundered it
> from parlor to garret, drank themselves drunk on the venerable trea-
> sure of the wine closet, and diverted themselves with soiling the car-
> pets, breaking the chairs, ripping up the sofas, and defacing the family
> portraits. Some gentle sentiment, perhaps a feeble love for the de-

parted young "missus," perhaps the passion of their race for music, had deterred them from injuring the piano, which was almost the only unharmed piece of furniture in the once handsome parlor. (252–53)

Reflecting on this sad ruin, Miss Ravenel's father feels a "little human sympathy, or at any rate a little poetic melancholy, on stepping thus into the ruins of a family." But he also thinks with malevolence that some "grand jury of future centuries will bring in the verdict, 'Served them right'" (254).

I wonder if those of war-hero Porgy's slaves who also fled into the swamps behaved in the same way to the big house at Glen-Eberley when their master was away? I am inclined to think so, notwithstanding their meekness on Porgy's return home or Mammy Sappho's ingratiating protestations of joy at the return of her unrecognizing "my chile . . . my son" (333). Whatever the case might have been, this is what Porgy first sees of his family place at the end of the plantation's dreary avenue, with its dark, enclosing, moss-hung live oak trees surrounded by vacant and unkempt fields: "The house was an ample one, of wood, on a brick basement. But it had been completely gutted. There was neither table nor chair, and our friends couched themselves upon the blankets of Mrs. Eveleigh, spread about the fireplace" (201).

Later, Porgy decides to take up residence again in his old bedroom. He looks on its interior wreckage tearfully, the returned soldier in a paternalistic mood now. His worries over his debt-ridden future are as much for the care of his comrades as they are for his impending loss of house and land. Here is what Porgy sees that first night in his old room. Again, I quote at some length, for here, in *Woodcraft*, Simms is writing at his graphically realistic best:

> for a long time he did not lie down. His eyes were bent upon the fire, or slowly wandered around the almost vacant chamber. It was a snug, but sufficiently capacious apartment, probably eighteen by twenty feet. The walls still exhibited proof of a degree of pride and state, which declared for a former wealth and taste, such as were strangely inconsistent with the present fortunes of the possessor. The panelling of wood over the fireplace still showed traces of two landscape paintings in oil, done upon the panels with no inconsiderable art. The framework around them consisted of heavy carved work, and the pillars of the mantelpiece were richly ornamented with carvings in similar style.

About the room still hung the dingy and shattered frames of pictures, probably portraits from which the canvas had been cut out. It had probably been found useful for the meanest purposes, and had been appropriated, with all other movables of any value, by the marauding British and tories. The glass was destroyed in the sashes of all the windows. The shutters were mostly torn from the hinges and carried off, probably destroyed for firewood. One of the planks of the floor had been taken up, and lay beside the opening, very much hewed and mangled by the axe. The fragments of an ancient mahogany bedstead lay piled up in one corner, but it was evidently no longer available for use. It had been that upon which Porgy had slept when a child: it was the bedstead of his mother. A bit of green cord still depended from a nail against the opposite wall. It had sustained the picture of his mother; that portrait of a fair young woman, taken when she was yet un-married, whose sweet smiling features, in the active exercise of mem-ory and fancy, seemed still to be looking down upon him. (220–21)

Like John William DeForest of Connecticut, then—and a little later that arch-realist William Dean Howells of New York—William Gilmore Simms of antebellum South Carolina has the clear eye of a literary photog-rapher and the innovative daring of a literary frontiersman. As much as it is DeForest's device in *Miss Ravenel's Conversion from Secession to Loyalty*, Simms's literary device in *Woodcraft* is the "untrodden path" of a consistent realism, and a first in American literature. It is time for readers of and com-mentators upon Simms's works to get off the fence and identify (I say pro-claim) him for what he certainly became in United States letters of the early 1850s, and not for what he started out as, in, say, *Guy Rivers*. Pablo Picasso, after all, did not start out painting in the mode of his later and era-indicating fragmented abstractionism. But it is as a groundbreaking artist that Picasso generally is recalled.

Simms did not start out as a realist in fiction. But his essentially realistic "taste and temperament," to use Vernon Louis Parrington's phrase in ref-erence to Simms (126, 134) in *The Romantic Revolution in America, 1800–1860* (1927), led him to become one in his culminating literary achieve-ment, *Woodcraft*. Indeed, even while hedging between finally identifying Simms as a romancer or a realist, in his welcome, informed, and elegant biography of Simms, John Caldwell Guilds states: "it seems safe to say, [he] was instinctively, and deliberately, a realist" (339). In its depictions of characters, actions, and scenes, *Woodcraft* is a true antebellum masterpiece of realistic human character and comedy, postwar crisis and crime, Southern community and commonplace. Furthermore, his realistic taste and temperament prevail in the direction of such other Twain-preceding tall and vernacular tales Simms also wrote, such as "Sergeant Barnacle: The Boatman's Revenge: A Tale of the Edisto" (1845), "Ephraim Bartlett, the Edisto Raftsman" (1852), "Paddy McGann; or, The Demon of the Stump" (1863), and "How Sharp Snaffles Got His Capital and Wife" (1870). No: the antebellum Southern fictionalizer William Gilmore Simms is American literature's first distinctly "realistic" writer—not the postbellum Northern fictionalizer, John William DeForest. And I assert this canon-revising position without equivocation.

NOTES

1. In one of his letters, Simms writes that his tales "aim at something more than the story." His rule is to "write truthfully, honestly, without affectation, as we feel and suppose we know." Always, in every age, he writes, "To seem like truth . . . has been . . . the object of fiction" (*Letters* 3 : 421, 11). To Philip C. Pendleton, editor of the *Magnolia* magazine, Simms wrote a letter dated August 12, 1841, in which he states that the goal of the writer is attained "if he takes care to speak the truth, the whole truth and nothing but the truth. In this, in fact, lies the whole secret of his art. *A writer is moral only in proportion to his truthfulness*" (*Letters* 1 : 259). In an article titled "Modern Prose Fiction," published in the *Southern Quarterly Review* eight years later, Simms says that "all literature faithful to truth serves a moral purpose . . . as truthfulness is never without its moral, and as the great end of the artist is approximation of all his fiction to a seeming truth so, unavoidably, he includes a moral" (43). True, here Simms would seem to be going along merely with the reader preference of his Victorian day for the inclusion of clear moral lessons as justification for producing and reading imaginative literature. But what he writes also precedes by many decades an observation made by another great Southern realist, William Faulkner, who somewhere has observed that all serious (that is to say, "true") writers of fiction are "moral teachers."

2. The second occurs when Porgy—"corpulent . . . like a young buffalo . . . emerging from the cover of his piazza . . . came forward, swelling and *splurging*—to employ the phrase by which Millhouse frequently described his assault afterward—his eyes glaring like meteors, his voice yelling a terrific slogan; his broad-sword waving like a broad tail of a fiery comet, at the advent of an earthquake. Porgy could not exactly rush or run, but he could roll forward with wonderful effect, and his

lungs were good" (505)—comes down from his house to his gate to arrest without bloodshed the gentlemanly sheriff who has come to Glen-Eberley to serve Porgy eviction papers for indebtedness to M'Kewn. For all his ungainly-comic appearance in his fat and headlong charge here, Porgy means business. Again Simms combines comedy with realism for an appealing and convincing effect. There is no comedy at all, however, in the first skirmish, when mounted Porgy and Millhouse rescue Widow Eveleigh and her son from the robbers.

WORKS CITED

Bakker, Jan. *Pastoral in Antebellum Southern Romance*. Baton Rouge: Louisiana State University Press, 1989.

Cooke, John Esten. *Mohun; or, The Last Days of Lee and His Paladins*. Ridgewood: Gregg, 1968.

DeForest, John William. *Miss Ravenel's Conversion from Secession to Loyalty*. Intro. Arlin Turner. Columbus: Charles E. Merrill, 1969.

Guilds, John Caldwell. *Simms: A Literary Life*. Fayetteville: University of Arkansas Press, 1992.

Hawthorne, Nathaniel. *The House of the Seven Gables*. New York: Norton, 1967.

Howells, William Dean. *Criticism and Fiction*. New York: Harper, 1891.

Parrington, Vernon Louis. *The Romantic Revolution in America, 1800–1860*. New York: Harcourt, 1927.

Simms, William Gilmore. *The Letters of William Gilmore Simms*. 5 vols. Ed. Mary C. Simms Oliphant, Alfred Taylor Odell, T. C. Duncan Eaves. Intro. Donald Davidson. Columbia: University of South Carolina Press, 1952–1956. (A sixth volume, *The Letters of William Gilmore Simms, Supplement [1834–1870]*, edited by Oliphant and Eaves, was published by the University of South Carolina Press in 1982.)

———. "Modern Prose Fiction." *Southern Quarterly Review* 15 (April 1849).

———. *Woodcraft; or, Hawks About the Dovecote*. Ed. and intro. Charles S. Watson. Albany: New College and University Press, 1983.

———. *The Yemassee: A Romance of Carolina*. 1835. New and rev. ed. New York: Redfield, 1854.

Stein, Gertrude. *The Autobiography of Alice B. Toklas*. New York: Vintage, 1990.

Tate, Allen. *The Fathers*. Athens: Swallow Press, 1990.

Trent, William Peterfield. *William Gilmore Simms*. New York: Haskell House, 1968.

CAROLINE COLLINS

Simms's Concept of Romance and His Realistic Frontier

When W. P. Trent characterized the Border Romances of William Gilmore Simms as being "marred by a slipshod style" and "by a repetition of incidents" (88), his distaste for the romance form set the tone for their critical reception ever since. For critics as early as Trent, the genre of romance was declining into what many perceived to be an outmoded tradition. The twentieth century has done little to recover the romance tradition and its conventions, and this has had serious implications for Simms, as Mary Ann Wimsatt notes: "it is not too much to claim that a general misunderstanding of this tradition coupled with ignorance of his work is in large measure responsible for the neglect or misinterpretation of his writing" (8). She asserts that Simms "theorized about romance throughout his life" (36), altering the romance patterns of Walter Scott and James Fenimore Cooper "sometimes in striking ways, in order to make plain the peculiar conditions of southern culture" (38). Unfortunately, as she observes, scholars have yet to explore or emphasize "the degree to which American novelists, working from a different set of cultural conditions, modified Scott's patterns in order to make distinctive historical statements of their own" (37). Indeed, according to Wimsatt, the trend is still to ignore the contributions of nineteenth-century Southern writers in general, and of romancers in particular:

> Ever since literary publishing established itself in the late eighteenth century, there has been a tendency in the country, encouraged by the emergence of New York as its publishing capital, to view northern traditions as the dominant American traditions and to assign to the South before the twentieth century an inferior role in literary history. This consensus of criticism has recently come under attack, yet authors of standard studies of American Romance continue to concentrate on Cooper, Hawthorne, Melville, and Brockden Brown while treating in detail no southern writers save Poe. (262–63)

Even proponents of Simms have been loath to recognize the romance as a valid form. Donald Davidson's judgment that "The prose romance—the only form available to Simms if he wished to derive income from his productions—was a highly unsuitable vehicle for a saga-man" (xlv) fails to acknowledge that Simms achieved the effects of saga through his use of the romance. Northrup Frye's *Anatomy of Criticism* is singular in avowing the integrity of romance: "a great romancer should be examined in terms of the conventions he chose. William Morris should not be left on the side lines of prose fiction merely because the critic has not learned to take the romance form seriously. Nor . . . should his choice of that form be regarded as an 'escape' from his social attitude" (305). Rejecting "the historical illusion" that the romance is "something to be outgrown, a juvenile and undeveloped form," Frye praises "its revolutionary nature": "however conservative he [a romancer] may be, something nihilistic and untamable is likely to keep breaking out of his pages" (305). Unfortunately, Frye offers little more than a general overview of what the romancer's own terms might be and leaves the reader to decide for himself what constitutes the revolutionary nature of romance.

Although twentieth-century criticism in America has neglected to examine the richness and potential of the romance tradition that was a vital resource not only for Simms, but also for Hawthorne, Melville, and others, Russian literary theorist Mikhail Bakhtin, writing approximately fifty years after Trent's assessment of Simms and twenty years before Frye's analysis of romance, recovered various types of Greek romance as well as their conventions and possibilities, thus divesting the genre of many negative associations and providing us with a concept of romance much closer to what Simms's must have been. Simms's own statement in *Views and Reviews of American Literature* that the American romance would differ from earlier forms solely in terms of subject matter has caused critics to assume that his view of the romance was at best simplistic; however, when we examine Simms's works in terms of Bakhtin's analysis of romance, the Border Romances emerge as highly sophisticated writings, interwoven with strands from various types of Greek romance.

In his essay "Forms of Time and of the Chronotope in the Novel," Bakhtin uses virtually the same words as Trent, not to condemn the romancer but to describe the stock elements of a particular type of Greek romance: "The plots of these romances . . . are remarkably similar to each other, and are in fact composed of the very same elements [motifs]: individual novels differ from each other only in the number of such elements, their proportionate weight within the whole plot and the way they are combined" (87).

For Bakhtin, as for Simms, the Greek romance represented "a very malleable instance of the novelistic genre, one that possesses an enormous life-force" (107). Nor is that genre separable from or inferior to realism. Indeed, Bakhtin insists that there must be something of "substance" to the romance, and Simms's own characterization of the romance as an "amalgam" of poem and novel in his preface to the 1854 edition of *The Yemassee* implies a recognition that the romance's tendency toward "a higher reality, a deeper psychology" constituted a kind of realism in and of itself and did not preclude the novel's "representative detail" or "'mimesis' in its narrow sense" (Wellek and Warren 216). If, as Gillian Beer has noted, the romances of Sir Walter Scott "increased the impulse toward *realism*" by virtue of "the accuracy of Scott's historicism, his sense of the temper of precise periods and their relationship to the time at which he writes" (66), certainly this is no less true of Simms's romances. And although twentieth-century readers still regard realism as something achieved in spite of the romance form, Bakhtin's suggestion that romancers used conventions and simultaneously undercut them argues for both the viability and realism of the genre. Clearly Simms learned the potential of romantic conventions not only through extensive reading but also through trial and error, moving from earlier and more conventional works like "The Maroon" into more complex romances. Indeed, in the Border Romances, especially in *Guy Rivers* and *Richard Hurdis*, he broke free of the confines of romance by selecting conventions from various types of romance and by learning to use those conventions in new and different ways. Combining them, reversing them, and playing them off each other, he thus achieved a tension under the surface of his works. Simms's realistic frontier, then, derives at least as much from his ability to exploit romantic conventions as from his graphic depictions of violence.

Bakhtin's notion of the chronotope affords us a useful way to observe how Simms used romantic conventions to realistic ends; it may also offer a specific example of the revolutionary nature of romance. The chronotope consists of the interconnectedness of space and time within a work of literature: "Time, as it were, thickens, takes on flesh, becomes artistically visible; likewise, space becomes charged and responsive to the movements of time, plot, and history" (84). *The Yemassee*, for example, displays the inseparability of time and space in a very unique way: we literally see the Indian lands receding and the settlers' lands growing, even as we see the ritual time of the Indian being replaced by a more chronological kind of time. Yet space is charged with historical time in all of Simms's novels, and the Border Romances are no exception. Bakhtin's praise of Balzac's unusual ability "to 'see' time in space" as well as his "marvelous depictions of houses as materialized history and his description of streets, cities, rural landscapes at the level where they are being worked upon by time and history" (247) could just as easily be applied to Simms's description of the Chestatee jail and courthouse in *Guy Rivers* or his portrayal of the fledgling town of Tuscaloosa in *Richard Hurdis*. For Bakhtin, however, the chronotope consists not only of the inseparability of time and space in a work of literature, but also of the events that happen in this realm of time and space together. Thus a literary work may contain a number of chronotopes, and these may be in dialogue with one another. In both *Guy Rivers* and *Richard Hurdis*, the surface chronotope of the Greek romance is undercut by the presence of other chronotopes erupting under the surface, pulling against each other.

Simms's own definition of the romance in the first edition of *The Yemassee* as a form that "hurries individuals through crowding events in a narrow space of time," puts "a human agent in hitherto untried situations," and "exercises its ingenuity in extricating him from them, while describing his feelings and fortunes in their progress" (vi–vii) seems not far afield of Northrup Frye's comic definition of romance at its most naive: "an endless form in which a central character who never develops or ages goes through one adventure after another until the author himself collapses" (186). The implication is that the reader suffers a similar exhaustion. Like Trent, Frye objects here to the overriding pattern of the Greek romance, which gives a deceptively simple surface to *Guy Rivers* and *Richard Hurdis*.

The chronotope of Greek romance stems from a type of romance Bakhtin calls "the adventure novel of ordeal," and this accounts for a number of the elements in *Guy Rivers* and *Richard Hurdis*. The most recognizable elements include a boy and girl of marriageable age, both beautiful and chaste, who suddenly fall in love and encounter barriers such as parental objections. They endure separation, but finally surmount all obstacles, reunite, and marry (87–88). We see this chronotope in the relationships of Ralph and Edith Colleton as well as Richard Hurdis and Mary Easterby. Certainly there is a sense of awkwardness to Simms's depictions of these relationships: even Bakhtin acknowledges that "the absolute irreproachability of the heroes" in such a form "results in a certain stiltedness" (107). In Simms's works, it results in artificial dialogues and oversimplified endings as well. Adding to the stilted or contrived nature of this kind of romance, at least in Frye's opinion, is the element of adventure-time, which controls the action. As Bakhtin describes it, this kind of time "is composed of a series of short segments that correspond to separate adventures; within each adventure, time is organized from without, technically. What is important is to be able to escape, to catch up, to outstrip, to be or not to be in a given place at a given moment, to meet or not to meet and so forth" (91). Time is measured in adventures rather than chronological time, and the elements of each adventure are linked by connectors like *suddenly* and *at just that moment*. As a result, the romance may indeed take on the semblance of endless adventure that Frye opposes. But for Bakhtin, the randomness of chance is crucial to the "adventure-time" contained within the "adventure novel of ordeal":

> "Suddenly" and "at just that moment" best characterize this type of time, for this time usually has its origin and comes into its own in just those places where the normal, pragmatic and premeditated course of events is interrupted—and provides an opening for sheer chance, which has its own specific logic. Should something happen a minute earlier or a minute later, that is, should there be no chance simultaneity or chance disjunctions in time, there would be no plot at all, and nothing to write a novel about. (91)

For Bakhtin, and for Simms, there is much more to the romance than this simple surface. Under the surface chronotope are other chronotopes, which Simms used effectively to undercut the conventions of Greek romance. Of these, perhaps the chronotope of the road is the most significant, for it brings other underlying chronotopes into opposition with the surface one. In both *Guy Rivers* and *Richard Hurdis*, the road is closely related to the chronotope of Greek romance. A number of major characters take to the road, whether to achieve independence and escape real or imagined obstacles to their own love relationships, as in the case of Ralph Colleton or Richard Hurdis, to flee from justice, as in the case of Mark Forrester, or to procure the means necessary to set up housekeeping with his betrothed, as in the case of William Carrington. Indeed, for both Forrester and Carrington, the road is bound up with the pursuit of the "capital" necessary to marry their loved ones. In their situations, and in Edward Eberly's as well, Simms explores the same themes that we see in "How Sharp Snaffles Got His Capital and Wife" without the comic treatment.

As in his other novels, Simms's roads in *Guy Rivers* and *Richard Hurdis* are fraught with ambiguity and peril, and peril often results from the ambiguity of an encounter. When Guy Rivers presses Ralph Colleton to pay the toll of the Pony Club, the young traveler is "almost led to doubt whether the whole was not the clever jest of some country sportsman, who, in the guise of a levyer of contributions upon the traveller, would make an acquaintance, such as is frequent in the South, terminating usually in a ride to a neighboring plantation, and pleasant accommodations" (16). Likewise, though Richard Hurdis objects to the manners of the New York dandies he meets, he cannot fault their "curiosity": "The custom of the country is to ask questions, and to ask them with directness" (122). Hurdis finds Mat Webber's demeanor just prior to the ambush even more deceiving: "the fellow played the part of humility in sundry instances to admiration; when we resisted him on any subject, he shrank from pursuing it, and throughout the interview exhibited a disposition to forbear all annoyance" (170). The initial ambiguity of such encounters allows Simms to build the suspense essential to romance: "everyday time" may become "adventure time" at any moment. With this treatment of time Simms breaks decisively from the conventions of Greek romance seen in the adventure novel of ordeal and draws on what Bakhtin calls "the adventure novel of everyday life." For Simms, "the mix of adventure time and everyday time" became a source of rich potential, a viable means of emphasizing the unpredictability of the frontier. It was particularly appropriate for the Border Romances, which, unlike the Revolutionary Romances, explore the development of society in times of crisis not formally declared as such. Indeed, life on the frontier roads of the Border Romances approaches the sheer unpredictability of what Bakhtin has termed "the chivalric romance": "The whole world becomes miraculous, so the miraculous becomes ordinary without ceasing to be miraculous. Even 'unexpectedness' itself—since it is always with us—ceases to be something unexpected. The unexpected, and only the unexpected, is what is expected" (152). When coupled with his decision to set the Border Romances in the present, that is, during his own lifetime, Simms's treatment of time appears no less than revolutionary.

In noting that the road is an especially good place for random encounters and events governed by chance, Bakhtin expresses a point of view remarkably similar to Simms's and Frederick Jackson Turner's:

> On the road . . . the spatial and temporal paths of the most varied people—representatives of all social classes, estates, religions, nationalities, ages—intersect at one spatial and temporal point. People who are normally kept separate by social and spatial distance can accidentally meet; any contrast may crop up, the most various fates may collide and interweave with one another. On the road the spatial and temporal series defining human fates and lives combine with one another in distinctive ways, even as they become more complex and more concrete by the collapse of *social distances*. The chronotope of the road is both a point of new departures and a place for events to find their denouement. (244–45)

Bakhtin's observation almost seems to echo Simms's description of the citizens of Chestatee in *Guy Rivers:* "They came, not only from all parts of the surrounding country, but many of them from all parts of the surrounding world; oddly and confusedly jumbled together; the very *olla-podrida* of moral and mental combination. . . . Here, alike, came the spendthrift and the indolent, the dreamer and the outlaw, congregating, though guided by contradictory impulses, in the formation of a common caste, and in the pursuit of a like object" (45). The difference, perhaps, is that for Bakhtin, writing in the 1930s, the concept of the road was largely a theoretical one. For Simms, however, the road and its implications were more historical and realistic than theoretical. As he notes in *Guy Rivers*, clashes between individuals were bound to occur both on the road and in the town, in Chestatee or elsewhere, because "the parts [of society] had not yet grown together" (46). It seems likely that Simms witnessed such encounters during his travels on the frontier and realized the dramatic and comic potential of such meetings for his own novels. The brief yet vivid glimpse of the Georgia stagecoach driver who offers to lick German duke Saxe Weimar for refusing to travel with the man snoring in the last seat on the coach in "Notes of a Small Tourist" is only one such example.

But the encounters that occur on the road in *Guy Rivers* and *Richard Hurdis* serve a higher purpose than mere comic or dramatic effect, for it is through the patterns of such encounters that Simms chronicles the development of the American frontier and achieves the effects of saga. This is especially true of the encounters of "frontier justice" in both novels, and perhaps the best way to view the underlying chronotopes is to examine the portrayals of frontier justice in *Guy Rivers* and *Richard Hurdis*. If we define frontier justice as "people on the frontier taking the law into their own hands," we see the motif of encounters connected with the chronotope of the road undercutting the surface chronotope of Greek romance.

The encounters in both *Guy Rivers* and *Richard Hurdis* bear out Bakhtin's concept of the road as both "a point of new departures and a place for events to find their denouement." Though Ralph Colleton is wounded in his first encounter with Guy Rivers, he escapes; after losing consciousness, he is discovered by Mark Forrester, who takes him to a doctor to have his wounds treated. Forrester is not so lucky. His anxiousness to protect the small savings he has laid up from gold-mining for his impending marriage to Kate Allen makes him especially vulnerable. Following his role in the clash with the Georgia Guard, he flees from justice, hoping to make his way to the Mississippi Valley, where Kate Allen and her family will join him. On the road, however, he is slain by Rivers. In *Richard Hurdis*, William Carrington's impending marital bliss accounts in part for his easy, trusting manner that results in his "singular lapse of thought" or fatal mistake of showing his large sum of money to strangers while playing cards. Though he escapes their ambush, he blunders into Ben Pickett's rifle sights on an unusually straight part of the road soon after, and is killed. Richard Hurdis, who is too quickly surprised by the ambush to attempt escape, lives to avenge the murder of his friend.

For twentieth-century readers and critics, such random, "on the road" encounters often seem aesthetically displeasing. It is ironic, certainly, that readers are most likely to reject what is most crucial for Simms. To be sure, incidents of chance tend to be better incorporated and more believable in Simms's Revolutionary Romances, while chance seems to come consistently out of nowhere in the Border Romances. Yet this emphasis upon the role of chance is a vital part of Greek romance. For both Bakhtin and Simms, there is a certain reality to the randomness of life, the randomness of nature. For them, the encounters on the road seemed more realistic than romantic, for the roads held more perils for them than they now hold for us.

The role of chance in *Guy Rivers* and *Richard Hurdis* derives from the "adventure novel of everyday time." According to Bakhtin, the role of chance in this type of novel is somewhat limited in its effects. In other words, characters are not entirely passive: individual responsibility and initiative play an equally important role. This is best demonstrated in *Guy Rivers:* Ralph Colleton ultimately accepts the fact that he is legally held responsible for Forrester's murder, and the minor characters who are brought into play to effect Colleton's acquittal represent Simms's conviction that the legal system will be successful only with the help of people who believe in it and are willing to take an active role to see justice done. Likewise, at Colonel Grafton's urging, Richard Hurdis assumes the responsibility of telling Emmeline Walker about her lover's death, as well as the responsibility of avenging his friend's death. Thus in both *Guy Rivers* and *Richard Hurdis*, as in Bakhtin's adventure novel of everyday time, the issues of metamorphosis and identity become no less significant than the role of chance: "The *primary initiative*, therefore, belongs to *the hero himself* and to his own *personality*. . . . The final link—the conclusion of the entire adventure sequence—is . . . not determined by chance" (116–17).

Nonetheless, the randomness of chance is important to Simms: it allows him to depict the grim realities of frontier life. Through his characterizations of Forrester, Carrington, and Edward Eberly and their random encounters on the road, Simms surpasses the dialectical structure typical of romance. His use of the stock device of doubles here is by no means new, but it takes on a new significance in this context. Generally, as Frye observes, characters in romance "tend to be for or against the quest. If they assist it they are idealized as simply gallant or pure; if they obstruct it they are caricatured as simply villainous or cowardly. Hence every typical character in romance tends to have his moral opposite confronting him, like black and white pieces in a chess game" (195). Certainly Colleton and Hurdis confront their moral opposites, but they also face their virtual "breathing doubles" in the persons of Forrester and Carrington, just as Gabriel Harrison faces his own image in Sanutee in *The Yemassee*. Forrester is no less virtuous and humane than Colleton: "There were few persons in that part of the world like Forrester. A better heart, or more honorable spirit, lived not; and in spite of an erring and neglected education—of evil associations, and sometimes evil pursuits—he was still a worthy specimen of manhood" (*Guy Rivers* 58). Both Forrester and Carrington share the hero's "noble" character, but lack his vigilance. Hurdis notes this early in his narrative, describing the easygoing manner that led to his companion's demise: "While my nature, helped by my experience, perhaps, made me jealous, watchful, and suspicious, his, on the other hand, taught him to believe readily, to trust fearlessly, and to derive but little value even from his own experience of injustice" (28). As John Caldwell Guilds notes in *Simms: A Literary Life*, "the frontier . . . thoroughly tests the character of a people" (85), and it tests the individual no less thoroughly. For Simms, the deaths of Forrester, Carrington, and even Eberly are not a matter of punishment for crime or sin as much as a matter of realism: individuals in close proximity to criminals are unlikely to emerge unscathed. (Contrary to what Arthur Hobson Quinn has said, perhaps the most unbelievable part of both novels is the fact that both Colleton and Hurdis walk away unharmed.) The deaths of these characters illustrate Simms's fidelity to realism: neither remorse nor bravery in saving the lives of others will save Forrester or Eberly, and both Colleton and Hurdis must acknowledge that. They must realize, too, that but for their vigilance, the same fate could have befallen them. On Simms's frontier, people pay dearly for their vulnerable moments. Through his emphasis on the parallel circumstances and opposite fortunes of these and other characters, Simms achieves a saga that is both unique and unflinching.

What happens literally on the road brings an almost anti-Greek romance chronotope into the picture, undercutting the surface chronotope of Greek romance. Here the issue of frontier justice becomes crucial to an understanding of Simms's point. The secret meetings with lovers in forests or other settings are balanced by random, brutal encounters on the road, and the lives of others are dramatically altered by the deaths that occur on the road. For each couple who lives happily ever after in *Guy Rivers* and *Richard Hurdis*, there are at least two couples whose love is ill-fated. In *Guy Rivers* there is an ominous, unsettling suggestion of an anti-Greek romance chronotope. Though the narration does not concern itself with the fate of Kate Allen, the reader may safely assume that Forrester's death changes the life and destiny of his beloved Kate Allen in certain ways, just as the suicide of Guy Rivers has serious implications for Ellen. Yet there is some hope for the lives of Kate Allen and the orphan Lucy Munro, who still have friends or relatives to sustain them. They may recover from their griefs and begin life anew, as it were, in a new setting.

In *Richard Hurdis*, however, the anti-Greek romance chronotope appears almost fatalistic. Against the relationship of Richard Hurdis and Mary Easterby, Simms juxtaposes the relationship of William Carrington and Emmeline Walker as well as that of Edward Eberly and Julia Grafton.

Again, the lives of others are dramatically affected by what happens on the road. After Carrington and Eberly are slain, both Emmeline Walker and Julia Grafton essentially die of broken hearts, in spite of the love and support of their families. Julia Grafton lingers for a few years, but Emmeline Walker's death occurs almost immediately after Carrington's. Certainly there is nothing more romantic than the lover who dies of a broken heart; yet, in this context, the novel approaches the proportions of Shakespearean tragedy in terms of the sheer number of bodies (especially the bodies of lovers) that have piled up at the end. (Including married couples makes for an even more fatalistic anti-Greek romance chronotope, as we can then add Ben Pickett to the death toll.) Here Simms's use of romance tends toward realism. Perhaps the deaths of these women are not entirely free of the melodramatic. Emmeline's madness seems rendered in overly romantic terms: "Her eyes were shooting from their spheres—the whites barely perceptible. . . . Purple blotches gleamed out upon and as suddenly disappeared from her face . . . her teeth and lips were set as resolutely as if death's last spasm had already been undergone. If they had opened at all, it was only when she uttered that heart-piercing moan—so faint, so low, yet so thrilling, that it seemed to indicate at every utterance the breaking of some vital string" (278). Hurdis describes Julia's ethereal beauty, as she gradually wastes away, in equally romantic terms: "Her sorrows had sublimed her beauty. . . . The worm was gnawing at her heart, and its ravages were extending to her frame" (401). Her expression of "an intense spirituality" indicates that she is already in another world. In spite of occasional melodrama, the use of the romance here is highly realistic, though not merely because of Emmeline's function as Hurdis's conscience and Simms's graphic portrayal of her death. The deaths of these young women are part of the larger pattern of random on-the-road encounters and their far-reaching effects. Again, through this emphasis on parallel circumstances and opposite fortunes, Simms chronicles the development of the frontier and taps the power of romance. For Bakhtin and for Simms, such randomness is a crucial kind of realism, and through his emphasis on this randomness, Simms skillfully depicts the realistic, ugly side of frontier life. The future of young couples and families, and of entire generations, Simms suggests, is made or broken by the vigilance of young men. The frontier environment demands extraordinary emotional endurance from men and women alike. Only those who are both psychologically and physically strong will survive. In this respect, *Guy Rivers* and *Richard Hurdis* go beyond the simple surface of the romance, the naive and artificial happy endings characteristic of the adventure novel of ordeal. Through skillful characterization and deft manipulation of the romance form, Simms achieves the effect of saga, capturing the epic sweep of history in a way that is both unique and unsettling.

By virtue of their very setting in the present, *Guy Rivers, Richard Hurdis*, and the other Border Romances display the "element of prophecy that is characteristic of romance" (Beer 79), not because they are absorbed with the ideal, like most romances, but because in them Simms was writing about events—like the Georgia gold rush and the Great Migration—that had not yet completely worked themselves out. How they would end was by no means a foregone conclusion, as it was in *The Yemassee* and the Revolutionary Romances. If we examine Simms's romances in terms of Bakhtin's analysis, we see that both *Guy Rivers* and *Richard Hurdis* display astonishing versatility and defy easy categorization. Thus it becomes impossible to see Simms as paralyzed by the romance form. With the help of Mikhail Bakhtin's concepts, perhaps, Simms and other romancers may be recognized for their challenging, ambitious, and innovative achievements in the romance form.

WORKS CITED

Bakhtin, Mikhail M. "Forms of Time and of the Chronotope in the Novel: Notes Toward a Historical Poetics." *The Dialogic Imagination: Four Essays.* Ed. Michael Holquist. Trans. Caryl Emerson and Michael Holquist. Austin: University of Texas Press, 1981. 84–258.

Beer, Gillian. *The Romance.* Ed. John D. Jump. The Critical Idiom series 10. London: Methuen, 1970.

Davidson, Donald. Introduction. *The Letters of William Gilmore Simms.* Ed. Mary C. Simms Oliphant, Alfred Taylor Odell, and T. C. Duncan Eaves. Vol. 1. Columbia: University of South Carolina Press, 1952.

Frye, Northrup. *Anatomy of Criticism: Four Essays.* Princeton: Princeton University Press, 1957.

Guilds, John Caldwell. *Simms: A Literary Life.* Fayetteville: University of Arkansas Press, 1992.

Quinn, Arthur Hobson. *American Fiction: An Historical and Critical Survey.* New York: D. Appleton-Century, 1936.

Simms, William Gilmore. *Guy Rivers: A Tale of Georgia*. 1855. Ed. John Caldwell Guilds. Fayetteville: University of Arkansas Press, 1993.

———. *Richard Hurdis: A Tale of Alabama*. New and rev. ed. New York: Redfield, 1855.

———. *Views and Reviews in American Literature, History, and Fiction. First Series*. Ed. C. Hugh Holman. Cambridge: Harvard University Press, 1962.

———. *The Yemassee: A Romance of Carolina*. 2 vols. New York: Harper and Brothers, 1835.

Trent, W. Peterfield. *Simms*. Ed. Charles Dudley Warner. American Men of Letters series. Boston: Houghton Mifflin, 1892.

Wellek, Rene, and Austin Warren. *Theory of Literature*. 3d ed. New York: Harcourt, 1949.

Wimsatt, Mary Ann. *The Major Fiction of William Gilmore Simms: Cultural Traditions and Literary Form*. Baton Rouge: Louisiana State University Press, 1989.

New Perspectives:
Simms and Current Literary Theory

THOMAS L. MCHANEY

Simms's *Border Beagles:*
A Carnival of Frontier Voices

Villiam Gilmore Simms's *Border Beagles* is in many respects a lesser novel than the other border novels—*Guy Rivers* or, especially, *Richard Hurdis.* But *Border Beagles* is instructive in many ways for serious study of Simms's life and art. It is, additionally, despite its limitations as compelling fiction, remarkably foresighted as an aesthetic gambit. In general, his novelistic *oeuvre* regarded as a whole, Simms took on for the developing American South of his day the same task, with the same energy, as his near contemporary Balzac took on for France a few decades after the revolution. Both writers have some of the same energies and the same faults, though Balzac, in a richer artistic tradition and allowed a freer spirit, had the advantage. Imagine trying to be the Balzac of a country still so much under development and undertaking to write a specific series of novels that moved west into those savage parts of the Old Southwest that were hardly half-formed.

Nonetheless, *Border Beagles*, even more than the earlier border novels, anticipates by a year or two Ralph Waldo Emerson's famous call, in his lecture and essay "The Poet," for new American writing. "We have yet had no genius in America," Emerson wrote, "with tyrannous eye, which knew the value of our incomparable materials, and saw, in the barbarism and materialism of the times, another carnival of the same gods whose picture he so much admires in Homer; then in the middle age; then in Calvinism. Banks and tariffs, the newspaper and caucus, methodism and unitarianism, are flat and dull to dull people, but rest on the same foundations of wonder as the town of Troy, and the temple of Delphi, and are as swiftly passing away." Emerson goes on to make a catalogue for an epic not yet written: "Our logrolling, our stumps and their politics, our fisheries, our Negroes, and Indians, our boasts, and our repudiations, the wrath of rogues, and the pusillanimity of honest men, the northern trade, the southern planting, the western clearing, Oregon and Texas, are yet unsung" (21–22).

These remarks originate in a lecture of 1841–1842; the essay Emerson eventually fashioned was announced as complete in February 1844. Interestingly enough, Simms of course was already at work on these incomparable materials about the barbarism of the times: in letters, essays, and the border novels. *Border Beagles* appeared in 1840, at which time Balzac was about a decade into his "Comedie Humaine."

So much of what Emerson cites appears in *Border Beagles* that we must credit the two authors with simultaneous generation. *Border Beagles* takes up banks and their problems during an era of speculation and worthless specie; Methodism; boasts and repudiation; the wrath of rogues and the pusillanimity of honest men; the Southern planting, the Western clearing; even Texas, at least as a place to which failed or dishonest men flee from Mississippi, leaving the famous slogan "GTT" (gone to Texas). But these subjects are not the only affinities between Simms's work and Emerson's vision for a new American poetry. From entries in his journals, we know that as Emerson contemplated the lectures into which "The Poet" ultimately fitted, he reflected frequently about language. He favored, in thought if not in use, the kind of strong speech Simms records in the novel: "What can describe the folly & emptiness of scolding like the word *jawing?* I feel too the force of the double negative, though clean contrary to our grammar rules. And I confess to some pleasure from the stinging rhetoric of a rattling oath in the mouth of truckmen & teamsters. How laconic & brisk it is by the side of a page of the *North American Review.* Cut those words & they would bleed; they are vascular & alive; they walk & run" (*Journals* 7:374).

These remarks from the great "man thinking" of Simms's times correspond to our modern perception of the singular expressions and violent events—the deliberate facing up to roughness—in *Border Beagles.* Despite the hero with the noble sentiments, as Stephen Crane might have mockingly described Harry Vernon, and a three-marriage ending that James Fenimore Cooper would have deplored, the rich mixture of backwoods characters in *Border Beagles* is, I think, more than an unapologetic portrait of the strife wrought by bandits and bankers in the old Yazoo Purchase of early-nineteenth-century Mississippi.

There are several points to admire in *Border Beagles.* I am struck, for example, by the similarity of Simms's instinct to that of Eudora Welty's brilliant little backwoods story "A Still Moment." Simms throws together the well-spoken bandit Saxon, modeled on the outlaw John Murrell; the doughty but ineffective and ridiculous backwoods Methodist Billy Badger, who appears so methodistical as to live in a perpetual camp meeting; and the frontier thespian Tom Horsey, gone a-fishing in his Hamlet costume and dunked like Ophelia, but with less tragic result. Welty's story, you may recall, brings together John Murrell, a renowned circuit-riding Methodist minister named Lorenzo Dow, and the wandering artist John James Audubon to provoke an epiphany in which Welty shows, among other things, that the violence of art may transcend and even surprise the violence of murderous banditry or of compulsive soul-saving on the old Natchez Trace. Simms's through-line is a bit different, because he has made theater, not graphic art, a ground metaphor in his work. But in both cases there is an affinity through absurdity: that the artist or the thespian should wander the backwoods. Simms emphasizes through his novel's plot that playacting is everywhere. Under a simple ruse, the circumspect and genteel hero Vernon pursues the fleeing banker Maitland, who appears under the false name Wilson; Maitland, his daughter Virginia realizes with full irony, has "sought safety in a region still wild, and still the abode of so much that was barbarous" (*Border Beagles* 2:51). Tom Horsey, the most inauthentic of strolling players, who spouts lines like a concordance to Shakespeare run wild, is flung falsely on Vernon's trail by outlaws in disguise. And all Simms's players are troubled by the masquerading bandits, who have a place in every household, except for that of the sturdy new men Wat Rawlings and Dick Jamison, whose plainness and honesty are a result of their lack of encumbrance with any sort of past. As Jamison says to the Irishman Denis O'Dougherty, "You're of too old a family, Dennis, to stand up with a young man from Alabam"—"the blood gets mighty thin going through three, or five, or seven generations, unless the breed is crossed mighty often. . . . In my state, all the men are of new families, and we've got the strength in us" (2:18). When O'Dougherty claims to be a gentleman by his mother's side, Jamison mocks him by suggesting that he therefore must be "a lady by his father's" (2:20).

Such wordplay in this topsy-turvy new world brings down inherited position and the established order. "The business of the squatter," we learn, "always carries him a little over the line" where the frontier risks impermanence. Along the Big Black River, there is "no more use naming little towns than little chickens," so perishable are they, but the people there can "frolic in a ditch" and are "fierce at poker, brave at brag" (1:37). The gamblers in this nest of speculators are numerous "as peas in a fair season" and "audacious"—but the quickest hand gets off with fewest scratches. It is not too much to say that something is meant by all this folk masquerade; and even theater, we soon learn, for all Horsey's critical language and pretense of legitimacy, invariably attracts the inappropriate credulity of the yokel, who enters the play with a speech or action and, though credulous, explodes the pretense.

Simms's writing of *Border Beagles* was as headlong as its action, as we know. Simms sent off the first half before he had written any of the second. But Simms still did better than he knew, partly by virtue of his integrity as a writer, partly by virtue of the energy of his prose, and partly because scenes and action in the land between the Big Black and the Yazoo rivers were sharply recalled from his three early trips to the Mississippi frontier. He had directly experienced the ingredients of a new literature of the sort for which Emerson would call. One of the chief requirements for a new literature that Emerson singled out in the 1840s, as Simms was making his own work, is represented by an old word that has taken renewed meaning in contemporary critical parlance. We must realize, Emerson said, that the barbarism and materialism of the times represent a *carnival* of the gods worth writing about. In his journals at the same time, Emerson reflects that the "poet cannot spare any grief or pain or terror in his experience; he wants every rude stroke that has been dealt on his irritable texture. I need my fear & my superstition as much as my purity & courage, to construct the glossary which opens the Sanscrit of the world" (*Journals* 7:390). Humankind requires polarity, Emerson writes; it needs to be struck by some fierce antagonism in living or in language to stimulate human vision:

> Who can blame men for seeking excitement? They are polar, & would you have them sleep in a dull eternity of equilibrium? Religion, love, ambition, money, war, brandy,—some fierce antagonism must break the round of perfect circulation or no spark, no joy, no event can be. As good can not be. In the country the lover of nature dreaming through the wood would never awake to thought if the scream of an eagle, the cries of a crow, or a curlew near his head, did not break the continuity. Nay if the truth must out, the finest lyrics of the poet come of this coarse parentage; the imps of matter beget such child on the Soul. (*Journals* 7:272)

The terms of Emerson's observations—the carnivalesque quality of America's rough strife, which fulfilled man's need for polarity, for dialectical stimulus—fit the plan of Simms's rude novel. They also have close counterparts in a rich contemporary criticism of the novel derived from the writings of the Russian formalist Mikhail Bakhtin—who was, we remember, a close contemporary of, say, Faulkner. Bakhtin based his celebration of the leveling and revealing power of long fiction upon studies in Rabelais—the jocund celebrator of carnivalistic reordering who worked the frontier between the Middle Ages and the Renaissance—and in Dostoyevsky, a rough contemporary of Simms who lived in a society in many respects akin to the one from which Simms himself came. Bakhtin has given us a new appreciation of the ways in which the novel form is truer to life by virtue of its rich polyphonic play of human voices, its rough grotesque realism, and its parodic displacement of all authority—secular and religious—through the replication, in narrative, of the carnivalization process carried out in folk celebrations.

The polyphony of Simms's novel—the play of folk voices against the staid and genteel—can be regarded, of course, as nothing more than evidence of Simms's close observation of local color "on the very skirts . . . of civilization" (*Border Beagles* 1:39). But Bakhtin's elaborations of the achievement of the nineteenth-century novel that he knew and loved can help us perceive an ulterior effect beneath Simms's realism. The play of voices in Simms is—even more than the richly dialectical variety that Mark Twain claims in his well-known note prefacing *Huckleberry Finn*—a play of forces. *Border Beagles* is a dramatization of the heteroglossia of a society in flux where, often, an individual voice is all that a single person owns for use in the struggle to claim a piece of action in a new section of a rapidly vanishing frontier. The frontier is vanishing not under the press of new ordinary men, but under the manipulations of law and money, the tools of the established order. Thus, in the genre of writing that Simms exploits, exists the presence of such mottoes as that of Alabamian Johnson Jones Hooper's Simon Suggs: "It's good to be shifty in a new country." In *Border Beagles*, capital, authority, and the genteel order are at men's backs as much as anything: the flatboatmen, for instance, the deceiver Hawkins tells Tom Horsey, who's sung one of their songs, "are done up now. These steam-sturgeons [powered riverboats] have cut up as pretty a bunch of business as ever needed a long pole, and deserved a glorious frolic" (1:76).

The slight varieties of dialect in the cognate tongues of *Border Beagles* express the spirit of Simms's times. Linguistically, it is a frolic. The forces of individuality and assurance often prove wrong or simply adversarial, but are rarely inauthentic—and that usually by intent to deceive. It is interesting that the two men most easily deceived in *Border Beagles* are the men of formal language: the old Methodist firm in his piety but surrounded by agents of the antithesis, even in his very bosom, and the tragedian Tom Horsey, spouting poetry that is always in fragments, never filled out, a man innocent of the consequences of his own vanity and profligacy. The other great master of language, of course, is Saxon, alias Foster, the secret force behind the mysterious brotherhood that is doomed, too, by its very variousness of voice—so that Bull, Jones, Stillyards, the Irishman O'Dougherty, and the corrupted boys Gideon Badger and Ned Mabry all still have voices of their own and waver, or provoke, or reveal, or strike out on their own, when wronged by the words of others—a veritable babel of backwoods renegades hoping to conquer a piece of the new unlanguaged land.

Emerson had put it this way in his journals: the speakers of the vernacular have "this elegancy, that they do not trip in their speech. It is a shower of bullets, whilst Cambridge men & Yale men correct themselves & begin again at every half sentence. . . . this profane swearing & bar-room wit has salt & fire in it. . . . *Guts* is a stronger word than intestines" (*Journals* 7: 374). "The best old poets," he thought, "smite & arouse me with the sharp fife, & . . . open my eye on my own possibilities. They clap wings to the side of all the solid old lumber of the world & I see the old Proteus is not dead" (7:524).

Thoreau may have believed later with some justice that Emerson had become too much a gentleman, but in the 1840s Emerson could lament, "What a pity that we cannot curse & swear in good society. Cannot the stinging dialect of the sailors be domesticated? It is the best rhetoric and for a hundred occasions those forbidden words are the only good ones. My page about 'Consistency' would be better written thus: Damn Consistency" (*Journals* 7:524). Simms must have had very similar feelings, and the result in *Border Beagles* was a dialogue between stinging dialect and genteel speech. *Border Beagles*, we can now tell, thanks to James Kibler's good work, is close in language and reflection of experience to Simms's first set of letters from the West, his brief correspondence back to Charleston about the 1826 trip that carried him to Mobile, New Orleans, Columbus, Mississippi, and the Pearl River Valley. This, his second trip into the frontier territory, produced an account that is a bit less self-consciously literary than the "Notes of a Small Tourist" in 1831, though both trips, and the impressions they made, as well as the initial trip of which there is not a corresponding record, influenced the border novels. The young man of the first account seems close to Harry Vernon of *Border Beagles*, and at the same time, like Tom Horsey, quotes poetry in the strange context of the raw frontier. He may be more of a moralist, or at least less worldly, than the traveler of 1831. Both accounts show, however, that Simms interests himself in the theater and actors of Mobile and New Orleans, providing material for the theatrical subplot of *Border Beagles*. We know, too, that Simms found much that was appalling in the frontier and that, in his 1831 report, he made the often quoted plea for closing the frontier until the country had developed a true society. He allows the question to be debated in an interesting way in *Border Beagles*. Saxon, whose dark plans we know, claims that the "wildness of the region will keep back the cold, the slow, the timid, and the wealthy," who will shrink from the Indian and the squatter, "who, rude, rash, violent and reckless as they are, are yet necessary men in all new countries" (2:6). Emerson had put it in a similar way: "Every nation to emerge from barbarism must have a . . . graft on the wild stock, and every man must. He may go to college for it, or to conversation, or to affairs, or to the successes & mortifications of his private biography, war, politics, fishing or love, some antagonism he must have as projectile force to balance his centripetence" (*Journals* 7:90).

For his part, Simms's character Harry Vernon is deliberately cautious in his encounter with the unknown Saxon, who has come to ride along with Vernon in much the way Murrell was said to accost unwary travelers before he revealed himself and murdered them. With his suspicions, perhaps this is why Vernon says, in response to Saxon's ironic warnings, that he doesn't take much stock in fearful tales of frontier violence. And yet, he puts it in a moderate way that also deliberately undercuts some of Simms's earlier negative criticism of the frontier: "The border is always beyond you; the country of the monsters . . . is still the country of the unknown . . . and mankind for ages have shrunk from the possession of the garden spots of earth, through dread of those multiplied terrors which have been made to guard them, simply through the industry of their own imaginations" (*Border Beagles* 2:16–17). The garden spots of *Border Beagles* are, interestingly enough, all subjected to the transforming hand of carnivalization: the inn at which Vernon spends the night with the sleepwalking Horsey has local bandits using what is almost a stage-floor trap door, to slightly burlesque effect. The rude camp of the beguiled old Methodist who cannot see the evil all around him, and the bandit's lair at Cane Creek, which Tom Horsey interprets as the encampment of a rambling theater group, are portrayed with equally complex flair, part masquerade, part humor, part genuine threat. Polyphony, as Bakhtin might see it, abounds.

In his discussion of the carnivalesque, Bakhtin says that gambling, for example, is carnivalesque because people are made equal by the rules of the game. In *Border Beagles*, it is pointed out that backwoods gamblers are numerous and audacious, but dice and cards aren't the only medium of the carnivalesque in Simms's novel. Backwoods theater is carnival, too, as is the bandit's witty rendition of a mock plan to bring into the frontier a host of great spellbinding orators to speak to great crowds and "pick the teeth" of the people "while their jaws are on the stretch, listening to these fine sayings" (2:230). The impish Stillyards's role is very carnivalesque, since by virtue of his grotesqueness and his position in society, he stands outside life's normal logic. His attempt to wrest sexual favors from the beautiful ruined woman whom Saxon has abandoned, as his price for betraying the bandit chief, casts him and Florence into the roles of the idiot and the madwoman, a carnival pair (Bakhtin 172–73). They succeed in bringing down the arch-villain's plan, for his disregard of both of them seals his fate. The paradoxical depravity and nobility of these two refract the lives of the novel's other couples, whose decency is repeatedly threatened by deceit and violence and whose virtue is always under attack. What Bakhtin observes about Dostoyevsky's *The Idiot* may, in some sense, be observed in *Border Beagles* as well: "hell and paradise in the novel intersect" (173).

It is not without significance that the outlaw's paradise, Cane Castle, set in the midst of a primordial swamp, is one of those savage Edens that reflects for its time some aspects of the true condition of America. It seems particularly apt that Tom Horsey's falsely aroused theatrical ambitions at Cane Castle include first of all a production of *A Midsummer Night's Dream*, with the outlaws reflexively cast as the rustic band of wandering players. Unbeknown to Tom, this savage arcadia hides a bruised Hippolyta and a moody and criminal Oberon. Tom's identity—his everyday garb—is stolen from him to prove that he is dead, murdered by the novel's noble hero, and so he is forced to go out in the everyday world wearing his theatrical raiment. He chooses to go out as Hamlet. Given all the missing or contrary fathers, and the duty imposed on Simms's hero Harry Vernon by one surrogate father to apprehend and bring another surrogate father to an accounting (not a punishment), Horsey's garb is interesting material for anyone who would take Simms—and Simms's biography—seriously.

These all too brief hints about the presence of the carnivalesque and the dialogic in Simms's novels deserve further attention, which even now they are beginning to receive, as other essays in this volume show. Such elements function, as Bakhtin observes, to give vitality and to weaken one-sided rhetorical seriousness or dogmatism (107). Simms, as we know from his essays and poems, as well as the border novels, was ready and willing to debate the frontier, seeing it from many sides. What was Simms's attitude toward the frontier? Did he abhor it? Or was the question, in some sense, open? Was the question also intertwined with his expectations and disappointments vis-à-vis his father? The evidence of his writing about it, all in all, is that his regard for the wildness and openness of the backwoods was, in a word, ambivalent—or, to put it in a more positive way, it was not one-sided or singular. On the larger philosophical plane, his perception acknowledged the duality of things, and it seems appropriate to say of Simms's work in *Border Beagles* what Bakhtin says of the prose artist in general: "For the prose artist the world is full of other people's words, among which he must orient himself and whose speech characteristics he must be able to perceive with a very keen ear. He must introduce them into the plane of his own discourse, but in such a way that this plane is not destroyed. He works with a very rich verbal palette, and he works exceptionally well with it" (201).

Simms may be most effective when he refracts the romanticism of his times through the polyphony of his most vernacular voices—-a feat well achieved, as we know, in a book like *Huckleberry Finn*, but achieved, as well, in *Border Beagles*. In the midst of the artificial gentility of his society, Simms's frontier voices give life to language and to described action. He portrays a vital disorder, an open society, a folk risibility that diminishes the artificial codes of the higher classes. For all that Simms's novel ends with so many marriages, its concentration on ruses, betrayal, deceived innocence, and violence make it a *Midsummer Night's Dream* that acknowledges the possible advantage in this world held by the dark power of the forest spirits for their arcane purposes, and the essentially ambivalent—that is to say, shifty and dialogic—character of humankind.

WORKS CITED

Bakhtin, Mikhail. *Problems of Dostoevsky's Poetics*. Ed. and trans. Caryl Emerson. Introd. Wayne Booth. Minneapolis: University of Minnesota Press, 1984.
Emerson, Ralph Waldo. *The Journals and Miscellaneous Notebooks of Ralph Waldo Emerson*. Vol. 7: 1838–1842. Ed. A. W. Plumstead and Harrison Hayford. Cambridge: Harvard University Press, 1969.

————. *The Journals and Miscellaneous Notebooks of Ralph Waldo Emerson.* Vol. 8: 1841–1843. Ed. William Gilman and J. E. Parsons. Cambridge: Harvard University Press, 1970.

————. "The Poet." *Essays: Second Series.* Vol. 3 of *Collected Works.* 24 vols. Cambridge: Harvard University Press, 1983. 1–24.

Simms, William Gilmore. *Border Beagles: A Tale of Mississippi.* 2 vols. Philadelphia: Carey and Hart, 1840.

————. *Guy Rivers: A Tale of Georgia.* New and rev. ed. New York: Redfield, 1855.

————. *Richard Hurdis: A Tale of Alabama.* New and rev. ed. New York: Redfield, 1855.

Welty, Eudora. "A Still Moment." *The Collected Stories of Eudora Welty.* New York: Harcourt Brace Jovanovich, 1980. 189–99.

Simms's Frontier:
A Collision of Cultures

In an oration delivered in August 1844, Simms argues that a nation cannot be independent unless it believes in itself and that it cannot believe in itself if it depends on other nations for its cultural traditions. In order to be an independent nation, America must nurture an awareness of itself as an evolving culture with a unique system of values, a unique ideology, a unique cultural identity. Simms suggests that the country's future depends on the development of this uniquely American cultural identity, for he writes: "Our development depends upon our faith in what we are, and in our independence of foreign judgment. A resolute will, a bold aim, and a spirit that courageously looks within for its encouragements and standards,—these are our securities for intellectual independence" (*Views* 12). America has declared herself independent and must now rely on her own judgments and her own values (not those of the British) for her intellectual and cultural development, or her independence, according to Simms, will never be true independence. A national identity unique to the country and the people must be developed; a new cultural tradition must be established.

Yet Simms finds the American identity of his time, in both thought and language, to be "wholly English," not reflecting the "self-speaking" of America any more than it reflects her "native progress and development" (*Views* 12). Simms recognizes the need to develop a unique intellectual voice that can encourage and establish this needed American identity and can reflect the uniquely American culture. He continues: "It is but to see these things as we should—to understand the world-wide difference between writing for, and writing from one's people. . . . To write from a people, is to write a people—to make them live—to endow them with a life and a name—to preserve them with a history forever" (*Views* 12). Simms understands that an American literature must reflect the American people in their entirety and diversity; it must reflect their values, their struggles, and the uniqueness of the American experience. Through this literary representation, the creation and development of an American cultural identity and American cultural tradition will be encouraged. Simms also recognizes the importance of the textual representation of American experience in maintaining that developing identity. Consequently, much of his work focuses on defining the American experience, and, through the textualization of this experience, he explores the progressive evolution of the national and cultural identity from its early stages.

One of the places where this emphasis is most obvious is in his frontier literature. As a defining element of the American experience, the frontier is particularly important to Simms. Much of his best work makes use of the frontier as a setting, but, in Simms, the frontier becomes much more than a location and much more than a boundary between the civilized and uncivilized. It can best be described as a center of cultural confrontation, a battleground where various cultural identities confront each other and where the American cultural identity is defined and eventually solidified. It is also the battlefield upon which some cultural identities are inevitably lost.

Simms's use of the frontier fits nicely within the context of Annette Kolodny's view of the frontier as a literary element. Kolodny defines a frontier as "a locus of first cultural contact, circumscribed by a particular physical terrain in the process of change because of the forms that contact takes, all of it inscribed by the collisions and interpenetrations of the language" (3). The frontier, as a literary element, has the potential, then, to represent a dialogic, textualized enactment of cultural conflict. As in Simms, the frontier is more than a boundary, more than a simple line that marks marginalization from society or that separates civilization from the wilderness. It is a demarcated zone in "which the relations among the peoples in the territory begin, develop, and eventually crystalize"[1] (Kolodny 4–5). Frontier literature textualizes this process; it captures these cultural collisions and defines the conflicting ideologies through language. As Kolodny describes, this defining of both culture and ideology occurs most clearly in the clash of discourses that refract "the collisions and negotiations of distinct cultural groups" and express them through "languages and texts" (5).

The literature that refracts this process of collisions and negotiations would, by its nature, lean toward Mikhail Bakhtin's dialogic model. Bakhtin sees the novel as a metaphoric battleground where conflicting value systems or ideologies come into contact. If the authorial voice, through narrative structure, technique, or some other means, denounces one ideology while supporting another, if it concludes that one ideology is correct, then the text is monologic. However, if the ideologies speak with their own voices, if they enter into a dialogue (or confrontation) with each other, and if the author intentionally does not subvert one to the other or if the attempt to subvert one ideology fails, then the text is dialogic (or multi-voiced).[2] According to Bakhtin, the dialogic text does not or cannot silence one voice or ideology with the domination of another. Whether the failure to silence is intentional or not is not a concern. Regardless of authorial intent, the differing ideologies continue to permeate the text, even if only in the margins, and the text calls attention to the dialogue and the power struggle the dialogue represents.

The frontier itself is in a continual state of dialogue and flux. Simms sees the frontier as "a wild, uncivilized region, caught in conflict between good and evil and torn by moral, social, and environmental forces, in the gradual yet violent process of becoming civilized" (Guilds 313). In this state of "becoming," conflict and opposition have the potential to define the ideology and eventual identity of the region. Frontier literature in general and Simms's work in particular refract through language these shifting cultural consciousnesses and identities. Different value systems compete within the demarcated region of the frontier text. Multiple cultural voices or ideologies are contained, clash, readjust, respond, and eventually realign themselves. The very nature of the interaction makes it difficult to completely silence one ideology in subordination to another. As long as the frontier is in the state of "civilizing," or of changing, the different systems of value, the ideologies, will be competing. As long as they compete, there will be a dialogic potential within the literature. Once the competition ceases, the region's identity has been defined, and it is no longer a frontier.

The significance of the frontier and of cultural identity to Simms and their importance as elements in his fiction would be difficult to doubt. Throughout his frontier literature, Simms displays an awareness of the frontier's impact on cultural identity and exhibits an active fascination with frontier interaction. Louis Rubin, in a study of Simms's *The Yemassee* and Cooper's *The Last of the Mohicans*, suggests that Simms and Cooper were the first two American novelists "to make important literary use of the frontier, the wilderness, and the Indians as shaping forces in the national history" (112). Here, Rubin calls attention to the power of the frontier "to shape" a national identity and to enter into a dialogue of textual ideologies. Yet, he sees Cooper as more effectively using the frontier, finds *The Yemassee* lacking "tension between nature and society," and concludes that Simms sees "the matter almost exclusively in terms of a social, historical confrontation," which Rubin views as a clear weakness in the work (116–17). Interestingly, what Rubin isolates as a weakness, when placed within the frame of Kolodny's definition of the frontier or within the frame of dialogism becomes a strength, for it is within the confrontation between peoples (the social-historical confrontation) that their cultural voices can be heard and the working out of their cultural relationship ultimately understood.

Though Rubin deals only with *The Yemassee*, others of Simms's novels are also set in the regions between the white man's civilization and the as yet untamed, unconquered wilderness of the Indian. Similarly, within these novels, the frontier is a defining element of cultural confrontation. As Rubin suggests, the border is clear and well-defined for Simms; a demarcated zone exists between cultural boundaries, and this zone separates two distinct ways of life. And it is true that in Simms's fiction cultural demarcations (boundaries of the frontier) are of social and historical as well as moral and ideological importance.

For example, in *Vasconselos* and *The Cassique of Kiawah* (as well as in *The Yemassee*), the boundary separates distinct people and different cultures, the Indian and the European; it is within this physical zone between the two (Simms's frontier) that the cultures meet and the relationship between cultures is developed and essentially worked out. Even though there is a victorious culture within these works and, consequently, one ideology appears to overcome, subvert, or somehow assimilate the other, the subverted culture is not truly silenced in the novels. It remains in the margins of the text, unwilling to surrender its identity.

This is Simms's dialogic frontier in its simplest form and as it is seen in his extremely culturally aware works. As the cultures clash, the voices of the conflicting ideologies enter into a dialogue and speak to each other; they echo throughout the texts. Even when the Yemassee are defeated, their voice (most clearly heard through their chief, Sanutee) is not silenced, because Simms's authorial voice does not justify the annihilation of the Yemassee people nor deny the validity of the Yemassee's culture or their stand to defend it. Consequently, the Yemassees' cultural identity lingers in the margins of the text, even after the destruction of their society. Similarly, in *Vasconselos*, the ideologies of the Spanish conquerors, the native American

Indians, and the Portuguese knight Philip Vasconselos speak in their own voices throughout the narrative, and, even though the authorial voice attempts to pass judgment, the ideologies in the text tend to defy that judgment and speak for themselves.

Since Simms is unable to silence the opposing values within his texts, the representations of these values and ideologies create powerful cultural identities that become controlling forces in the novels. Within the novels, each culture has a strong identity or characterization of its own, and it is the characters' perception and understanding of their cultural identities (or their lack thereof) that control the characters' responses and the movements of the novels. Since cultural identification is so very powerful, Simms's heroes are not generally highly individualistic; instead, his best creations are mythic in scope, often cultural figures who ascertain (or attempt to ascertain) the continuation of their cultures against all odds. Clearly, an individual's cultural identity is also an important element in his work. For Simms, history (and thus fiction) is a study of the struggle of cultures, of the survival of their traditions, and of the individual as a cultural entity, and the frontier, as Simms represents it, is the classroom.

Simms's interest in the cultural identities of his characters and his exploration and development of the tensions between colliding cultures are both prevalent in the framing of the frontier romances that narrate the westward movement of the white man, especially in the Indian trilogy. These three works (*The Yemassee*, *The Cassique of Kiawah*, and *Vasconselos*) particularly show a level of cultural awareness found in few other nineteenth-century writers. The collision of cultures and the impact of this collision on members of each culture is a continuing theme in the Indian trilogy, and it is a powerful theme that Simms handles well.

Cultural collision is continually seen in the inability of two differing cultures to coexist as equals. In *The Yemassee*, for example, the expanding white civilization has collided with the traditional Yemassee way of life. Though the Indians are treated sympathetically throughout the novel, the authorial voice acknowledges early in the novel's structure that the two cultures cannot coexist: "It is the nature of civilization to own an appetite for dominion and extended sway, which the world that is known will always fail to satisfy. . . . Conquest and sway are the great leading principles of her existence, and the savage must join her train, or she rides over him relentlessly in her onward progress" (*Yemassee* 76). One culture, one controlling ideology, must prevail. Not only will the Yemassee be defeated, but the authorial

voice suggests that they will be destroyed if they refuse to acknowledge the
ideological and cultural superiority of the white man. In order to survive,
the Yemassee must be absorbed into the white culture, surrendering their
native identity. Yet, if absorbed, they will lose their unique cultural identity,
becoming only a part of the white man's civilization. Since the authorial
voice has set out this premise, whether the Yemassee culture is absorbed or
destroyed, the text would appear to be a monologic enactment of cultural
collision. But the Yemassee refuse to be absorbed and, through the words
of their chief, justify their refusal as a defense of their very essence. The
text of the novel traces the resulting confrontation of the two cultures
through the voices of the Yemassee, the whites, and the author. The multi-
voicing results in a dialogic treatment of conflicting cultures and ideologies.

Thus cultural collision seen in Simms's work becomes literary cultural
dialogism. In addition, the difficulties encountered by the character who
tries to move between cultures, live within multiple cultures, or live outside
of his native culture become still another form of cultural collision that
reflects the importance of cultural identity for the individual. The resolution of the character's situation and of his cultural dilemma is another way
that the cultures engage each other in dialogue within the text.

Mostly without exception, all characters in Simms's work are governed
by their cultural identity. They act as their place within their culture demands. Even his evil or dark characters are governed by the cultural conception of what they are. Simms creates characters who often struggle with
cultural limitations and expectations, but few of his characters exist outside
of cultural boundaries, especially in the frontier fiction. Fewer still try to
break from or exist outside of their cultural heritage; few attempt to move
from one culture to another. Those who do find it a nearly impossible task
and one that has serious, generally devastating, ramifications.

In *The Yemassee*, the westward expansion of the white civilization has en-
croached to such an extent on the Yemassee territory and lifestyle that the
noble chief Sanutee, who originally befriended the white man, realizes that
the two cultures can no longer coexist and acknowledges that inevitable
cultural conflict must come:

> The evidence rose daily before his eyes in the diminution of the
> game—in the frequent insults to his people, unredressed by their ob-
> trusive neighbours—and in the daily approach of some new borderer
> among them, whose habits were foreign, and whose capacities were

obviously superior to theirs. The desire for new lands, and the facility with which the whites, in many cases, taking advantage of the weaknesses of the Indian chiefs, had been enabled to procure them, impressed Sanutee strongly with the melancholy prospect in reserve for the Yemassee. (76)

The Yemassee stand in the way of the expansion and progress of the white culture, which is already, little by little, taking from the Yemassee part of their identity. The text becomes a dialogue between the opposing ideologies, the opposing value systems, each voiced through different characters. As Grayson, one of the Carolinians, explains the conflict to Reverend Matthews: "It is utterly impossible that the whites and Indians should ever live together and agree. . . . after a while, they [the Indians] must not only be inferior, but they must become dependent. When this happens, and it will happen with the diminution of their hunting lands, circumscribed, daily, more and more, as they are by our approaches, they must become degraded, and sink into slavery and destitution. A few of them have become so now; they are degraded by brutal habits" (291). The two views represent different ideologies that are present in the text. Grayson's solution is a monologic one, one that Sanutee, his people, and Simms reject. The absorption of the Yemassee into the white culture and the loss of their cultural identity, as Sanutee has come to understand, is the inevitable outcome of the white colonists' expansion. He acts for the preservation of his race and of their culture. At his death at the end of the novel, he acknowledges the loss: "The well-beloved has no people. The Yemassee has bones in the thick woods, and there are no young braves to sing the song of glory. . . . We may not drive [the white man] away. It is good for Sanutee to die with his people. Let the song of his dying be sung" (405–6). It is not only the death song of Sanutee but the death song of a people that is heard. The cultural identity of the Yemassee begins to fade; yet, within Simms's dialogic frontier text, their cultural voice can still be heard echoing in the margins, and their ideology (cultural belief) is not silenced, even at their death.

Occonestoga, the son of Sanutee, is a victim of the cultural collision. He is seduced by the "white man's poison" and speaks for "the chiefs of the English" to convince the Yemassee to sell the English more land (79). Occonestoga is caught in the transition of cultural power and loses his Yemassee cultural identity when he tries to move between the Indian and white cultures. His actions, both his attempt to change cultures and his eventual failure, can be seen as another part of the ongoing dialogue between the two cultures.

The Yemassee, as punishment for his betrayal, plan to exile him from their race. His totem, the identifying mark of the Yemassee, will be cut from his arm. Without this totem, the Yemassee has no identity "for, without this totem, no other nation could recognise them, their own resolutely refused to do it, and, at their death, the great Manneyto [the Indian god] would reject them" (96). The punishment for cultural betrayal in the Yemassee ideology is cultural rejection, not death. Occonestoga's future is bleak because he will live in total isolation and lose his identity within his culture. Yet Simms, in a dialogue of values within the Yemassee culture itself, redeems him. Matiwan, his mother, kills Occonestoga before the totem is removed. Before she strikes the killing blow, she assures, "I strike thee but to save thee, my son:—since they cannot take the totem from thee after the life is gone" (200). By dying with his totem still intact, Occonestoga dies within the culture and retains his cultural identity.

In *Vasconselos*, a novel narrating De Soto's march to the Mississippi, the treatment of cultural collision is more complex. Simms places a Portuguese hero in a Spanish expedition going among the Florida Indians. The most obvious cultural conflict in the novel is seen, of course, between the Spanish and the Indians. Again, two opposing lifestyles (Indian and European) come into conflict. Though the Indians at first welcome the Spanish explorers, they soon find that the Spanish have no respect for Indian culture or values, and the Indians realize that the two cultures cannot coexist. Again, cultural conflict comes as the Indians attempt to drive the Spanish from their lands in order to ensure their own survival as a nation. And, again, the conflict is dialogic due to the voicing in the novel.

Throughout the novel, in both Spanish Cuba and the wilderness of America, the center of cultural collision revolves around the third cultural voice, Philip Vasconselos, the Portuguese knight. The Portuguese cultural identity is brought into conflict with the Spanish cultural identity with the introduction of Philip to Cuba. It is clear that Philip, as a true chivalric knight of Portugal, holds to a different ideology than the Spanish. Though seen throughout the Cuban sequence, the Spanish rejection of Philip is most emphatically presented when De Soto delays in acknowledging Philip as winner of the tournament. Philip has defeated all the native Spanish knights rather easily, and yet he finds that: "The feeling was everywhere adverse to his claims and expectations; and it was with something of con-

tempt, not unmixed with bitterness, that our knight of Portugal was reminded of the national prejudice which felt reluctant to do justice to the
achievements of the stranger" (*Vasconselos* 234). Philip is a "stranger" because he is outside the "national" or cultural identity of the people. There
is a racial element here, and Simms reminds the reader that racial identity
is an important part of cultural and national identity.

Unlike other of Simms's heroes, Philip seems to struggle with cultural
identity throughout the novel. The crest on his shield was "a ruined tower,
from which a falcon was about to fly," with a device reading "Having the
wing, I no longer need the nest," which was "a sufficient allusion to his
homeless fortunes, and to the independent courage which enabled him to
soar above them" (221). The homelessness of the ruined tower along with
the flying falcon symbolizes an existence outside of a culture. And Philip is
true to this symbolic exile; he is always somewhat isolated: from his brother,
from his proposed lover, from his Spanish comrades, and even from the
Indians he helps. Yet Philip is an admirable character, and one Simms sees
as a hero.

After a long, rather drawn-out chain of events, Philip joins the Spanish
expedition to Florida where he is tricked, secretly arrested, and unjustly
accused of treason by one of Simms's black villains, Don Balthazar.
Though the treasonous act is one of chivalry, an act dictated by Philip's
ideology (he prevents two Spanish guards from raping an Indian princess
and then allows her to escape), Philip is condemned for betraying the Spanish. As in *The Yemassee*, Philip's punishment for cultural betrayal is not
death but cultural exile. De Soto sentences him to be exiled from "Chris-
tendom" through the "proper laws of chivalry, which he holds in such ven-
eration" (445). He will be stripped of all chivalric symbols, "driven with
blow and buffet from the army, and, tied to a tree of the forest," where "he
shall be left to the mercies of these red savages of Appalachia, to whom he
hath shown such favor" (445). The extremity of the punishment is empha-
sized in Philip's reaction: "then was soul thrown back upon itself, without
being able to find support"; and he pleads for "Death! Death, rather than
such doom as this!" (445).

The loss of the chivalric code is similar to the loss of the Yemassee totem;
it strips Philip of his identity. Though his cultural identity is Portuguese,
not Spanish, Philip has held that identity through his chivalric values and
the physical elements that symbolize those values. Moreover, since he is
removed from and outside of his culture, he needs these symbols of chivalry

(the reminders of cultural values he holds dear) to give him that identity. Removal of the symbols (like removal of Occonestoga's totem) would be "the obliteration of the whole previous life! It inured to the future. It tainted the name of fame forever! It was the death of the soul, and of all the hope, and pride, and glory, which the spirit of chivalry held most precious in esteem!" (445). Chivalric degradation becomes the symbolic death of Philip's ideology.

Unlike Occonestoga's case, however, the sentence is carried out. Philip is tied to a tree, stripped of the outward symbols of his chivalric code, and left to the mercy of the "red savages." The process takes away all outside emblems of his chivalry and, in doing so, symbolically exiles him from civilized humanity. Though death imagery is predominant in the description of Philip's sufferings, he does not physically die. Rather, he is transferred or reborn into a new culture when he is rescued by Cocalla (the Indian princess he saved). But cultural transfer is painful and costly, and as a result of this cultural exile and cultural rebirth, Philip undergoes "a fearful change of character," becoming a "vulture of revenge . . . waiting his moment when to swoop down in blood upon the quarry" (472). He is essentially reborn as the Indian chief Istalana and becomes the Indians' great leader against the Spanish.

Philip does clearly break with his culture, and he does adopt a new cultural identity. Both are as uncommon in Simms's fiction as they are in reality. However, it is important to note that Philip's native cultural identity (represented by his chivalric code) is taken from him; he does not surrender it. Consequently, the break with the native culture is forced and unwilling. His betrayal of the Spanish culture is not a true cultural betrayal because the Spanish are not his native people (unlike Occonestoga's cultural betrayal). Furthermore, Philip, again unlike Occonestoga, does not initiate the break; he himself is betrayed. Therefore, Philip can live in a partially redeemed state whereas Occonestoga could not. Yet, though he lives, Philip is never truly fulfilled in his new culture. As the novel ends, he has only "a fond embrace, the memory of which, in long years after, sweetened greatly the solitude to the heart of the knight of Portugal" (530). His isolation, a result of the loss of his native cultural identity, is never totally reversed.

In *The Cassique of Kiawah*, the cultural conflict is again between South Carolinian and Indian ideologies. As in *The Yemassee*, the white culture is advancing and threatening the Indian way of life, and the Indians resist the white expansion. Cussoboe, the chief, plants his son, Iswattee, within the barony so that he can let the Indians in to massacre the whites on the day of the insurrection. Iswattee, realizing that the success of the Indian attack rests on his actions and yet wanting to save the people of the barony, struggles with the cultural responsibility his father has given him. He searches in vain through Indian mysticism for an answer to his dilemma, but there is none.

Iswattee is unsuited for the cultural responsibility he is given. He is described as having a "soul, of less masculine nature than that of his people," and it "shrinks as he contemplates the results of his action" (*Cassique* 515). His totem that comes to him during his mystic initiation into manhood is "a little white bird," and his instincts tell him that Grace, one of the barony's occupants, is "the very creature which had been imaged to his dreaming senses as the bird whose totem he should bear!" (516). While remaining with the cassique, he begins "to feel, more and more, how terrible was the duty which had been set him by his sire" (516), and he wishes to find a way "to save the little white Bird and her people" (517). However, Iswattee's cultural identity rests on his ability to fulfill cultural expectations. But there is no way to remain loyal to his people and to save the whites. Consequently, he fails and finds himself, like Occonestoga and Philip Vasconselos, on the outside of his culture and in conflict with its ideology and with his cultural identity.

Unlike Philip and Occonestoga, however, Iswattee is not formally exiled from his people by a cultural ceremony, suggesting still another level of cultural values and dialogue within the text. Though he is renounced and nearly killed by his father, there is no definite cultural renunciation. Yet, for Iswattee, his cultural awareness of what he has done and what he has failed to do is too much for him: "He was a madman. His constant narcotic potations, his frenzied dreams, his wild and hopeless passion, the misery occasioned by his own consciousness of treachery to his people, and the stunning blow of his father's tomahawk upon his head, had utterly wrecked [his] intellect. . . . In a week he was dead" (596). While both Occonestoga and Vasconselos are redeemed in some sense, Iswattee is not; he is offered no cultural redemption, even within the margins of the text. His cultural exile, though not as formal nor as explicitly detailed as Vasconselos's or Occonestoga's, seems more complete. The boy dies alone, outside of both his native culture and the white culture he tried to save.

As a whole, these three novels emphasize a cultural and ideological struggle taking place on the frontier. They show a progressive awareness of the importance of cultural conflict and cultural identity and an awareness of the importance of the frontier as a locus for resolving the arising conflicts.

They also show a growing disillusionment with the hope of cultural compromise and with the hope of a compromise in ideologies. In *The Yemassee*, published in 1835, the cultural separation is clear; the conflict is inevitable; the cultural ideologies are clearly incompatible. However, the defeated culture is not silenced and retains a redemption through Sanutee. Occonestoga, though he betrays his people and defies their ideology, is also redeemed, like his people, and allowed to die within his culture, which restores his cultural identity. In *Vasconselos*, published in 1857, Philip Vasconselos is betrayed by the culture he tries to join, is stripped of the symbols of his true cultural identity, and is transferred to a third, more barbaric culture to live out his life. Though he does not die, his new cultural identity cannot fulfill his expectations; consequently, his redemption is not as complete as Occonestoga's. Finally, in *The Cassique of Kiawah*, published in 1859, the outcome of cultural conflict is harsher, for there is no compromise. Iswattee loses his cultural identity through his own awareness of his failure and dies unredeemed and alone.

In spite of this growing disillusionment with cultural or ideological compromise, all three novels retain a cultural dialogue, refracting the negotiation of conflicting ideologies through a dialogic treatment of the characters and their cultural identities. The inherent inability of two cultures to coexist on equal footing and the consequences individuals trying to change cultures must face both emphasize the complexities that Simms saw in cultural, as well as individual, survival on the American frontier and provide one view of the beginning of the evolution of an American cultural identity.

NOTES

1. Kolodny quotes Howard Lamar and Leonard Thompson, acknowledging that her definition of *frontier* incorporates their definition in "Comparative Frontier History."

2. See M. M. Bakhtin, "Discourse in the Novel," 259–422; Gary Saul Morson and Caryl Emerson, *Mikhail Bakhtin*, 49–62, 234–46.

WORKS CITED

Bakhtin, Mikhail M. "Discourse in the Novel." *The Dialogic Imagination: Four Essays*. Ed. Michael Holquist. Trans. Caryl Emerson and Michael Holquist. Austin: University of Texas Press, 1981.

Guilds, John Caldwell. *Simms: A Literary Life.* Fayetteville: University of Arkansas Press, 1992.

Kolodny, Annette. "Letting Go Our Grand Obsessions: Notes Toward a New Literary History of the American Frontiers." *American Literature* 64 (1992): 1–18.

Lamar, Howard, and Leonard Thompson, eds. "Comparative Frontier History." *The Frontier in History: North America and Southern Africa Compared.* New Haven: Yale University Press, 1981.

Morson, Gary Saul, and Caryl Emerson. *Mikhail Bakhtin: Creation of a Prosaics.* Stanford: Stanford University Press, 1990.

Rubin, Louis D., Jr. "The Romance of the Colonial Frontier: Simms, Cooper, the Indians, and the Wilderness." *American Letters and the Historical Consciousness: Essays in Honor of Lewis P. Simpson.* Ed. J. Gerald Kennedy and Daniel Mark Fogel. Baton Rouge: Louisiana State University Press, 1987. 112–34.

Simms, William Gilmore. *The Cassique of Kiawah.* 1859. Ed. David Aiken. Gainesville: Magnolia, 1989.

———. *Vasconselos.* New York: Redfield, 1857.

———. *Views and Reviews in American Literature, History, and Fiction.* Ed. C. Hugh Holman. Cambridge: Belknap, 1962.

———. *The Yemassee: A Romance of Carolina.* 1835. Ed. Alexander Cowie. New and rev. ed. New York: Redfield, 1853.

DAVID W. NEWTON

Voices Along the Border:
Language and the Southern Frontier
in *Guy Rivers: A Tale of Georgia*

We learn very soon in life—indeed, we are compelled to learn, in our
own defence, at a very early period—to go into the world as if we were
going into battle. . . . We watch every erring thought—we learn to be
equivocal in speech; and our very hearts, as the Indians phrase it, are
taught to speak their desires with a double tongue. We are perpetually
on the lookout for enemies and attack; we dread pitfalls and circum-
ventions, and we feel that every face which we encounter is a smiling
deceit—every honeyed word a blandishment meant to betray us. These
are lessons which society, as at present constituted, teaches of itself.
—RALPH COLLETON, *Guy Rivers: A Tale of Georgia*

In 1834, at the age of twenty-eight, William Gilmore Simms
published the first of his Border Romances, *Guy Rivers: A Tale of Georgia*.
Although Simms had published his first work of prose fiction, *Martin Faber:
The Story of a Criminal*, a year earlier, *Guy Rivers* was, as Simms describes
in his dedicatory epistle to Charles R. Carroll in the 1854 edition, "the first
of my regular novels," whose publication "commenced a professional career in literature which has been wholly unbroken since" (xxviii, xxv).[1] Set
on the border regions of the North Georgia wilderness, *Guy Rivers* tells the
story of a young Southerner named Ralph Colleton who leaves his plantation home in South Carolina and ventures into the chaos of the North
Georgia frontier. Colleton soon discovers that the frontier is a dangerous
and vastly different world than the well-ordered plantation society he has
left behind. His travels eventually take him to the frontier settlement of
Chestatee, where he meets a variety of backwoods settlers and social outcasts. While he is there, he helps expose and defeat an infamous band of
criminals called the Pony Club, led by the renegade lawyer-turned-outlaw

Guy Rivers, before finally returning once again to the world of his plantation home.

Guy Rivers was Simms's first fictional work to deal specifically with the subject of the Southern frontier.[2] In the novel Simms vividly depicts the violence and instability that occur when individuals from different social classes encounter one another along an open frontier where social order is weak and where territorial and economic claims are in dispute.[3] Unfortunately, many scholars have ignored the novel's literary value because of these specific qualities, insisting that its propensity for melodrama and violence—while giving *Guy Rivers* great popular appeal—limits its potential for developing or exploring more serious literary themes. One aspect of *Guy Rivers* that has received criticism and praise is Simms's use of language, specifically his representations of speech. Simms's ability to depict the dialect of many of his backwoods characters in the novel represents one of his finest accomplishments as a writer and contributes significantly to the realistic portrayal of the frontier. However, scholars have been critical of Simms's romance heroes and heroines—like Ralph and Edith Colleton in *Guy Rivers*—for they speak in artificial voices that are filled with the traditional rhetoric and sentimental clichés of the romance. Despite Simms's success in portraying the vernacular speech of his frontier characters, many critics have concluded that Simms's ability to imagine other possibilities for the use of language was aesthetically restricted by the conventions of the romance genre.

Nevertheless, biographical evidence suggests that Simms was aware of the imaginative possibilities of language, particularly in the power of the spoken word. While Simms never wrote a formal treatise on language, his personal life, his correspondence with others, and his fiction reveal a continuing fascination with the sounds of human voices and an interest in how language contributed to the social and cultural landscape of the American South. As one of antebellum America's preeminent and most prolific men of letters, Simms spent much of his adult life exploring the complexities of the written and spoken word. However, Simms also lived during an era when the spoken word had significant social and political power. Oratory and other public speech acts were not only carefully developed forms of art, they were also one of the primary means through which individuals like John C. Calhoun and Daniel Webster achieved and maintained their power as political leaders.[4] Within the cultural context of the antebellum South, Simms would have certainly recognized the power of words to direct public

opinion and shape the patterns of social discourse. John Guilds even suggests that Simms perhaps used his mastery over the spoken word to assert
his own social power and control over others: "Simms felt a need, almost
an obsession, to be in charge and his unusual verbal facility made it possible
for him, by effective speaking or writing, to take control of situations
through his ability to explain, interpret, clarify, or make plausible to others,
who looked to him for leadership. At times, this compulsiveness led to the
manipulation of the thoughts and actions of those around him" (Guilds,
Simms 332). While Guilds's statement does not provide conclusive evidence, it is compelling from the perspective of Simms's fiction, for in many
of his works, like *Guy Rivers*, Simms creates characters whose authoritative
voices and mastery over words give them significant, if not potentially dangerous, social power.

A variety of emerging critical perspectives in the fields of linguistics, literary theory, and American cultural criticism provide new ways of assessing
the literary value of antebellum texts like *Guy Rivers*.[5] As Jane Tompkins observes, "Reconstructing sympathetically the discourse out of which
[antebellum] fiction springs . . . requires a considerable effort of imagination" (120). Tompkins's emphasis on the importance of the critical imagination is crucial to the reading of texts like *Guy Rivers* because, ironically, it
is Simms's own artistic imagination that has often been overlooked in the
study of his fiction. While continuing to affirm the significance of realism
in Simms's linguistic representations, it is also important to examine how
Simms uses language imaginatively in works like *Guy Rivers* to explore particular social and cultural relationships.[6] While Simms is using language to
say some very specific things about the social conditions of the frontier
and the South in general, he also uses the resources and materials of language in highly imaginative ways to create and comment upon the frontier
in *Guy Rivers*. By exploring the different ways Simms imagines language in
Guy Rivers, I intend to reestablish the vital connection between Simms's
impulse toward realism and the deep linguistic resources of his own artistic
imagination.

Given the frontier setting of *Guy Rivers*, one might legitimately wonder
whether the novel really has anything significant to say about language.
The story is one of frontier adventure, filled with breathtaking action, violent confrontations, and dark criminal conspiracies. The novel is set on
the border regions of the Georgia frontier, and one can easily imagine that
this harsh, unforgiving environment is a place where action and physical

strength would be valued far more highly than words. However, from the very beginning of the novel Simms focuses our gaze on the medium of language, drawing attention again and again to the presence of particular words and phrases, as well as to the sound of different human voices. Using a variety of linguistic tropes and images, Simms begins his Border Romance by contrasting the silence of the wilderness with the cacophony of voices that have intruded upon the stillness of the forest. The wilderness is characterized by "unbroken silence" and solitude "that send out no voices, and hang out no lights for the encouragement of civilized man" (2). This "solemn hush" is disrupted only by the sound of human voices, by backwoodsmen and settlers, criminals and other social outcasts who have fled into the wilderness to avoid either the social restraints or punishments of organized society (6). As Simms observes, the wilderness is "infested with many with whom the world had quarrelled—whom it had driven forth in shame and terror" (10). The very presence of language seems to transform the landscape, turning the silence of the wilderness into a noisy, chaotic frontier where men argue over the ownership of land and mineral rights and where primitive settlements arise overnight.

Throughout *Guy Rivers*, Simms frequently reminds the reader that the open frontier that shares its border with the well-ordered, established society of the plantation South is a dangerous and unfamiliar place. One of the primary ways in which Simms imagines the unsettled landscape of the frontier is through the medium of language. He does this by depicting the frontier as an uncharted linguistic space, an alien territory that requires interpretation if it is to be understood. At several points in the narrative, Simms temporarily suspends his telling of the story to define words and explain unfamiliar terms related to life on the frontier to the reader. For instance, he momentarily interrupts the story of Ralph Colleton's narrow escape from an ambush to explain the following frontier terminology: "The *trace* (as some public roads are called in that region) had been rudely cut out by some of the earlier travellers through the Indian country, merely *traced* out—and hence, perhaps, the term—by a *blaze*, or white spot, made upon the trees by hewing from them the bark. . . . It had never been much travelled, and . . . had, therefore, become, at the time of which we speak, what, in backwood phrase, is known as a *blind-path*" (274). This process of interpretation occurs throughout the novel; for instance, we see evidence of it when Simms pauses to introduce or define words such as "stands," "thrip," "fugleman," and "sulkey" (283–84), when he translates vernacular expressions like "considerably up a stump" (380), or when he interrupts to tell the reader about appropriate forms of greeting on the frontier, where "[t]he society and the continued presence of Nature . . . put aside all merely conventional distinctions, and men meet upon a common footing" (306).

Similar acts of translation and interpretation appear in connection with different vernacular speaking characters. For example, consider the speech of Mark Forrester, one of the frontiersmen who lives near Chestatee, as he describes Jared Bunce, a Yankee peddler who has been selling defective goods and housewares to the residents of the village: "His rascality ain't to be measured. Why, he kin walk through a man's pockets, jest as the devil goes through a crack or a keyhole, and the money will naterally stick to him, jest as ef he was made of gum turpentine. His very face is a sort of kining [coining] machine. His look says dollars and cents; and its always your dollars and cents, and he kines them out of your hands into his'n. . . . He cheats in everything, and cheats everybody" (52).

Similar representations of dialect appear throughout the novel, and they give Simms's portrayal of the frontier a realistic texture. Words like *naterally*, *kines*, and *back'ards* are comprehensible to the reader, but they deviate enough from conventional standards of spelling and pronunciation to suggest that Forrester's speech, like the frontier itself, represents a different kind of linguistic space. These linguistic differences are further reinforced by Simms's own direct editorial intrusions. On several occasions, Simms inserts translations of words or interpretations of colloquial expressions directly into the speech of his frontier characters. For example, in the midst of Forrester's speech, Simms intrudes to provide translations of *kining* [coining], *'scuse* [excuse], and *cutting dirt* [flight] (52–53). In instances such as this, Simms is not simply recording colorful forms of frontier speech in an objective fashion; instead, his editorial comments provide a visual contrast between Forrester's speech and an authoritative linguistic standard that Simms and the reader presumably share. Simms's editorial intrusions heighten our perception of the frontier as an unfamiliar space characterized by elements of social and linguistic instability. Representations of speech in this context reinforce our awareness as readers of just how malleable language actually is, how the forms of words are susceptible to change, especially along the Southern frontier where social conventions and cultural institutions have little power to fix established forms and meanings.

Of course, Simms's imaginative use of language in evoking the unsettled status of the frontier is not limited to isolated speech acts or representations of individual words and phrases. In fact, it is the chaotic interaction of voices along the frontier—the struggle between different voices to speak and to be heard—that most powerfully evokes the frontier's social instability. Simms describes the frontier as a region where social organization is relatively weak and where social institutions—such as education, religion, and the law—have very little power or value. As Simms observes, "The wild condition of the country—the absence of all civil authority, and almost of laws" frequently creates an unsettled environment where struggles for social power erupt between individuals or competing social groups (46). Without stable forms of social order and civil authority, the conventions governing public discourse and social interaction are subject to challenge and even disruption.

The absence or instability of social order is particularly evident in Simms's description of the frontier village of Chestatee, where many of the events in the novel take place. Despite the presence of a tavern and a blacksmith shop, which represent the most basic forms of social interaction and economic commerce, Simms's description of Chestatee suggests that the villagers who live there are defined more by their differences than by any common goal or collective purpose. Indeed, the village remains little more than an uneasy mixture of individuals with different interests and ambitions. Simms refers to them as an "incoherent" mixture, "[a] mass so heterogeneous" that strife and conflict are continually breaking out among them (46). He notes that "[t]hey came, not only from all parts of the surrounding country, but many of them from all parts of the surrounding world; oddly and confusedly jumbled together; the very *olla-podrida* of moral and mental combination" (45). In the textual notes to *Guy Rivers*, Guilds observes that the Spanish word *olla-podrida* literally means "melting pot."[7]

Simms's use of an unfamiliar foreign word in this context is interesting because it seems to suggest the polyglossia or unfamiliar heteroglossic impulses that are always present within any language.[8] Just as the heterogeneous social composition of the village literally creates different physical and social forms of organization, the heterogeneity of the frontier also affects the way language is used and appropriated. Indeed, Simms reveals that this heterogeneous confusion is not only social, but linguistic, and soon influences the different forms of social discourse that occur within the village.

When Ralph Colleton arrives at Chestatee, the village is—quite literally—in an uproar over the capture and upcoming trial of Jared Bunce, a traveling Yankee peddler who has for years sold the settlers defective

housewares and swindled them out of their money. The shouts and conflicting arguments coming from the tavern reflect an atmosphere of linguistic confusion that affects the trial itself. Simms's decision to focus on
Bunce's trial is significant within this chaotic linguistic context because the
law represents social discourse in its most precise, rational, and objective
form. Within organized society, the court of law ensures that the process
of language and the meaning of words are carefully controlled. The institution of the judicial court allows all voices in a dispute to be heard and the
verbal testimony of each witness to be carefully scrutinized; it constitutes
a social space where the precise meaning of words can be measured and
where truth can be reasonably determined.

However, at Bunce's trial the precise social order that language ordi-
narily provides is absent, and nothing but confusion prevails; different
speakers emerge out of the tavern crowd, struggle to be heard above the
roar of the mob and, in turn, are interrupted and silenced by other speakers. Simms observes that just as quickly as one of Bunce's accusers stands
to make charges against him, "[a]nother and another followed with like
speeches in the most rapid succession, until all was again confusion" (58).
Separated from the well-ordered, institutional structures that give language
its civil authority to organize and control, social discourse begins to rupture
into little more than noisy cacophony, and words begin to lose their meaning entirely. For instance, when Ralph Colleton and Mark Forrester are
discussing whether or not Bunce will get a fair trial, Colleton suggests that
if law and order are to be upheld, "justice should be administered only by
the proper hands" and not by mob rule (54). Forrester replies that Colleton
is "speaking according to the social standards of a different region" (54).
In essence, words like *justice* have no fixed meaning on the frontier but
are open to individual interpretation. As Forrester concedes, "It's a regular
court, though we make it up ourselves, and app'ints our own judges and
juries, and pass judgment 'ccordin' to the case" (53).

No character at the trial better epitomizes the disruptions at work in the
social discourse of the frontier than the lawyer Pippin, who is called upon
by the tavern crowd to sit as judge in the case against Bunce. Pippin, quite
literally, makes his living off of words, and he takes great pride in his abilities as an orator, to the extent that "an opportunity for a speech . . . was not
suffered to pass without due regard" (57). However, for the most part Pippin's mastery of language is little more than a comic parody of legal eloquence and refined speech. Pippin's language possesses the ornamentation

of legal discourse but has little meaningful substance: "[T]he lawyer knew how to make the most of his learning among those who had none. Like many other gentlemen of erudition, he was grave to a proverb when the occasion required it. . . . He relied greatly on saws and sayings—could quote you the paradoxes of Johnson and the infidelities of Hume without always understanding them, and mistook, as men of that kind and calibre are very apt to do, the capacity to repeat the grave absurdities of others as proof of something in himself" (56–57).

Pippin's command of language is largely a mastery of legal or rhetorical jargon that has no effective meaning at all and certainly does not have the social power to bring order to the chaotic judicial proceedings taking place in the tavern. As a result, Pippin is unable to use language or his superficial talents as an orator to control the mob in the tavern or establish order during the trial. His speeches are repeatedly interrupted by other voices from the crowd who are in direct competition with him to be heard. Throughout the trial, Simms draws the reader's attention to the struggle between different speakers to be heard and the linguistic chaos that ensues:

> [Pippin] had long since seemingly given up all hope of exercising, in their true spirit, the duties of the station which he held. For a while, it is true, he battled with no little energy for the integrity of his dignity, with good lungs and a stout spirit; but, though fully a match in these respects for any one, or perhaps two of his competitors, he found the task of contending with the dozen rather less easy, and, in a little while, his speeches, into which he had lugged many a choice *ad captandum* of undisputed effect on any other occasion, having been completely merged and mingled with those of the mass, he wisely forbore any further waste of matter, in the stump-oratory of the South usually so precious; and, drawing himself up proudly and profoundly in his high place, he remained dignifiedly sullen. (63)

Within the frontier village of Chestatee, Pippin's social position as judge provides him with very little, if any, linguistic authority. Although the crowd has called upon Pippin to serve as judge, they demonstrate very little interest in hearing what Pippin has to say; their main interest in his eloquent facility with legal jargon is to create an atmosphere—to use Simms's term, a verbal "fabric"—of institutional authority, which will sanction their accusations against Bunce.

Most of the time, Pippin's public eloquence seems only comic, if not entirely harmless; however, Simms indicates there is another, more private aspect to Pippin's facility with language that serves a different function. While Pippin's attempts at public speaking are often comic and ineffective, he is quite adept at using words behind the public scene to create social conflict and, hopefully, turn a small profit. Simms states:

> [A]mong the arts of his profession, and as a means for supplying the absence of more legitimate occasions for its employment, he was reputed as excessively expert in making the most of any difficulty among his neighbors. The egg of mischief and controversy was hardly laid, before the worthy lawyer . . . watched and warmed it without remission; and when fairly hatched, he took care that the whole brood should be brought safely into court, his voice, and words, and actions, fully attesting the deep interest in their fortunes which he had manifested from the beginning. Many a secret slander, ripening at length into open warfare, had been traced to his friendly influence. (57)

In essence, Pippin profits by sowing seeds of linguistic discord among the settlers, manipulating and misrepresenting their words so that legal action—and hence, a lawyer—will be required to resolve the disputes. While Pippin's abilities as a public speaker are portrayed as comic, his subtle understanding of how to use words enables him to thrive in a region where social disputes create ideal conditions for linguistic manipulation and deceit.

Interestingly, Pippin's deceptive use of language closely identifies him with Jared Bunce, the Yankee peddler who is on trial. Bunce is a master at manipulating language to deceive unsuspecting settlers and escape from punishment. As Forrester observes, his linguistic talents are legion: "[H]e can blarney you so—and he's so quick at a mortal lie—and he's got jest a good reason for everything—and he's so sharp at a 'scuse [excuse] that it's onpossible to say where he's gwine to have you, and what you're a gwine to lose, and how you'll get off at last, and what way he'll cheat you another time. . . . The regilators have swore a hundred times to square off with him; but he's always got off tell now; sometimes by new inventions—sometimes by bible oaths—and last year, by regilarly *cutting dirt* [flight]" (53).

Even though Bunce has been caught by the settlers at Chestatee and has good reason to fear for his life, he continues to use language during his trial to create confusion and avoid the charges against him. With almost comic precision, Bunce seizes upon every opportunity to use his evasive linguistic skills. When Pippin asks him whether or not his name is Jared Bunce, the peddler artfully evades the question. Later, Bunce is accused of selling a clock to Dick Jenkins's wife that "began to whiz . . . and commenced striking, whizzing all the while, and never stopped till it had struck clear thirty-one, and since that time will neither whiz, nor strike, nor do nothing" (59). Bunce's response is, once again, a circuitous one, which confuses events so badly that he is able to imply that Mr. Jenkins broke the clock by striking it with a hammer. Finally, Bunce is accused of selling a coffee pot to Colonel Blundell that melted "at the very sight of hot water" (61). In what must surely be one of the novel's best examples of linguistic misdirection, Bunce explains: "Well, lawyer, it stands to reason I can't answer for that. The tin wares I sell stand well enough in a northern climate: there may be some difference in yours that I can't account for; and I guess, pretty much, there is. . . . Who knows, again, but you boil your water quite too hot, as in not boiling it hot enough. Who knows? All I can say is, that the lot of wares I bring to this market next season shall be calkilated on purpose to suit the climate" (61).

Ironically, it is Pippin—presiding as judge over the trial—who is most easily deceived by Bunce's dissembling responses. The dialogue that ensues between them contrasts Pippin's linguistic self-importance with Bunce's more subtle ability to control the direction of the trial with his words. "There does seem to be something in this," Pippin says, speaking "with a gravity corresponding with the deep sagacity he conceived himself to have exhibited" (61). As this comic dialogue about boiling water in the North continues, Bunce skillfully uses his words to flatter Pippin, concluding that the lawyer "must have travelled pretty considerable down east in your time and among my people, for you seem to know all about the matter jest as well and something better than myself" (61). "The lawyer," Simms observes, "not a little flattered by the compliment so slyly and evasively put in, responded to the remark with due regard for his own increase of importance" (61). Before long, their dialogue has completely interrupted the proceedings of the trial, as they engage in a lengthy discussion of whether or not it is possible to boil water in the North during the winter months.

The tavern mob, however, familiar with Bunce's deceptive use of language, is not so easily taken in by his evasive words. As the mediating bonds of social discourse slowly begin to rupture, the crowd in the tavern—angered now by all of the talking—erupts into a riot of physical activity, setting fire to Bunce's wagon and "howling over it, at every successive burst of flame that went up into the dark atmosphere, a savage yell of triumph that tallied well with the proceeding" (67). "The scene," Simms observes, "was one of indescribable confusion. The rioters danced about the blaze like so many frenzied demons" (67). Significantly, the chaos that ensues allows Bunce to escape from the regulators, and we also discover that Pippin is making plans to bring a civil suit against the tavern mob in Bunce's favor for the destruction of his wagon. By focusing on all of these different aspects of language in his description of the frontier and in his narration of the events taking place in the village of Chestatee, Simms heightens the reader's ability to imagine the region's social instability, as well as the struggles for power that erupt along its borders.[9]

These comic scenes of frontier justice clearly illustrate Simms's interest in realistic depictions of frontier life and speech; however, they also reveal how Simms focuses imaginatively on language to enrich his portrait of the Southern frontier. Simms's attentiveness to language also links the comic figures and events in the village of Chestatee to the major characters and events in the novel. For instance, the trial of the Yankee peddler Jared Bunce provides a comic parallel to Ralph Colleton's trial later in the story, when he is accused of murdering Mark Forrester. Pippin's occupation as a lawyer and his comic misuse of language also establish several important points of comparison and contrast to the lawyer-turned-outlaw, Guy Rivers. Specifically, Simms depicts Pippin's comic eloquence as a parody of Guy Rivers's more powerful rhetorical skills. In contrast to Pippin, Guy Rivers clearly presents a more dangerous threat to the social order. While Pippin's eloquence has little success in establishing social order or controlling the tavern mob at Chestatee, Rivers has the capacity to dominate and command others through the persuasive power of his own voice.

Although secondary characters like Pippin and Bunce reveal how Simms focuses on the social role of language in his presentation of the frontier, it is the outlaw Guy Rivers who most compellingly demonstrates the dangerous potential of language to disrupt the bonds of society and destroy individual lives. Rivers's verbal eloquence and cunning mastery of speech make him an extremely dangerous figure on the frontier. Throughout the novel, Guy Rivers wields language like a powerful weapon, using his subtle skill with words to coerce, seduce, and manipulate other people. Through the commanding power of his own voice, Rivers becomes leader of the band of outlaws and wages frontier warfare against society, particularly against those members of the planter class, like Ralph and Edith Colleton, who have rejected his claims of political power and equal social status.

Simms's portrait of Guy Rivers is by far the most complex of any character in the novel. While Rivers is not the story's romance hero, it quickly becomes evident why Simms names the novel after him. Rivers's violent criminal behavior and complex psychological motivations give the story much of its dynamic energy. Furthermore, Simms succeeds in creating this complex psychological portrait by focusing on how Rivers's desire for social and political power and his eventual fall into a life of frontier crime are determined by language. As a young, aspiring lawyer, Rivers's facility with words and his eloquent power as a speaker readily distinguish him from his fellow lawyers. Recalling his days as a lawyer serving in the Gwinnett County courthouse, Rivers says, "I ruled without competitor, riding roughshod over bench, bar, and jury, dreaded alike by all" (243). As his comments suggest, Rivers uses his rhetorical skills to dominate others and establish his own authority even when he is a young lawyer. Rivers's observation about his own linguistic powers is confirmed by his criminal companion, Wat Munro, who recalls, "I sometimes look back and laugh at the manner in which you used to bully the old judge, and the gaping jury, and your own brother lawyers, while the foam would run through your clenched teeth and from your lips in very passion" (243). Munro's description of Rivers's linguistic power and his impassioned rhetorical style evoke images of the fiery rhetoric of real-life antebellum orators like William Preston, William Yancey, and John C. Calhoun, who used their superior rhetorical skills to acquire political power and to rise within the ranks of the Southern aristocracy. From the beginning of his career, Rivers believes that his ability to wield language can lead to greater social and political power.

Rivers acknowledges that professional ambition and personal pride are behind his desire to rise above his legal peers and beyond the narrow social confines of the Gwinnett County courthouse, where he serves as a lawyer. And it is his power over words that becomes the primary means through which Rivers seeks to realize his social and political aspirations. Although he begins his career as a poor country lawyer, Rivers believes his rhetorical skills and superior intelligence are signs that he is destined for a higher social station in life. Consequently, Rivers envisions language not simply as a means of communication but as a form of power intimately connected to social status. However, Rivers's rise to power is interrupted when he runs for election to the legislature against a wealthy member of the planter class. Rivers describes his opponent as the most "shallow and insignificant fop and fool . . . [who] yet dared to thrust his head into a deliberative assembly" (246). While his opponent is no match for Rivers's intelligence or his rhetorical skills, Rivers soon learns that his natural abilities are worth very little without the influence of wealth and social position. Rivers is outraged by these rejections and is convinced that he has been treated unfairly by society, particularly by those members of the Southern aristocracy who do not possess his own abilities. His decision, therefore, to retreat into the frontier and enter into a life of crime becomes a means of rebellion against the society that has rejected him.[10]

The peculiar linguistic focus that informs Rivers's description of his rise to social prominence and his fall into a life of crime is striking. Indeed, at first it seems unusual that Rivers would regard his talents as a lawyer— particularly his rhetorical skills—as any kind of marker of social status. However, there is evidence within the novel to support this particular attention to language as an important factor in determining social status. Near the beginning of *Guy Rivers*, Ralph Colleton and his uncle become involved in a violent argument over whether Ralph is socially suitable to marry his cousin, Edith Colleton. Interestingly, most of Colonel Colleton's misgivings about the union have to do with the social status of Ralph's father, who, Colonel Colleton reveals, married a "miserable peasant . . . a wife from the inferior grade, who, without education, and ignorant of all refinement, could only appear a blot upon the station to which she had been raised" (37). Although Ralph has been brought up as the son of a planter, is heir to his father's estate in Tennessee, and has the appropriate education and social refinements to warrant entry into the planter class, his true social status is suspect. If Ralph is to marry his cousin Edith, he must prove himself and his worthiness to become a member of the planter class. As Colonel Colleton explains: "The man who seeks my daughter must not look for a sacrifice; she must win a husband who has a name, a high place,—who has a standing in society. Your tutors, indeed, speak of you in fair terms; but the public voice is everything in our country. When you have got through your law studies, and made your first speech, we will talk once more upon this subject" (36).

This argument between Ralph and his uncle represents a crucial turning point in the course of the narrative, since Colonel Colleton's rejection forces Ralph to leave his plantation home and venture into the border regions of the Southern frontier. However, what almost goes unnoticed in the passage quoted above is Simms's image of the powerful position of language in determining social status. Colonel Colleton's concern over his nephew's unproven social standing does not focus simply on traditional signifiers such as inherited wealth, land ownership, or a suitable profession. Instead, Colonel Colleton speaks openly about Ralph's need to win the approval of the "public voice." The choice of this particular linguistic trope seems especially relevant within this context, for the public voice marks a rite of social passage—the public recognition of Ralph's entry into the social hierarchy of the planter class—that is also designated by a particular linguistic performance, Ralph's first public speech.[11]

The significance of this linguistic event and its relationship to the social order of the antebellum South is not simply a fictional creation by Simms. A number of Southern historians have written about the important relationship between ritual forms of language and the structure of plantation society in the antebellum South. In *Intimacy and Power in the Old South: Ritual in the Lives of the Planters*, Steven M. Stowe describes "the shared mentality [among planters] that lies between observable behavior . . . and formal systems of thought . . . in order to show how the planters made sense of both behavior and intellect" (xiii). Stowe argues that forms of linguistic discourse played a vital role in the organization and stability of plantation society:

> The planters followed certain [linguistic] forms in the name of correctness or pleasure. . . . Elite children were taught the use of language with explicit attention to the social order and to family continuity. . . . [P]olitical talk among men followed conventions of deference and equality; courtship letters showed controlled usages of language . . . ; an affair of honor could not proceed without strict adherence to linguistic form. Moreover, these and other kinds of expression were joined to certain social relations which the elite assumed were part of the natural world and thus not easily open to change. (2–3)[12]

Stowe's analysis reveals the remarkable extent to which language can be used to regulate social behavior and define social status, and it also reinforces the social significance of language and the power of speech acts in *Guy Rivers*. Within the linguistic economy of the novel, Colonel Colleton's references to the public voice and to Ralph's first speech convey larger patterns of meaning that heighten the role language plays in imagining the social world presented in the novel.[13]

Given the relationship that Simms establishes between language and social power in the novel, Guy Rivers's awareness of language takes on heightened social significance. Indeed, his attentiveness to language reveals deeper layers of meaning in Rivers's actions throughout the novel. For example, soon after his defeat in the legislative elections, Rivers commits his first act of violence when he murders a member of the planter class. In recalling the event Rivers confesses that "[m]y first great crime proved my nature" (246). In fact, in this act of violence, which initiates Rivers into a life of crime, we see how his description of the event is connected to his rejection by society and his belief that social power is inscribed within language: "He was a poor coward; made no struggle, and begged most piteously for his life; had the audacity to talk of his great possessions, his rank in society, his wife and children. These were the enjoyments all withheld from me; they were the very things the want of which had made me what I was—what I am—and furiously I struck my weapon into his mouth, silencing his insulting speech" (246). Initially, Rivers sets out only to rob the man. But his victim has "the audacity to talk of his great possessions, his rank in society" (246). Rivers literally becomes enraged by his words, and—as if to make the event symbolic of his initiation into a life as a criminal outcast—he sticks a gun into the man's mouth, "silencing his insulting speech."

Throughout *Guy Rivers*, Simms focuses on language—particularly speech acts—in imagining Rivers's rejection by society and his disruptive social influence. One of the most disturbing instances of Rivers's rhetorical power takes place during the bloody massacre of the Georgia Guard. In the novel, the Georgia Guard represents the forces of social order and stability that attempt to regulate and control the chaotic environment of the frontier. The Georgia Guard enters the frontier to protect the state of Georgia's holdings and to reclaim lands taken over by different groups of frontier settlers. When the Georgia Guard arrives on the scene, the settlers from the village of Chestatee are involved in a feud with a rival gang of squatters over disputed claims to nearby mineral mines; however, the two groups of squatters soon band together against the state militia to defend their claims to the mines and to the surrounding land.

The squatters' claims to land and mineral rights are considered illegal by the state, but the squatters are determined to defend their property. However, Guy Rivers, who is present among the squatters, has no interest in the land disputes. He is motivated only by his desire for revenge against society and his thirst for social chaos; therefore, he uses the encounter with the Georgia Guard to create an atmosphere of violent anarchy. Working behind the scenes, Rivers uses his rhetorical skills to arouse the unrestrained anger of the squatters. Following a plan designed by Rivers, the squatters prepare an ambush for the militia, which traps them in a narrow gorge. When the guard enters the gorge most of the troops are killed by an avalanche caused by the squatters.

The squatters soon recognize that they have been manipulated into committing a senseless act of violence. Simms states that Guy Rivers, "by whose black and devilish spirit the means of destruction had been hit upon" (157), is responsible for persuading the squatters to participate in the assault against the Georgia Guard. Even Mark Forrester, who possesses many of the positive virtues traditionally associated with the frontier, falls victim to Rivers's rhetorical seduction. After the massacre occurs, Rivers confidently confesses to his companion, Wat Munro, "I aroused him [Forrester] and set him on. His hot blood took fire at some little hints that I threw out, and the fool became a leader in the mischief" (202). Forrester echoes a similar sentiment when he tells Ralph Colleton, "I was mad, 'squire, mad to the heart, and became the willing tool of men not so mad, but more evil than I!" (172). As a result of what Simms calls the "deficiencies of education" and the "denials of birth" (162), the settlers living in Chestatee become easy victims of Rivers's linguistic powers of persuasion. The adventurous spirit and self-reliant nature evident in backwoodsmen like Mark Forrester represent qualities that have made America strong as a nation; nevertheless, Forrester is easily manipulated by Guy Rivers, who seems to thrive on linguistic and social chaos.

For Guy Rivers, the frontier remains an unstable linguistic space where he uses his rhetorical skill to manipulate and control others. However, there are characters in the novel—like Ralph Colleton and Lucy Munro—who are able to resist, in part, Rivers's subtle powers of persuasion and verbal coercion because they possess social attributes such as a formal education, higher social status, or ties to organized society beyond the frontier. Ralph Colleton is perhaps the most important figure in this respect because his relationship with Rivers represents the central dramatic conflict in the novel. Rivers, on the one hand, is obsessed with destroying Colleton, because of his jealousy of the love Ralph shares with his cousin Edith. However, Rivers also hates Colleton because he belongs to the planter class that has rejected him. Consequently, the conflicts that take place between the two men are social as well as personal.

The threat of impending physical violence hangs over virtually every encounter between Guy Rivers and Ralph Colleton in the novel. However, what is fascinating about these different confrontations is their peculiar linguistic context. Simms consistently uses language to imagine the personal conflicts and struggles for power and control between the two men. This linguistic focus is evident in Simms's description of the encounters between Rivers and Colleton as verbal games, rhetorical attacks, and speech contests. In George Steiner's study of the relationship between language and social power, he observes, "Where there is not true kinship of interests, where power relations determine the conditions of meeting, linguistic exchange becomes a duel" (202). This trope of the linguistic duel is evident in the first confrontation between Guy Rivers and Ralph Colleton in the novel. As the story opens, Colleton is found wandering through the North Georgia frontier, having left his plantation home in South Carolina after a violent argument with his uncle. His progress is suddenly interrupted by the appearance of another man blocking the trail in front of him. Later in the story, the narrator reveals that the figure is Guy Rivers. However, during the first encounter between Rivers and Colleton, they do not recognize each other.

Because of the remote frontier setting where the encounter takes place, Colleton immediately becomes suspicious that the man blocking the trail before him is a backwoods outlaw who intends to rob him of his horse and possessions. Rivers does plan to rob the young rider and steal his horse; however, instead of simply calling upon the members of his gang to ambush Colleton from the underbrush along the trail, Rivers pauses to engage Colleton in conversation. Colleton is prepared for violence; therefore, the linguistic nature of the encounter strikes him as unusual:

> [Colleton was] curious to see how far the love of speech in his assailant might carry him in a dialogue of so artificial a character. . . . [Yet] he found it excessively difficult . . . to account for the strange nature of the transaction so far as it had gone; and the language of the robber seemed so inconsistent with his pursuit, that, at intervals, he was almost led to doubt whether the whole was not the clever jest of some country sportsman. . . . If, on the other hand, the stranger was in reality the ruffian he represented himself, he knew not how to account for his delay in the assault—a delay, to the youth's mind, without an object. (16)

Rivers's fondness for talking seems strangely out of place, given the wilderness location where their encounter occurs. However, the focus on language heightens our awareness that Ralph is in an unfamiliar environment and that he is outside the boundaries of society. As if to emphasize this point, Rivers tells Colleton, in a tone that is both sarcastic and subtly threatening, "I hate to part over-soon with company that talks so well; particularly in these woods, where, unless such a chance come about as the present, the lungs of the heartiest youth in the land would not be often apt to find the echo they seek, though they cried for it at the uttermost pitch of the pipe" (13).

Simms signals the adversarial nature of the encounter early in the dialogue between the two men when he observes that Colleton is aware that a "contest awaited him which would try his strength" (12). For Rivers, the conversation is part of a dangerous game, for he is interested not only in robbing his adversary but in overpowering him with words. However, Ralph Colleton is not like Rivers's first victim, the wealthy planter who had cowered before Rivers, begging and pleading for his life. Colleton quickly takes up the challenge of the rhetorical "game." Rivers quickly discovers that his adversary has "caught up the spirit of the dialogue" (17). The linguistic duel that ensues is full of dramatic tension, with both men provoking each other with subtle insults and countering with forays of carefully veiled threats and rhetorical taunts. The confrontation becomes a dangerous verbal competition between the two men to see if one can subdue or overpower the other through the force of words. In many respects, the encounter resembles the ritual of dueling prominent among Southern gentlemen during the antebellum era. Like dueling, which operates within the framework of very rigid linguistic codes, the verbal game between Rivers and Colleton is not simply a matter of physical prowess, but a test of will to see whose spirit can be overpowered and to see whose nerve can be broken. In *Southern Honor: Ethics and Behavior in the Old South*, Bertram Wyatt-Brown observes that dueling rituals were carefully linked to precise forms of linguistic behavior as a means of settling disputes among gentlemen and insuring social stability. The duel frequently took place to resolve social disputes between two gentlemen, or as a means of responding to verbal insults or threats that placed one's honor into question. The lengthy sequence of events leading up to the actual duel was composed of a series of highly ritualized linguistic encounters that provided opportunities for the dispute between the gentlemen to be satisfied. The entire ritual performance of the duel, therefore, was both caused and regulated by a sensitivity to the precise meaning of words.

A similar sensitivity to speech acts is evident in the encounter between Guy Rivers and Ralph Colleton. Both men exhibit a striking attentiveness, not only to what is said, but to how things are said, to verbal nuances and tones of voice. As their dialogue begins, the narrator observes that "the manner, rather than the matter" of Rivers's speech "proved offensive" to Colleton (12). In response to Rivers's threats Colleton warns, "unless you will be pleased to speak a little more respectfully, our parley will have a shorter life, and a rougher ending, than you fancy" (13). Throughout the conversation, Rivers plays upon Colleton's emotions and uses words in an attempt to establish his own rhetorical authority over his opponent. He repeatedly refers to Colleton's youthful inexperience and to his social status as a "young gentleman." When Colleton calls Rivers "impertinent," Rivers responds by warning him, "Softly, softly, young sir. Be not rash, and let me recommend that you be more choice in your adoption of your epithets. Impertinent is an ugly word between gentlemen of our habit" (13). Rivers's own anger is most evident whenever Colleton attempts to use his superior social position to command the outlaw or to question him about his intentions. Indeed, Rivers seems acutely aware of how the use of language communicates and reinforces different levels of social power and authority. From a social and linguistic perspective, questions and commands imply superior and inferior positions of power between speakers; therefore, when Ralph begins to question Rivers, the outlaw warns, "Look you, young fellow, I am better able to ask questions myself, than to answer those of other people. In respect to this matter of answering, my education has been woefully neglected" (12–13).

This attentiveness to language is difficult to explain, given the frontier setting of the novel. After all, one would imagine that physical strength and action would have greater value on the frontier than mere words. Indeed, Guy Rivers's criminal companions—including Wat Munro—are perplexed by his curious preoccupation with words. After Ralph Colleton escapes from the trap set by the outlaws, Munro observes: "[S]ince this youth, who got out of the scrape so handsomely, has beat you at your own game, it may cure you of that cursed itch for tongue-trifling, upon which you so much pride yourself. 'Twould have done, and it did very well at the county sessions, in getting men out of the wood; but as you have commenced a new business entirely, it's but well to leave off the old, particularly as it's now your policy to get them into it" (102). Rivers's obsession with language suggests that Simms's focus is not simply on portraying the violent action and criminal activities that take place on the frontier. He is also interested in exploring the linguistic construction of social relationships and the complex dynamics of social power within the antebellum South.

Throughout the novel, Simms continues to link the use of language to explorations of power and social status. In fact, virtually every confrontation between Guy Rivers and Ralph Colleton centers on struggles for social power that are expressed through language. Furthermore, the social and linguistic dynamics between Rivers and Colleton change during the course of the novel. After their initial encounter in the wilderness, Colleton realizes that Rivers is nothing but a common criminal. When he confronts Rivers again later in the novel, he positions himself in a superior linguistic relationship to Rivers, thus reinforcing Rivers's inferior social status. Instead of speaking directly to Rivers—a linguistic act that would imply that Rivers is a social equal—Ralph issues a public proclamation:

> "Hear me!" was the exclamation of the youth—his voice rising in due effect, and illustrating well the words he uttered, and the purpose of his speech:—"I charge this born and branded villain with an attempt upon my life. He sought to rob and murder me at the Catcheta pass but a few days ago. Thrown between my horse's feet in the struggle, he received the brand of his hoof, which he now wears upon his cheek. There he stands, with the well-deserved mark upon him, and which, but for the appearance of his accomplices, I should have made of a yet deeper character. Let him deny it if he can or dare." (163)

Significantly, Colleton also insists, "Until the ruffian . . . had answered the penalties of the laws for his . . . more heinous offence against them, he should be silent" (166). Rivers is outraged and "insulted" by the charges Colleton makes against him. Although Colleton refuses to address him, Rivers poses a direct challenge:

> "I have not done with *you*, young sir," was the immediate speech of Rivers—his self-confidence and much of his composure returned, as, with a fierce and malignant look, and a quick stride, he approached the youth. "You have thought proper to make a foul charge against me, which I have denied. It has been shown that your assertion is unfounded, yet you persist in it. . . . I now demand redress—the redress of a gentleman. You know the custom of the country, and regard your own character, I should think, too highly to refuse me satisfaction. You have pistols, and here are rifles and dirks. Take your choice." (166)

Ralph Colleton's accusations and verbal insults demand a physical response
by Rivers, but rather than physically attacking Colleton, Rivers demands
the dispute be settled through dueling. However, Colleton knows that a
duel involves a dispute between two gentlemen of the same social status.
Therefore, he refuses to grant Rivers the recognition he seeks as his social
and linguistic equal. Colleton's precise adherence to the social and linguistic codes of his class keeps the encounter from erupting into chaotic violence. However, Forrester finds Colleton's behavior perplexing:

> "Come, 'squire, how's this? Don't give way—give him satisfaction,
> as he calls it, and send the lead into his gizzard. It will be no harm
> done, in putting it to such a creature as that. Don't let him crow over
> old Carolina—don't, now, squire! You can hit him as easy as a barn-
> door, for I saw your shot today; don't be afraid, now—stand up, and
> I'll back you against the whole of them."
>
> "You mistake me greatly, Forrester, if you suppose for a moment
> that I will contend on equal terms with such a wretch. He is a common
> robber and an outlaw, whom I have denounced as such, and whom I
> can not therefore fight with. Were he a gentleman, or had he any pre-
> tensions to the character, you should have no need to urge me on, I
> assure you." (167–68)

Forrester's comments suggest that Colleton's sensitivity to social differences has no practical place on the frontier, where each individual is judged
by his physical prowess and by his ability to back up his words with physical
action. Nevertheless, Colleton's insistence on social and linguistic differences indicates the crucial role that language performs within Southern
society to maintain social order and stability.

Guy Rivers reveals Simms's continuing interest in exploring the social
power of words and in the capacity of language to create as well as disrupt
the bonds of social organization. Simms recognized that the radical democratic atmosphere and the spirit of self-reliance on the frontier made many
important contributions to the continuing expansion and development of
America and the South. However, his portrayal of the frontier in *Guy Rivers*
also reveals his anxieties about this sparsely settled region. Although it may
seem unusual for a writer like Simms, whose career was so dependent upon
the production of the written word, *Guy Rivers* reveals Simms's underlying
anxieties about the dangerous power that words can have in a democratic
society. For language to function properly, strong social order is needed.

Or, perhaps one should say that language and society strengthen and reinforce one another, creating a stable social framework that enables human communities to develop.

Although the examples provided in this essay are not exhaustive, they begin to suggest some of the ways in which Simms uses language to imagine the physical and social landscape of the frontier in *Guy Rivers*. By focusing on the relationship between language and the literary imagination, one begins to see more fully the complex artistry of Simms's fiction and his talent for taking the materials of life—like language—and using them for the imaginative purposes of art.

NOTES

1. Quotations in this essay are from the recently published Arkansas edition of *Guy Rivers*, prepared and edited by John Caldwell Guilds, which is based on the copy-text of the 1855 edition, hereafter cited in parentheses within the text. *Guy Rivers* was originally published sometime in either June or July 1834 in two volumes by Harper and Brothers of New York. In 1855 Simms revised and edited *Guy Rivers* and condensed it into one volume for publication in the uniform edition of his *Works*, published by J. S. Redfield of New York. In preparing the research for this essay, I have consulted both the 1834 two-volume edition and the revised 1855 edition; however, my primary reading of the text is based on the 1855 Redfield edition, which includes Simms's own changes and revisions.

2. Simms wrote four novels that he described as Border Romances. They are *Guy Rivers* (1834), *Richard Hurdis* (1838), *Border Beagles* (1840), and *Helen Halsey* (1845). Several other works written by Simms share similar themes or fictional settings with these particular Border Romances. Among these are *Confession* (1841), *Beauchampe* (1842), *The Wigwam and the Cabin* (1845), *Charlemont* (1856), *Voltmeier* (1869), and *The Cub and the Panther* (1869). All of these works are set on either the Southwestern or trans-Appalachian frontiers, indicating that Simms was interested in the subject of the frontier throughout his career.

3. Although *Guy Rivers* is Simms's first fictional work to deal specifically with the rapidly developing Southern frontier, he had already taken three trips to the Southwestern territories by the time the novel was written. On the first of these two trips, he was accompanied by his father, who had moved to Mississippi when Simms was a child. While Simms was there, he witnessed the chaotic settlement and rapid economic expansion occurring in the Southwest. James Kibler notes that in letters written in 1826 while visiting such frontier towns as Mobile, Alabama, and Columbus, Mississippi, Simms expresses his "disgust with materialism and

greed on the frontier" ("The First Simms Letters" 81). Simms took a third trip to the Southwestern frontier in 1831 when he traveled to Mississippi to settle his father's estate. On this trip he commented on the remarkable changes and social developments that had occurred along the frontier since his first visits.

Simms wrote two series of letters describing his experiences and impressions while traveling through the Old Southwest. The first series, "Letters from the West," was published in 1826 in *The Album* and was only recently rediscovered by Kibler and printed in "The First Simms Letters: 'Letters from the West' (1826)." See Kibler, "*The Album* (1826): The Significance of the Recently Discovered Second Volume," for an analysis of Simms's travels through the Southwest in 1826. Also, see John Caldwell Guilds, "Simms's First Magazine: *The Album*." A second series of letters, "Notes of a Small Tourist," was first published in 1831 in the Charleston *City Gazette* and is reprinted in *Letters* 1:10–38.

4. One of the best studies of oratory and other forms of public address in the antebellum South remains Waldo W. Braden, *The Oral Tradition in the South*. See especially 1–44. While Braden argues that no generalizations can be made regarding Southern oratory or the figure of the Southern orator, his analysis indicates the powerful social and political function of the spoken word during the antebellum era. Also, see Waldo W. Braden, ed., *Oratory in the Old South: 1828–1860*; and Cal M. Logue and Howard Dorgan, eds., *The Oratory of the Southern Demagogues*.

5. For example, see Jane Tompkins, *Sensational Designs*; Michael Kramer, *Imagining Language*; David Reynolds, *Beneath the American Renaissance*; and Philip Fisher, *Hard Facts*. For an excellent introduction to some of the emerging critical perspectives and their relationship to American literary studies, see Donald Pease, "New Americanists," 1–37.

6. For more on the imaginative use of language among American writers during the nineteenth century, see Michael Kramer, *Imagining Language*. In his excellent study, Kramer uses the critical trope of "imagining language" to explore how the linguistic imagination functions in a variety of Northeastern writers like Walt Whitman and Nathaniel Hawthorne. As Kramer states, "[M]y concern is not only with ideas about language but with the language that expresses those ideas—the literary forms in which they are presented and the cultural presuppositions that underlie them" (ix). In this essay, I show how Simms uses language—particularly tropes of speech and voice—imaginatively to describe the unstable social context of the Southern frontier and to represent different social relationships.

7. *Guy Rivers* contains an unusually large number of foreign words and phrases. The French word *dernier* appears in the same paragraph with *olla-podrida*. Other words, such as *outre, fusee, ad captandum, soi-disant medico, sui generis,* and *lese majeste*, also appear. For an extended discussion of how the presence of foreign words can be used to create disruptions in the social coherence of language, see George Steiner, *After Babel*.

8. The reference here to the presence of polyglossia (different languages) and heteroglossia (different social and regional dialects or other specialized forms of speech identified with a particular individual or group) emerges from my reading of Mikhail Bakhtin's seminal work on heteroglossia in the novel. While it is difficult to categorize *Guy Rivers* as a "dialogic novel"—at least in the terms Bakhtin describes in his studies of the novel—his understanding of how forms of social discourse become destabilized along the frontier and how different characters in the novel participate in a struggle for power through the spoken word has informed my reading of Simms's work. For more on Bakhtin's ideas about language and the novel, see *The Dialogic Imagination*. Also see Morson and Emerson, *Mikhail Bakhtin*.

9. This particular analysis of language in *Guy Rivers* reinforces the connection between Simms and the antebellum Southern humorists that Mary Ann Wimsatt and other Simms scholars have previously explored. See Wimsatt, "The Evolution of Simms's Backwoods Humor" and *The Major Fiction of William Gilmore Simms*. Simms shares with the Southern humorists an awareness of the disruptions in social discourse that often occur along the Southern frontier, and the unsettling of linguistic forms and conventions created by the instability or absence of social institutions. As antebellum writers like Joseph Glover Baldwin and Johnson Jones Hooper observe, language along the frontier is often used by confidence men and other hucksters to assume different personas, conceal their criminal intentions, and deceive others for economic gain. Some of the most memorable characters in the antebellum humor tradition—like Simon Suggs, Sut Lovingood, and Ned Brace—intentionally draw upon the resources of language and use their own rhetorical skills to create a comic atmosphere of social chaos that disrupts conventional forms of social authority.

10. It is striking how much Rivers's words echo Satan's own peculiarly linguistic rebellion in *Paradise Lost*. Rivers believes he has been denied his true social birthright and rebels against society. Similarly, in *Paradise Lost* Satan falls because of his overweening pride and the arrogant belief in his own superiority. More importantly, both Guy Rivers and Satan rely on their subtle skills with language to create social chaos and to corrupt those around them. Satan, for example, uses his seductive rhetoric to convince some of the other angels in heaven to follow him in rebellion against God and later uses his linguistic guile to deceive Eve. Like Satan's, Rivers's fall also centers on aspects of language. Rivers literally is cast out of society and into the frontier, where he continues to use his powerful command of language in his warfare against society. Rivers's linguistic seduction of Ellen—a frontier maiden who desperately loves him—and his attempts to seduce Lucy Munro and Edith Colleton also echo Satan's verbal seduction of Eve. At several key points in the novel, Rivers is explicitly referred to as a "devil," a "serpent," and a "demoniac" (247). While specific textual evidence linking Rivers to the figure of Satan in *Paradise Lost* is difficult to find in the novel, John Guilds notes that Simms does refer to

"Mammon" and "Moloch" in *Guy Rivers*, two fallen angels who also appear in *Paradise Lost* (Afterword 478).

11. Although Ralph Colleton and Guy Rivers are presented throughout the novel as moral opposites, it is important to note that the two men share many similarities. Like Guy Rivers, Ralph is trained in the rhetorical discourse of the law. Colonel Colleton, in fact, states that Ralph is finishing his law studies (36). Like Rivers, Ralph is also rejected (by his uncle) as a socially appropriate suitor for Edith. Ralph also retreats into the frontier after losing a heated argument with his uncle, which centers on the question of Ralph's uncertain social status.

12. In presenting Stowe's ideas on the relationship between language and the social life of the antebellum South, I do not intend to argue for any precise historical correlation between Simms's representation of speech-acts in *Guy Rivers* and the actual sociolinguistic behavior of planters in the antebellum South. Rather, I am interested in how Simms uses such images to construct the social world and define social relationships within the fictional text of *Guy Rivers*. It should be noted, however, that many of the studies on the social and intellectual life of the planters suggest that the characteristics of their worldview would have an affect on how language was used to define social relationships and regulate social behavior. For an extended analysis of these relationships see Michael O'Brien, *The Idea of the American South*, and "On the Mind of the Old South and Its Accessibility" in *Rethinking the South: Essays in Intellectual History*, 19–37; and Lewis P. Simpson, *The Dispossessed Garden*. For a particularly fascinating look at intellectual life of the antebellum South that focuses specifically on Simms, see Drew Gilpin Faust, *A Sacred Circle*. Another important study that reinforces many of Stowe's observations on the relationship between language and social behavior is Bertram Wyatt-Brown, *Southern Honor*.

13. Edward Sapir has observed, "It is quite an illusion to imagine that . . . language is merely an incidental means of solving specific problems of communication or reflection. The fact of the matter is that the real world is to a large extent unconsciously built up on the language habits of the group." See Sapir, "The Status of Linguistics as a Science," 69. Structuralist critics have also contributed to the development of this particular type of literary and linguistic analysis. While structuralist criticism differs considerably from the approach I take here, many structuralist critics focus on how forms of language within culture assume particular shapes to fit the specific context of human affairs.

WORKS CITED

Bakhtin, Mikhail. *The Dialogic Imagination: Four Essays.* Ed. Michael Holquist. Trans. Caryl Emerson and Michael Holquist. Austin: University of Texas Press, 1981.

Braden, Waldo W. *The Oral Tradition in the South*. Baton Rouge: Louisiana State University Press, 1983.

———, ed. *Oratory in the Old South: 1828–1860*. Baton Rouge: Louisiana State University Press, 1970.

Faust, Drew Gilpin. *A Sacred Circle: The Dilemma of the Intellectual in the Old South, 1840–1860*. Baltimore: Johns Hopkins University Press, 1977.

Fisher, Philip. *Hard Facts: Setting and Form in the American Novel*. New York: Oxford University Press, 1987.

Guilds, John C. Afterword. *Guy Rivers: A Tale of Georgia*. By William Gilmore Simms. Rev. ed. 1855. Ed. and intro. John C. Guilds. Fayetteville: University of Arkansas Press, 1993.

———. *Simms: A Literary Life*. Fayetteville: University of Arkansas Press, 1992.

———. "Simms's First Magazine: *The Album*." *Studies in Bibliography* 8 (1956): 169–83.

Kibler, James. "*The Album* (1826): The Significance of the Recently Discovered Second Volume." *Studies in Bibliography* 39 (1986): 62–78.

———. "The First Simms Letters: 'Letters from the West' (1826)." *Southern Literary Journal* 19, no. 2 (1987): 81–91.

Kramer, Michael. *Imagining Language in America: From the Revolution to the Civil War*. Princeton: Princeton University Press, 1992.

Logue, Cal M., and Howard Dorgan, eds. *The Oratory of the Southern Demagogues*. Baton Rouge: Louisiana State University Press, 1981.

Morson, Gary Saul, and Caryl Emerson. *Mikhail Bakhtin: Creation of a Prosaics*. Stanford: Stanford University Press, 1990.

O'Brien, Michael. *The Idea of the American South, 1920–1941*. Baltimore: Johns Hopkins University Press, 1979.

———. *Rethinking the South: Essays in Intellectual History*. Baltimore: Johns Hopkins University Press, 1988.

Pease, Donald E. "New Americanists: Revisionist Interventions into the Canon." *Boundary* 2 (spring 1990): 1–37.

Reynolds, David. *Beneath the American Renaissance: The Subversive Imagination in the Age of Emerson and Melville*. Cambridge: Harvard University Press, 1988.

Sapir, Edward. "The Status of Linguistics as a Science." *Culture, Language, and Personality*. Ed. David G. Mandelbaum. Berkeley: University of California Press, 1949.

Simms, William Gilmore. *Guy Rivers: A Tale of Georgia*. Rev. ed. 1855. Ed. and intro. John C. Guilds. Fayetteville: University of Arkansas Press, 1993.

———. *The Letters of William Gilmore Simms*. 5 vols. Ed. Mary C. Simms Oliphant, Alfred Taylor Odell, and T. C. Duncan Eaves. Columbia: University of South Carolina Press, 1952–1956. (A sixth volume, *The Letters of William Gilmore Simms: Supplement [1834–1870]*, ed. Oliphant and Eaves, was published by the University of South Carolina Press in 1982.)

————. *Voltmeier.* Columbia: University of South Carolina Press, 1969.

Simpson, Lewis P. *The Dispossessed Garden: Pastoral and History in Southern Literature.* Athens: University of Georgia Press, 1980.

Steiner, George. *After Babel: Aspects of Language and Translation.* New York: Oxford University Press, 1975.

Stowe, Steven. *Intimacy and Power in the Old South: Ritual in the Lives of the Planters.* Baltimore: Johns Hopkins University Press, 1987.

Tompkins, Jane. *Sensational Designs: The Cultural Work of American Fiction, 1790–1860.* New York: Oxford University Press, 1985.

Wimsatt, Mary Ann. "The Evolution of Simms's Backwoods Humor." *"Long Years of Neglect": The Work and Reputation of William Gilmore Simms.* Ed. John C. Guilds. Fayetteville: University of Arkansas Press, 1988.

————. *The Major Fiction of William Gilmore Simms: Cultural Traditions and Literary Form.* Baton Rouge: Louisiana State University Press, 1989.

Wyatt-Brown, Bertram. *Southern Honor: Ethics and Behavior in the Old South.* New York: Oxford University Press, 1982.

Simms and Folklore: Southwest Humor and the Oral Tradition

MARY ANN WIMSATT

Frontier Humor and the "Arkansas Traveler" Motif in *Southward Ho!*

Setting: The backwoods of Arkansas near the middle of the nineteenth century

Characters: A wet, bewildered traveler on horseback and a native or squatter

Traveler.—Halloo, stranger.

Squatter.—Hello, yourself.

T.—Can I get to stay all night with you?

S.—No, sir, you can't git to—

T.—Have you any spirits here?

S.—Lots uv 'em; Sal seen one last night by thar ar ole hollar gum, and it nearly skeered her to death.

T.—You mistake my meaning; have you any liquor?

S.—Had some yesterday, but Ole Bose he got in and lapped all uv it out'n the pot.

T.—You don't understand; I don't mean pot liquor. I'm wet and cold and want some whiskey. Have you got any?

S.—Oh, yes—I drunk the last this mornin.

T.—I'm hungary; havn't had a thing since morning; can't you give me something to eat?

S.—Hain't a durned thing in the house. Not a mouffull uv meat, nor a dust uv meal here. . . .

T.—As I'm not likely to get to any other house to night, can't you let me sleep in yours; and I'll tie my horse to a tree, and do without anything [to] eat or drink?

S.—My house leaks. Thar's only one dry spot in it, and me and Sal sleeps on it. . . .

T.—Why don't you finish covering your house and stop the leaks?

S.—It's been rainin' all day.

T.—Well, why don't you do it in dry weather?

S.—It don't leak then.

—JAMES MASTERSON, *Tall Tales of Arkansaw*

Setting: The stormy seacoast of North Carolina near the middle of the
nineteenth century
Characters: Several steamboat passengers who go ashore near a little
town called Smithville in search of an oyster, and a native. One of the
passengers describes what ensues.

"We met a fellow seven feet high, with his back against a bank of sand
that kept off the wind, while the fragment of an old cutter's deck,
hanging over the bank, covered him from the rain—all except drippings
and leakage. . . . We questioned him about oysters.

"'Reckon it's hard to find 'em now.'

"'Why?'

"'Why, you see, we've done cleaned off all a'top, and them down low
in the water's mighty hard to come at. Don't get much oysters at
Smithville now. Reckon there mought have been a right smart chance of
'em long time ago—'bout the Revolution.'

"'Well, do you think we can get any broiled chickens anywhere?'

"'Chickens don't do so well at Smithville. I'm thinking they drink too
much of the salt water, and the gravel's too coarse for 'em, but they die
off mighty soon, and there's no cure for it.'

"'Eggs?'

"'Well now, as for eggs, somehow the hens don't lay as they used to.
Folks say that there's a sort of happidemic among the poultry of all kinds.
They don't thrive no more in Smithville.'

"'And what *have* you got in Smithville?'

"'I reckon there's pretty much all the Smiths here that was here at the
beginning. Old granny Pressman Smith lives thar in that rether old
house that looks a'most as if it was guine to fall. 'Lijah Smith keeps
opposite. He had the grocery, but he's pretty much sold out. . . . Rice
Smith owns that 'ere flat, you sees thar' with its side stove; and the
old windmill yander with the fans gone b'longs to Jackson W. Smith,
the lawyer. He's pretty much broke up I hear, by buying a gold mine
somewhere in the South. . . . I'm a Smith myself—my name's Fergus
Smith, but I'm the poorest of the family. I don't own nothing, no how,
and neer did.'"

—WILLIAM GILMORE SIMMS, *Southward Ho!*

$\mathbf{B}$ecause the University of Arkansas generously hosted the inaugural meeting of the Simms Society, it seems appropriate in this essay to examine some parallels between what is perhaps the most celebrated specimen of folk humor from the state—the famous story of the Arkansas Traveler[1]—and the lively passage from Simms quoted above as a way of illuminating certain things that Simms was doing with Southern frontier humor in his midcentury writing, particularly in one of his most neglected volumes, *Southward Ho!*, published by J. S. Redfield in 1854. A careful study of the Smithville passage in that volume suggests that Simms was either appropriating several elements from the Arkansas Traveler yarn, which was widely circulated in oral form from 1840 onward, or that, drawing on his own extensive knowledge of the Southern frontier and its humor, he was inventing a dialogue remarkably similar in content and design to that of the yarn a few years before it appeared in print between 1858 and 1860 (Masterson 186). The issue of whether Simms invented or adapted the passage in question, like many such issues in his fiction, cannot be settled with any certainty; and in fact it is not necessary *that* it be settled. What is important instead is an analysis of the correspondences between Simms's Smithville story and the Arkansas Traveler legend as these correspondences illuminate Simms's command of Southern frontier humor near midcentury.

When studied closely, the two accounts reveal several similarities: the contrast of civilization and frontier that is rendered through a sophisticated traveler and a canny squatter or native; the indolence and alleged poverty of the latter, which he uses to deny the traveler food or drink; the rainy weather and leaky roof that he stubbornly ignores; his use of prevarication as a means of duping or gulling the traveler in order to keep him at bay; and the dialogue format involving a question-and-answer structure depending on a time-honored device in backwoods humor, the thrust-and-parry procedure. Described another way, what is obvious in both versions of the story are the native's clever manipulation of the traveler through lies and tricks; his implicit defense of his homestead and way of life through his refusal to offer aid or accommodation; and—perhaps most interestingly—his clever use of tall tale elements involving *understated* or negative exaggeration, rather than the more familiar type of tall tale employing *overstated* or extravagant exaggeration, in order to throw the traveler off the track. These and other resemblances between the Arkansas Traveler legend and the Smithville story invite us first to take a closer look at the composition and history of the famous folk story and then to examine the various kinds of frontier humor in *Southward Ho!* that form the context for Simms's anecdote of Smithville.

Numerous humor and folklore scholars—among them Walter Blair, Norris Yates, James Masterson, Catherine Marshall Vineyard, and Gene Bluestein—have speculated about and studied the discomfited traveler, his squatter-opponent, and the various versions of the yarn in which they appear. These scholars arrive at several similar conclusions, perhaps the most prominent of which is that the saucy dialogue forming one of the most striking features of the yarn is not entirely original: it incorporates comparable passages of dialogue found in printed works dating at least from the 1830s, and in oral form from probably well before that time. These passages typically involve an educated speaker whose rural counterpart responds to questions or instructions with sarcastic remarks, stupid rejoinders, or both. In 1835, for instance, in Augustus Baldwin Longstreet's *Georgia Scenes*, speaker Lyman Hall asks a "smerky little fellow" to "[G]ive me your name." The fellow replies, "[T]ake it—take it, and welcome" (215, 216). In 1836 William T. Porter of the *Spirit of the Times* printed a brisk short dialogue that foreshadows the deliberately misleading comments that form a major motif in "The Arkansas Traveler": "Stop that cow,"—"I have got no stopper," "*Head* her,"—"her *yead* is on the right end,"—"*Turn* her,"—"Her *skin* is on the right side"—"D--n it! speak to her,"—"*Good morning, Mrs. Cow!*"[2]

Somewhat closer to Simms's Smithville story and the Arkansas Traveler legend is the type of thrust-and-parry exchange that centers on the poverty and ignorance of poor whites in the backwoods and their reluctance to offer hospitality or speak courteously to travelers. Two particularly notable yarns of this sort were printed in the New York *Knickerbocker* magazine in 1839 and partially reprinted in the *Spirit of the Times* (Yates 108). The yarns anticipate several important elements in the passages quoted above from the traveler legend and Simms, including importunate travelers, inhospitable natives, inclement weather, and poor accommodations—all of which are presented humorously, with liberal use of dialect and exaggeration. In the first of the *Knickerbocker* stories, two lawyers traveling in backwoods Georgia come upon a "clumsy, ill-shapen log hut" that boasts chinks "wide enough to throw a sizeable bear through." A fire of lightwood knots blazes in the chimney; a gaunt woman, many children, and the squatter himself huddle near the fire. When one of the lawyers, after greeting the squatter, observes, "Fine situation you have here," the squatter responds, "Fine h-ll! . . . [W]hat's it fine for?" The lawyer replies, "Why, I should suppose you would have good sport here, in hunting." The squatter rejoins, "Then you'd suppose a d--n lie! You can't hunt, 'cepting you got something to hunt at, kin you?" After several further exchanges, during which the squatter's account of his circumstances grows more and more negative, the lawyer inquires, "Why do you stay here?" The lazy squatter rejoins, "Oh, 'cause the lightwood knots are so 'mazin' handy!" (*Knickerbocker* 141).

The second yarn in the *Knickerbocker* shows even closer resemblances to the situation in the Arkansas Traveler legend and the Smithville story. The two lawyers, further along in their travels, find another hovel, where rain pours "in torrents through the roof" and the "only dry spots [are] near the bed and the fire-place." The lord of this dwelling sits in a backless chair fiddling a tune that has "no beginning, no middle, no end." One of the lawyers inquires, "Why do n't you stop that cursed fiddle? Why do n't you stop the leaks in your roof?" The squatter responds, "You would n't have me go out in the rain, would you?" The lawyer rejoins, "No; but why do n't you stop them when it do n't rain?" "Oh, *they do n't leak then!*" (*Knickerbocker* 142–43).

Simms, who was familiar with backwoods Georgia, corresponded with Longstreet, and contributed in the 1830s to the *Knickerbocker* (and probably to the *Spirit of the Times* during his many visits to New York), may have known these or similar pieces.[3] Or he may have heard a version of the Arkansas Traveler story on his travels through the rural Southern countryside and especially on his several trips to the Gulf South, which he visited in the 1820s, the 1830s, and the early 1840s, well before he composed the Smithville passage in *Southward Ho!*[4] The Arkansas Traveler yarn in oral form, as already noted, began to be widely circulated around 1840, near the time of what was apparently Simms's final visit to the Gulf South or Old Southwest.[5] Folklorist James Masterson attributes the version of the yarn quoted at the beginning of this essay to Colonel Sandford (or Sanford) C. Faulkner, a native of Kentucky who had moved to Arkansas and acquired a sizable plantation (Masterson 186; Vineyard 51). A noted raconteur, Faulkner became so famous for his many retellings of the story that when he visited New Orleans he was given a special hotel room with "The Arkansas Traveler" in gilt letters above the door (Vineyard 50). Because the tale consists almost entirely of dialogue and because several of its many versions make

reference to plays and theaters, Vineyard suggests that it may have originated on the stage. She speculates, moreover, that the fiddle music that
figures prominently in sections of the yarn (from which I have not quoted)
may have arisen independently of the dialogue in the playing of a noted
violinist along the Ohio River (51–54).

The wide dissemination of the story and its persistent popularity derive,
in fact, almost as much from its association with music, painting, theater,
and the media as from its intrinsic appeal. Throughout much of the story,
the native—like the squatter in the second *Knickerbocker* story—plays and
replays a single monotonous tune upon his fiddle. When the traveler inquires, "[W]hy don't you play the balance of that tune?" the native rejoins,
"[E]f you think you can play any more onto that thar tune, you kin just try
it." The traveler then takes up the fiddle and completes the melody. This
so-called "turn of the tune" is also the turn of the story. The native, over-
joyed at hearing the remainder of the melody, reverses his behavior toward
the traveler, showers him with courtesy, offers him deer meat and whiskey,
asks him to spend the night, gives him directions for further travel, and
invites him to return to the house, "whar you kin cum and play on thar 'ar
tune as long as you please" (Masterson 188–89).

In light of the important role of music in the Arkansas Traveler story, it
is worth observing that the yarn achieved its greatest circulation in the
nineteenth century through its inclusion in a collection called *The Arkansas
Traveller's Songster* (Masterson 191–92).[6] It also inspired two widely known
paintings by artist Edward Payson Washburn called "The Arkansas Traveler" and "The Turn of the Tune" that were lithographed late in the nineteenth century by Currier and Ives (Vineyard 57–60). The story, moreover, furnished the title for a magazine published for about ten years, and,
in an interesting development, it was made into a skit and a play that not
only helped to spread its fame but also returned it to the stage from which
it had perhaps originally sprung (Vineyard 55–56). Living on into this century, the legend appeared in books, anthologies, or song collections in
1900, 1913, 1917, 1918, 1926, 1932, 1936, and 1944, acquiring wide circulation through the works of B. A. Botkin, an indefatigable accumulator
of folk and humorous lore, and even wider circulation as a staple of "the
country music repertoire on radio, television, and recordings" (Bluestein
80). In short, the story of the Arkansas Traveler is "one of those creations
that has straddled folk and popular levels of culture" because it reflects "the

tensions which still exist between rural and urban life in the United States"
(Bluestein 80).

Let us turn now to some evidence involving Simms's knowledge of
comic, rural, oral and written lore, particularly the kind of lore resembling
the Arkansas Traveler story, in order to see how it influenced the sort of
frontier humor that went into *Southward Ho!* Simms's exposure to such material, which began through his travels, continued through his self-styled
"insatiate" reading from childhood on in the work of Longstreet, James
Hall, James Kirke Paulding, Davy Crockett, William Alexander Caruthers,
William Tappan Thompson, and other authors who regularly employed
native humor in their writing (Simms, *Letters* 1 : 161). That he was broadly
familiar with several of the elements that appear in the Arkansas Traveler
story is suggested by his use of similar elements in his own writing. Early
in his career, for instance, using the thrust-and-parry method he incorporated passages of dialogue into his second Revolutionary War romance,
Mellichampe (1836). Here patriot scout Thumbscrew Weatherspoon del-
uges loyalist scout Ned Blonay with questions about British army movements and supplies, responding evasively or feigning stupidity when Blonay
questions him in turn. Thumbscrew observes:

> "They gits a-fighting every now and then in these here parts, and they
> do say they're a-mustering now above, the sodgers."
>
> "What soldiers?" demanded Blonay, with an air of interest.
>
> "Eh! what sodgers?—them that carries guns and swords, and shoots
> people, to be sure—them's sodgers, a'n't they? . . . Talking about
> horses now, I've hear'd say that they were getting mighty scarce down
> in your parts. . . . Some say that they were buying and stealing all they
> could, to bring troops up into this quarter. You ain't hear'd any say
> about it, I reckon? . . ."
>
> "What troops?" [Blonay] asked, carelessly.
>
> "Why, them that fights, to be sure. . . ."
>
> "Yes, troopers," said Blonay, tired, seemingly, of putting questions
> so unprofitably answered.
>
> "Ay—troopers, is it?—I always called them troops." (*Mellichampe* 1 :
> 48, 49–50)[7]

Giving the convention of artful questions a different twist, in the lively,
comic *Border Beagles* (1840)—set in frontier Mississippi—Simms draws

upon the tradition of inquisitive backwoods natives investigated by Walter
Blair and other scholars when he has a settler pepper a traveler with queries:
"[M]y name's John Horsey . . . but yours—what's your name? . . . Harry,
Harry Vernon! . . . The old people living, Mr. Vernon? Your health, sir, in
the meantime. . . . Did I hear you, Mr. Vernon? The old people, you said
they were living [?]" (1:23–24).

By midcentury, as evidenced by books ranging from *The Wigwam and the
Cabin* (1845) to *As Good as a Comedy* (1852), Simms had mastered such standard elements of Southern frontier humor as the frame structure, the dialect narrator, inventive, colorful backwoods language, and the tall tale. It
is therefore scarcely surprising that he incorporates these elements into
Southward Ho!, which he called "a Southern Decameron—a Christmas Decameron," a "good book for the traveller & for the Holidays" (*Letters* 3:
314, 340). *Southward Ho!* consists of a number of stories emerging from a
framing narrative that centers on a group of characters traveling from New
York to South Carolina by steamboat—a trip that Simms himself had frequently made, as he indicates by basing some of the characters on his real-
life friends. Reviewers of the book called it "a lively, sketchy, and most sug-
gestive work, in the very best style and manner of the author" and claimed
that Simms had written "few more attractive volumes," while according to
William P. Trent, the author's friends "found it charming, because, as they
said, it was written just as Simms talked." [8] Simms's own offhand comments
about the volume in his published correspondence—"a thread of circum-
stance, upon which I scattered fabrications"—may have encouraged his
twentieth-century readers to rank *Southward Ho!* somewhat lower in his
canon than perhaps it should be ranked; but not even the most ardent
Simms devotee can claim that the book is a masterpiece (*Letters* 3:355).
What one may legitimately claim, however—and the claim may be but-
tressed by ample evidence drawn from the frame—is that in *Southward Ho!*,
as in other less-than-perfect midcentury Simms productions, certain aspects of Simms's considerable comic talent, particularly his talent for frontier humor, stand forth clearly. From the tall tales about mosquitoes that
grace the early pages of the book to the elaborate narrative of Smithville
that enlivens its central chapters, the frame affords rich evidence of Simms's
genius for the kind of humor—humor with a distinctly tall cast—that cul-
minates in his masterworks, "How Sharp Snaffles Got His Capital and
Wife" and "Bald-Head Bill Bauldy."

At this point it will be helpful, before taking up the matter of frontier humor in *Southward Ho!* in detail, to look more closely at the origin and nature of Simms's framing narrative in order to understand his conception of the work and the setting from which his humor emerges. In 1847, Simms had broached the idea for the frame in a letter to his New York friend and informal literary agent, Evert Duyckinck: "How would you like a volume of sketches of the South,—its scenery & traditions entitled 'Slopes and Summits of the South?' I have the materials for such a vol." (Simms, *Letters* 2:273).[9] Shortly thereafter, these materials became the basis for a series of sketches titled "Spells of Sunshine; or, a Summer in the South" that Simms published in the *Charleston Evening News* during June and July of 1849. When he decided to use the sketches for the framing narrative of *Southward Ho!*, he revised them very slightly—thereby causing one of the major flaws in the printed volume, its failure to tie frame and stories firmly together.

Viewed at its broadest, the framing narrative reflects Simms's insistent emphasis upon the virtues of Southern culture during a period that had seen an enormous acceleration of sectional strife. It also shows his solid knowledge of Northern and Southern Atlantic seaboard states, including New York, New Jersey, Virginia, North Carolina, and South Carolina, and it reveals—at least in its early chapters—his reasonable impartiality in speaking of the North. It shows his understanding of Southern geography, his desire to overcome unflattering stereotypes about the South that were held by Northerners and Southerners alike, and his concomitant desire to educate his countrymen about the South's many attractive features, including its diverse landscape, its advantages for travel, and its local legendry. The frame, moreover, reflects Simms's passionate Southern patriotism, his equally passionate belief that the North was economically exploiting the South, his conviction that Southern planters were not practicing the best current scientific agricultural methods, and his developing secessionist sentiments.

In several passages in the frame of *Southward Ho!* Simms treats the last of these beliefs in a humorous backwoods manner that both sharpens and lends charm to his sociopolitical commentary. Near the middle of the book, for instance, a passenger from South Carolina recounts a conversation he once had with a "hale and rather pursy old farmer" who told him, "I'm a-thinking there's no chance for us in the eend, unless we cut loose from the whole Yankee consarn. Old Isaac Coppidge, one of my neighbors, he said, more than twenty years ago . . . that the Union was jest a sort of Union between a mighty fat frog and a hungry blacksnake—that the fat frog was the South, and the hungry snake the North. And, says he, it's because the frog is so big and so fat, that the snake kaint swallow him all at once. But the snake's got fast hold, and the frog's a-gitting weaker every day—and every day a little more of him goes down; when the day comes that the frog gives up and lies quiet, the snake'll finish him" (175, 176).

The steamboat setting that Simms employs for the frame of *Southward Ho!* had been a staple in Southern humor at least since Thomas Bangs Thorpe's "The Big Bear of Arkansas," published in the *Spirit of the Times* in 1841 and republished in 1845 as the title story of *The Big Bear of Arkansas*, Porter's collection of sporting and humorous yarns culled from the *Spirit*. The setting allows Simms—through his knowledgeable narrator, a Charlestonian like himself—to emphasize the diversity of Southern landscape and culture; and it also allows him to shape the characters in the frame to represent Northern as well as Southern regional types. Like Thorpe he is at pains, in fact, to designate certain figures by regional origin in addition to, or instead of, by name: the Gothamite, the machinist from Maine, the North Carolinian, the Alabamian, the Mississippian, the Texan, and so forth. This feature of the frame enables him to emphasize the rivalry between regions that was a standard feature of much native humor and that, in his work and that of his fellow authors, typically involves comic exaggeration about the virtues of a given region, especially its fertility and beauty (Blair and Hill 158–60).

Hence in the first chapter of the frame, Simms's narrator defends his native state against the New Yorker's playful charge that the South Carolina low country is ridden with mosquitoes. "Twenty miles from the coast," the Carolinian insists, "I can carry you to the most delicious pineland settlements and climate. . . . where a musquito [*sic*] is such a rarity, that people gather to survey him. . . . When one happens there, driven by stress of weather, he pines away in a settled melancholy, from the sense of solitude, and loses his voice entirely before he dies. He has neither the heart to sing, nor the strength to sting, and finally perishes of a broken heart. His hope of safety, it is said, is only found in his being able to fasten upon a foreigner, when he is reported to fatten up amazingly" (*Southward Ho!* 4–5). That comparable tales about mosquitoes involving comparable regional rivalry circulated in frontier humor near midcentury is corroborated by a passage in "The Big Bear" in which Thorpe's protagonist, Arkansan Jim Doggett, after boasting that Arkansas is "The creation state, the finishing-up country," insists that it is "a state without a fault." When a Hoosier, taking issue with these statements, complains about the Arkansas mosquitoes, Doggett retorts that though the insects are enormous, "they never stick twice in the same place." With pointed regional reference, he continues, "I never knew but one case of injury resulting from them, and that was to a Yankee" (Porter 17–18).

In the third chapter of the frame of *Southward Ho!*, oysters, another staple of Southern frontier humor, furnish the topic for an untitled tall tale designated "Oyster Wars" by an early student of Simms's short fiction (Morris 26). It is narrated by the New Yorker, whose subject is a bloody battle between Jerseyites and Gothamites over oyster beds—a subject he presents in mingled mock-heroic, tall-tale manner.[10] "[W]ere you to have," he says, "proper portraits of the fierce Sam Jones, the redoubtable Pete Pinnock, Ben the Biter, Barney the Diver, Bill the Raker, Ned the Devourer, and a score or two more, on both sides, who distinguished themselves in the field during this bivalvular campaign, you would feel that there are still provinces for the epic muse." The hero of "Oyster Wars," the huge Sam Jones, is clearly a fellow to be reckoned with. "Very fearful," says the New Yorker, "had been Sam's experience. He had slept upon a circle of six feet, on an oyster-bed, with the Atlantic rolling around him. He had enjoyed a hand-to-hand combat with a shark, of sixteen feet, in five-fathom water. He had ceased to know fear. . . . The Greeks at Troy, under the conduct of Ajax the Buffalo, never darted under the hills and towers of Ilium with more defiant demeanor" (22, 24).

Somewhat later in the frame, Simms develops the character simply called "the Alabamian" as a wag and eccentric who wears green spectacles, engages in facetious conversations, and indulges in outlandish (and outlandishly long) orations. Throughout these passages, Simms emphasizes the Alabamian's strength, courage, and audacity in details that increase the humorous backwoods ambience of the frame. The Alabamian amuses himself, for instance, by twitting a "peppery little fellow" from North Carolina, who responds snappishly. During their encounter, the Texan—who has yelled, "Go ahead, old Bile!" to the Alabamian—says to the North Carolinian, "I say, young hoss . . . don't you see that old Bile is just putting the finger of fun into the green parts of your eye[?]" When the Carolinian, undeterred, proposes a fight, the Alabamian rejoins, in language smacking of the frontier, "I am apt to be *riled* . . . feel skin and hair both raised unnaturally—when I am threatened; and, as for a fight, it sounds to me rather like an invitation than a warning. . . . I should whip you out of your breeches, without unbuttoning mine" (*Southward Ho!* 312, 317, 326, 327).

Midway through *Southward Ho!* the Alabamian and the North Carolinian engage in a protracted verbal sparring match that, extending over
many chapters, reveals Simms's ability—rarely sufficiently commended—
to combine several strands from the literary and cultural traditions behind
him. To bedevil his fellow passenger, the Alabamian engages in bantering
derogatory commentary on North Carolina, which was familiarly known
throughout the nineteenth century as "Lubberland" and "the Old North
State." It is commentary of a sort that would be natural to a South Carolinian such as Simms's narrator or for that matter Simms himself, and it reflects Simms's knowledge of the William Byrd tradition of satiric commentary on "Lubberland," Byrd's term for North Carolina. Three of
Byrd's volumes—*The History of the Dividing Line Betwixt Virginia and North
Carolina, A Journey to the Land of Eden,* and *A Progress to the Mines*—had
been edited by Simms's friend Edmund Ruffin as *The Westover MSS* and
published in 1841. In passages relevant for Simms's presentation of North
Carolina in *Southward Ho!,* Byrd remarks:

> Surely there is no place in the World where the Inhabitants live with
> less Labour than in N Carolina. It approaches nearer to the De-
> scription of Lubberland than any other, by the great felicity of the
> Climate, the easiness of raising Provisions, and the Slothfulness of the
> People.

> Indian Corn is of so great increase, that a little Pains will Subsist a
> very large Family with Bread, and then they may have meat without
> any pains at all, by the Help of the Low Grounds. . . . The Men, for
> their Parts, just like the Indians, impose all the Work upon the poor
> Women. They make their Wives rise out of their Beds early in the
> Morning, at the same time that they lye and Snore, till the Sun has run
> one third of his course, and disperst all the unwholesome Damps.
> Then, after Stretching and Yawning for half an Hour, they light their
> Pipes, and, under the Protection of a cloud of Smoak, venture out into
> the open Air; tho', if it happens to be never so little cold, they quickly
> return Shivering into the Chimney corner. When the weather is mild,
> they stand leaning with both their arms upon the corn-field fence, and
> gravely consider whether they had best go and take a Small Heat at the
> Hough: but generally find reasons to put it off till another time.
>   Thus they loiter away their Lives, like Solomon's Sluggard . . . and
> at the Winding up of the Year Scarcely have Bread to Eat.

To speak the Truth, tis a thorough Aversion to Labor that makes People file off to N Carolina, where Plenty and a Warm Sun confirm them in their Disposition to Laziness for their whole Lives. (Byrd, 90–92)

Simms's familiarity with Byrd is shown by his reference to "the Westover Manuscripts" in a footnote in *Southward Ho!*, in which he describes Byrd as "a genuine wit and humorist, and a frank and manly Southron." His reference to Byrd in the text of *Southward Ho!* is even more illuminating, at least as it bears on the Smithville story. North Carolina, Simms says, has never been satisfied with "the high head [that Virginia] carries, from the day when that malicious Col. Byrd, of Westover, made fun of his commissioners" (323; see also 319–20).

That in the frame of *Southward Ho!* Simms draws on Byrd as well as on the tradition of gulling naive travelers found in the Arkansas Traveler legend and related tales is evident in long passages in which the Alabamian mercilessly gulls the North Carolinian, just as the native gulls the traveler in the exchange involving Smithville. The exchange in its entirety indicates that Simms's familiarity with frontier humor, his knowledge of Byrd, and the story about Smithville are connected, as will shortly become clear. The Alabamian's initial sallies against the North Carolinian contain little flashes of tall tales that, echoing Byrd while alluding to Jonathan Swift, prepare for some particularly extravagant portions of the Smithville exchange. The Alabamian says, "I have tried as much as possible to see something along your Carolina routes, but to little profit. . . . The whole country, so far as its agriculture is concerned, seemed wretchedly unpromising. . . . The cornfields were few, I could have covered half of them with a table cloth, and the crops raised seem all destined for the markets of Laputa" (*Southward Ho!* 312, 313).

Naively, the North Carolinian inquires, "Laputa? Where's that, I wonder?" The Alabamian waggishly replies, "Somewhere north of Brobdignag [*sic*], I believe, and west of the tropics, between the equator and the Frozen sea, and crossed by the central fires of the Equinox, which enables the people to raise potatoes and barley with equal facility, but prevents them from growing corn. This commodity, of which they are passionately fond, eating an ear at a mouthful, and chewing the cob at their leisure, is brought to them only once a year by one Captain Gulliver, a native of Cape Cod, the only known trader between Laputa and North Carolina. I should not be surprised if he is even now taking in a cargo at Wilmington." When the

North Carolinian snorts, "I never heard of the man. . . . Just say now, if you can remember, what's the vessel called that he navigates," the Alabamian replies, in direct if subtle reference to the fact that he is spinning a tall tale, "The Long Bow. . . . a great craft for shallow waters" (313).[11]

"[P]assing from the cornfields of your state," the Alabamian continues, "I am sorry to say that I can say as little for its habitations. The dwellings were all of the rudest construction, and signs of gardening, or culture of any kind, were as rare, almost, as you will find them along the waste places of the Tigris and the Dead sea." Next he narrates the opening part of the saga of Smithville quoted at the beginning of this essay. Upon hearing it, the North Carolinian objects, "But Smithville is not North Carolina." After further byplay, the Alabamian alleges, "This place, Smithville[,] . . . I have studied with great industry. It was settled—perhaps you have heard— by the first man of the name of Smith that came out of Noah's ark. It is supposed, indeed, to be the very spot where the ark rested where the waters subsided. . . . The people here, of course, are all named Smith" (313, 316, 329).

The North Carolinian exclaims, "Oh, that's a mistake, my dear fellow . . . I know the place, and know that the Buttons live here, and the Black family." But his opponent interrupts, "[I]t is you who are mistaken. They are really all Smiths, however much they may disguise and deny. There's a family likeness running through all of them which nobody can dispute." Then, in passages that indicate Simms has William Byrd in mind, the Alabamian continues, "The wonder is, that, boasting such a great antiquity, they are so little ambitious. Their enterprise is limited to an occasional visit to the oyster-bank, where it is said they will feed for some hours at a stretch, but they never trouble themselves to carry any of the fruits away." Next, in a particularly outrageous sally, he alleges, "Smithville . . . is a study for the ethnologist . . . all the children here are old when they are born. The period of gestation seems to be about eighteen years. The child is invariably born with a reddish mustache and imperial, and a full stock of reddish hair" (329, 330).

The North Carolinian sputters, "Bless me, what a story! Why, how they have imposed on you, old fellow! I tell you, I myself know the families of Button and Black, and—and they all have children—real children, just like any other people's children—little, small, helpless, with hardly any hair upon their heads, not a sign of a moustache, and the color of the hair is whitish, rather than reddish, when they are born."[12] The poker-faced Alabamian replies, "How a man's own eyes may deceive him! My dear friend, you never saw a child in Smithville of native origin at all. The natives are all full grown. If you saw children there—ordinary children—they were all from foreign parts, and grievously out of their element, I assure you. Your supposed facts must not be allowed to gainsay philosophy" (330).

And what do these exchanges, however ingenious, have to do with the story of the Arkansas Traveler? Simply this: that in the first part of the Smithville story—involving rainy weather, hungry travelers, lazy natives, and sparse provisions—Simms is apparently drawing either on the Arkansas Traveler material or on something very similar to it. But, by the point he has not reached, he has gone far beyond whatever his sources may have been. In other words, Simms has by this stage in *Southward Ho!* begun to spin inventive, imaginative fantasies out of his own wonderfully fertile comic imagination—meanwhile drawing upon, or drawing in, William Byrd, Jonathan Swift, various sorts of folk material, his own travels in the Old Southwest in the 1820s and thereafter, and his extremely wide knowledge of such traditions in frontier humor as dupes and duping; gulls and gulling; lies, hoaxes, and deceptions; civilized travelers, squatters, and natives; and tall tales and other matters.

Speaking of tall tales, the Alabamian gets in one particularly memorable "stretcher" of a somewhat different sort from the Smithville story. Midway through his exchanges with the North Carolinian, he interrupts himself to tell a snappy little story that, like the Arkansas Traveler legend, was widely recycled in nineteenth-century folk material. After claiming in a statement reminiscent of Davy Crockett that he was "born in a cloud and suckled by the east wind," he boasts that he has been in several fights:

"The last I had was with seven Apache Indians. I had but one revolver, a six-barrel—"

"Well?"

"I killed six of the savages."

"And the seventh?"

"He killed me!" (Simms, *Southward Ho!* 329).[13]

NOTES

1. According to Masterson 189, this is the earliest, best, and most authentic of the dozen or more versions of the yarn. Irregularities in spelling, as of *hungary* and *havn't*, are in the text as transcribed in Masterson. Blair, "Inquisitive Yankee" 20,

notes that much of the Arkansas Traveler story is derivative, a point that the re-search of Masterson, Vineyard, and Yates supports.

2. Irregularities in punctuation are the *Spirit*'s. In the quotation, I have emended the spelling *D--u* in the *Spirit*, which is probably a printer's error, to *D--n*.

3. Simms's first novel, *Guy Rivers*, is set in the mountainous region of north-western Georgia. Simms corresponded with Longstreet, called the humor of *Geor-gia Scenes* "the best specimens in this field that the American genius has produced," and secured the second series of the *Scenes* for *The Magnolia; or, Southern Appala-chian*, which he edited during 1842–1843. For his correspondence with Longstreet, see *Letters* 1:344–45; 2:68; and 6:205, 209. His praise of *Georgia Scenes* appears in his essay "The Humourous in American and British Literature" 178.

4. Simms describes his two trips in the middle 1820s to the Gulf South, where he visited his father in Mississippi, in "Letters from the West," Album 2 (March 4, 11, April 1, May 20, 1826), 68–69, 76–77, 100–101, 157–58. James E. Kibler dis-covered these documents in the long-missing second volume of the Album and pub-lished them as "The First Simms Letters." On Simms's trips to the region in the 1830s, see chiefly his letter sequence "Notes of a Small Tourist," published in the *Charleston City Gazette* in March–May 1831 and republished in *Letters* 1:10–38. He traveled to Tuscaloosa, Alabama, in 1842 to deliver the oration "The Social Principle" at the University of Alabama, from which he received an honorary LL.D.; see *Letters* 1:332 n. 111.

5. Simms's final visit to the Gulf South was apparently the trip to Alabama in 1842 described in note 4, above. Vineyard 49–50 and Botkin 346 date the oral circulation of the Arkansas Traveler yarn from the early 1840s.

6. The dates for printed versions of the "Arkansas Traveler" derive from Mas-terson, passim. Vineyard 57–58 corrects Masterson on a number of important points about the pictorial depiction of the yarn.

7. Irregularities in spelling (as of *ain't*) in the passage are Simms's or his printer's.

8. The reviews of *Southward Ho!* quoted in the text are from the *Charleston Courier* November 28, 1854: 2, and from *Graham's American Monthly Magazine of Literature and Art* 46 (March 1855): 287 (Trent 210). The passages are quoted at greater length in Keen Butterworth and James E. Kibler, *William Gilmore Simms* 96, 100.

9. The editors of the *Letters* observe that this passage "is doubtless the germ of Southward Ho!" (2:273 n. 58).

10. The New Yorker, Edgar Duyckman, is Simms's lighthearted portrait of his friend Evert Duyckinck. For the prominence of oysters in frontier humor, see, for instance, John S. Robb's well-known sketch "Swallowing an Oyster Alive."

11. "The Long Bow" is a metaphor for "tall tale." The reference to "shallow waters" may be the Alabamian's way of mocking the shallow wits of the North Carolinian, who does not understand how thoroughly he is being gulled.

12. Irregularities in the spelling of *mustache* in the quotations in the text are Simms's or his printer's.

13. Penrod 31 notes that this tale is of "widely diffused folk origin." He does not, however, cite Simms's version of the story.

WORKS CITED

Blair, Walter. "Inquisitive Yankee Descendants in Arkansas." *American Speech* 14 (1939): 11–22.

Blair, Walter, and Hamlin Hill. *America's Humor: From Poor Richard to Doonesbury.* New York: Oxford University Press, 1978.

Bluestein, Gene. *The Voice of the Folk: Folklore and American Literary Theory.* Amherst: University of Massachusetts Press, 1972.

Botkin, B. A., ed. *A Treasury of American Folklore: Stories, Ballads, and Traditions of the People.* New York: Crown Publishers, 1944.

Byrd, William K., ed. *William Byrd's Histories of the Dividing Line Betwixt Virginia and North Carolina.* Raleigh: North Carolina Historical Commission, 1929. With a new introduction by Percy Adams. New York: Dover, 1967.

Butterworth, Keen, and James E. Kibler. *William Gilmore Simms: A Reference Guide.* Boston: G. K. Hall, 1980.

Kibler, James E. "The First Simms Letters: 'Letters from the West' (1826)." *Southern Literary Journal* 19, no. 2 (1987): 81–91.

The Knickerbocker, or New-York Monthly Magazine 14 (August 1839): 140–43.

Longstreet, Augustus Baldwin. *Georgia Scenes, Characters, Incidents, &c. in the First Half Century of the Republic.* Augusta: The S. R. Sentinel Office, 1835.

Masterson, James R. *Tall Tales of Arkansaw [sic].* Boston: Chapman and Grimes, 1943.

Morris, J. Allen. "The Stories of William Gilmore Simms." *American Literature* 14 (1942): 20–35.

Penrod, James H. "Characteristic Endings of Southwestern Yarns." *Mississippi Quarterly* 15 (1961–1962): 27–35.

Porter, William T., ed. *The Big Bear of Arkansas, and Other Sketches, Illustrative of Characters and Incidents in the South and South-West.* Philadelphia: Carey and Hart, 1845. New York: AMS, 1973.

Robb, John S. "Swallowing an Oyster Alive." *Streaks of Squatter Life, and Far-West Scenes.* Philadelphia: Carey and Hart, 1847. Ed. John Francis McDermott. Gainesville: Scholar's Facsimiles and Reprints, 1962.

Simms, William Gilmore. *As Good as a Comedy: or, The Tennessean's Story.* Philadelphia: Carey and Hart, 1852.

———. *Border Beagles: A Tale of Mississippi.* 2 vols. Philadelphia: Carey and Hart, 1840.

————. *Guy Rivers: A Tale of Georgia*. Rev. ed. 1855. Ed. and intro. John C. Guilds. Fayetteville: University of Arkansas Press, 1993.

————. "The Humourous in American and British Literature." *Views and Reviews in American Literature, History and Fiction*. Second series. New York: Wiley and Putnam, 1845.

————. *The Letters of William Gilmore Simms*. 5 vols. Ed. Mary C. Simms Oliphant, Alfred Taylor Odell, and T. C. Duncan Eaves. Columbia: University of South Carolina Press, 1952–1956. (A sixth volume, *The Letters of William Gilmore Simms: Supplement [1834–1830]*, ed. Oliphant and Eaves, was published by the University of South Carolina Press in 1982.)

————. *Mellichampe. A Legend of the Santee*. 2 vols. New York: Harper and Brothers, 1836.

————. *Southward Ho! A Spell of Sunshine*. New York: J. S. Redfield, 1854.

Trent, William Peterfield. *William Gilmore Simms*. American Men of Letters Series. Boston and New York: Houghton Mifflin, 1892.

Vineyard, Catherine Marshall. "The Arkansas Traveller." *Backwoods to Border*. Ed. Mody C. Boatright and Donald Day. Texas Folk-Lore Society Publications 18. Austin: Texas Folk-Lore Society, and Dallas: Southern Methodist University Press, 1943. 11–60.

Yates, Norris W. *William T. Porter and the "Spirit of the Times": A Study of the "Big Bear" School of Humor*. Baton Rouge: Louisiana State University Press, 1957.

MOLLY BOYD

Southwestern Humor in
The Wigwam and the Cabin

In a 1955 *Georgia Review* article entitled "Three Streams of Southern Humor," Edd Winfield Parks complained about the omission of William Gilmore Simms from anthologies of frontier humorists.[1] Since that time, many scholars have looked with renewed interest at Simms's late comic tales, especially "How Sharp Snaffles Got His Capital and His Wife" and "Bald-Head Bill Bauldy."[2] Yet the first of these tales was published posthumously in *Harper's Magazine* for October 1870, and the second was not published until over one hundred years later when Simms's *Stories and Tales* were collected in the centennial edition of his works. By contrast, the Simms tales such as those collected in *The Wigwam and the Cabin* that were written and published during the heyday of frontier humor, the twenty-five years immediately preceding the Civil War, have received very little of the same critical attention, primarily because they are not viewed as tales of frontier humor. In fact, the standard notion of what constitutes frontier humor is not broad enough to accommodate Simms's stories in *The Wigwam and the Cabin*, a limitation that in recent years has led scholars such as James B. Meriwether to call for a more accurate definition of the array of writings of such authors as Longstreet, Thorpe, Lewis, and Hooper under the more descriptive appellation of "Southwestern humor."[3] If a better description of frontier humor were developed, William Gilmore Simms might be found to occupy a high place among the Southwestern humorists, as he does among so many other groups of writers from the nineteenth century.

The frontier humorists are currently defined as a group of writers who recorded orally transmitted anecdotes and fables from the Southwestern border areas of Georgia, Alabama, Louisiana, Arkansas, Kentucky, Mississippi, and Tennessee during the first half of the nineteenth century. Beginning with the publication in 1835 of Augustus Baldwin Longstreet's collection *Georgia Scenes*, a partial list of the best-known works of these humorists includes: *Major Jones's Courtship* (1843) by William T. Thompson, *Some Adventures of Captain Simon Suggs* (1845) by Johnson Jones Hooper, *Theatrical Apprenticeship* (1845) by Sol Smith, *The Mysteries of the Backwoods* (1846) by Thomas Bangs Thorpe, *Odd Leaves from the Life of a Louisiana "Swamp Doctor"* (1850) by Madison Tensas (pseudonym of Dr. Henry Clay Lewis), *Flush Times of Alabama and Mississippi* (1853) by Joseph G. Baldwin, and *Sut Lovingood's Yarns* (1867) by George Washington Harris.[4] Two important contemporary anthologies of frontier humor, *The Big Bear of Arkansas* (1845) and *A Quarter Race in Kentucky* (1846), were both edited by William T. Porter, the man who "more than any other was responsible for encouraging this vein of writing by giving it a national circulation through his weekly journal, the New York *Spirit of the Times* (1831–1861)" (Inge 3).

According to the information provided in the groundbreaking studies of such humor scholars as Walter Blair, Franklin J. Meine, M. Thomas Inge, and Hennig Cohen and William Dillingham, Simms differed radically from the standard profile of frontier humorists, most notably in his choice of setting and in his mode of publication. C. Hugh Holman writes that the humorists "reported to a society back home on what was happening on the wild frontier" but that "these reports became historical only after the westward movement had passed and had left them as its records" (Holman 90). By contrast, only two of Simms's tales in *The Wigwam and the Cabin* can be said to have been set in contemporary times, "The Snake of the Cabin" and "Those Old Lunes!" and these only because the period of the tales is unspecified. The remaining eleven tales represent Simms's intent to provide a historical report of legends, events, and persons of the past, most frequently of South Carolina, a state whose frontier and border tales had already become faded legends. Therefore, whereas the frontier humorists tended more toward realism by recording events and characters immediately at hand (or which were made immediate through oral relation), Simms's removal from the immediate time and scene of his narration gave him an aesthetic distance that allowed him to filter his narration through his own polished perspective and to use established romance techniques in constructing his tales.

Simms also differed from the standard profile of the frontier humorist in the mode of publication of his stories, which dictated three significant differences in audience, tone and material, and purpose. Simms records in the dedication to the 1856 edition of *The Wigwam and the Cabin* that the tales collected therein "were mostly written for the annuals" (iv). These annuals, more appropriately termed "gift books," were "table decorations of the . . . age, bought as much for their bindings and their richly engraved illustrations as their contents," which were aimed at a large, genteel, parlor-room variety of readers (Shelley 40). On the other hand, Cohen and Dillingham state that the humorists wrote for newspapers and weeklies, such as *The Spirit of the Times* (subtitled "A Chronicle of the Turf, Agriculture, Field Sports, Literature and the Stage"), whose readers were primarily "gentlemen of some means with a leisurely interest in masculine pursuits" (x).

These disparate differences in audience might justifiably produce striking differences in tone and material. M. Thomas Inge writes that the best word to describe the frontier humorists is "masculine," and further, that their tales deal with "'comic sin,' trickery, and knavery" in a manner that required a "'willing suspension of morality' . . . for a full appreciation of the unbridled humor" (5). Cohen and Dillingham also note that the frontier tales were "characterized by stark, realistic details and off-color, bawdy comments," were marked by "their lack of respect for delicate sensibilities," and "portrayed relationships between the sexes as directly as . . . gory accidents and fights" (xiv–xv). One would expect such tales to be unacceptable in the ladies' parlors where the gift books containing Simms's tales were prominently displayed. Simms's own comment that such frontier tales comprised "[j]ust the sort of volume to snatch up in railway and steamboat, and put out of sight in all other places" suggests the possible social censure possession of such tales might provoke in polite society (*Views and Reviews* 2 : 178).[5] And yet, Simms himself was plagued by criticism and social outrage over the indelicacy of some of his works. For instance, reviewers of *The Partisan* objected to the "preponderance of low and vulgar personages," and readers of "Caloya" reacted with "horrified" and "nasty" criticisms of its sexual content when it first appeared in the *Magnolia* (Parks, *Literary Critic* 21).

The third aspect of differences caused by the varying modes of publication relates to the purposes of the authors themselves. M. Thomas Inge writes: "In a day when writing was not a means by which one could earn a living, none of the humorists were professional authors. Their sketches were the products of amateur effort and leisure hours" (3). On the other hand, Simms, as "the leading exemplar of literary activity in the South," was a professional author who diligently worked to earn his living through his writings (Wimsatt, *Major Fiction* 1). Furthermore, Cohen and Dillingham note that "humor correspondents" to the newspapers such as *The*

Spirit of the Times "were not paid but were lavishly thanked and praised for their contributions" (x). By contrast, the annuals "published and paid for contributions by native authors" and, thus, "fostered the native literature at a time when professionalism in American arts was scarcely possible" (Shelley 40).

When the financial panic of 1837 severely reduced the remunerative outlets for works by American authors, Simms wrote to a correspondent, "These are begging times for authordom, but it is well to publish—well to keep yourself occasionally & creditably, even if not profitably, before the eye of the public" (*Letters* 1:425). In the aftermath of the panic, when he himself recorded a loss of two-thirds of his annual income from publishing, Simms was more than ever conscious of what was popular, what would sell, and what was most likely to keep him "before the eye of the public."[6] Therefore, although "[m]ost of the humorists were not writing for a literary public, and knew little about contemporary literary fashions," Simms was and did the very opposite (Inge 7).

In short, according to the standard definition, Simms is not a frontier humorist. In his choice of setting, his mode of publication, his audience, his tone and material, and his purpose, Simms differed from other humor writers such as Longstreet, Thorpe, and Lewis. But how many of these differences can be traced to the limitations of critical generalizations that fail to take into account the wide range of works produced by writers of humor during the era? For, despite the differences in the choice of setting and the mode of publication, some of Simms's tales exhibit striking similarities to other contemporary frontier humor tales in subject, format, characterization, and diction.

The thirteen tales Simms collected in *The Wigwam and the Cabin*, published in 1845 in two volumes, represent a variety of forms and literary modes. In them he explores such topics as the ghost story, local legends, folklore, and Gothic legends, most of them filtered through Simms's predilection for romance forms and liberally sprinkled with elements of tragedy and comedy. In *The Wigwam and the Cabin*, four tales are worth reviewing by aficionados of frontier humor—"Grayling; or 'Murder Will Out,'" "The Two Camps: A Legend of the Old North State," "The Lazy Crow; A Story of the Cornfield," and "Caloya: or, The Loves of the Driver." "Grayling" concerns the young Revolutionary War soldier James Grayling, who discovers the murder of his former commander, Major Spencer, and with the aid of a supernatural dream vision brings to justice the murderer, a Tory sympathizer named McNab. "The Two Camps" involves the adventures of an early settler in the Carolinas, Daniel Nelson, whose beneficent ministrations to a wounded young Indian, Lenatewà, bear fruit in later years as the recovered Lenatewà repeatedly saves the settler and his family from harm during the subsequent Indian wars. "The Lazy Crow" narrates from a white planter's perspective the clash between the "rival principals of African witchcraft, the Gullah and the Ebo fetishes," as the Ebo shaman Methuselah works to thwart the malicious spell cast by the other shaman, Gullah Sam, on a field hand (348). And finally, "Caloya" relates the amorous attentions of a swaggering African American slave driver named Mingo as he struggles to win the attentions of the virtuous Catawba woman Caloya from her degenerate and drunken husband, Enefisto, also known as Richard Knuckles.

The plots of the *Wigwam and the Cabin* tales take up many of the same common themes that concerned the frontier humorists—the conditions and circumstances surrounding a group of people meeting at the point at which an advancing civilization confronts a receding one. Augustus Baldwin Longstreet writes that his aim in *Georgia Scenes* was "to supply a chasm in history which has always been overlooked—the manners, customs, amusements, wit, dialect as they appear in all grades of society to an eye and ear witness of them" (Parks, "Ante-bellum Southern Humorists" 164–65). Similarly, Simms writes in the dedication to the 1856 edition of *The Wigwam and the Cabin* that the material for "these legends" is "local, sectional," and "represent[s], in large degree, the border history of the South" (iv). Simms further explains that "[t]he life of the planter, the squatter, the Indian, and the Negro—the bold and hardy pioneer, the vigorous yeoman—these are the subjects" (v).

In these stories, Simms employs many of the same situations and subjects as the frontier humorists. In the oft-cited introduction to the anthology *Humor of the Old Southwest*, the editors, Hennig Cohen and William Dillingham, list the twenty most commonly used subjects in frontier humor, which include frontier medical stories, sketches of law circuits and political life, and humorous descriptions of oddities in character (xiii).[7] Surprisingly, each of Cohen and Dillingham's twenty topics can be found in some part of the narration or plot of the thirteen tales in *The Wigwam and the Cabin*. In fact, most of the tales incorporate three or more of these topics. For instance, "The Two Camps" describes courting practices, militia drills, Indian fights, and a bear hunt, while "The Lazy Crow" portrays sickness and curses, tricks, religious experiences, local eccentrics in the persons of the witch doctor Gullah Sam and his rival Methuselah, and a parody of hunting yarns in the hexed slave Scipio's attempts to rid himself of the voodoo-bewitched crow.

The tales not only delineate similar themes and subjects but also describe stock frontier humor characters, such as the simple but brave and honest backwoodsman Daniel Nelson in "The Two Camps," and the handsome but comically conceited braggart Mingo in "Caloya." These tales also employ a format similar to that in many Southwest tales—that of the frame or box narrative enclosing a central story. The box narrative, generally speaking, consists of an outer frame in which a cultured and sophisticated gentleman observer establishes the circumstances or setting of the tale and an inner story in which a second, vernacular speaker takes over the narration of the primary tale. Establishing the frame narrative enabled the frontier humorists to describe the doings of uneducated rustic characters while maintaining their own cultural and social distance from such figures.

In "Grayling," "The Two Camps," and "The Lazy Crow," the box framework allows the educated, rational narrator to maintain a dignified distance from the central tale in which the power of supernatural or visionary experiences is explored. In the outer narrative, Simms gives expression to the ideals of the ruling or planter class, discusses the state of authorship in America, and describes in a tone of nostalgia people or events remembered from his youth. In the interior narrative, he relates the experiences of common soldiers, backwoodsmen, Native Americans, and African Americans. However, although the box framework allows him to distance the educated reader from the supernatural experiences and superstitions of the uneducated protagonists of the interior narrative, the weight of the combined tales validates and reinforces the beliefs of the common folk. For instance, in the ghost story "Grayling," the educated narrator resists his father's rational explanation of the supernatural events described in the inner tale, and declares, "I continued to believe in the ghost, and . . . to reject the philosophy" (36). Likewise, the rationalistic planter-narrator of "The Lazy Crow," who condescendingly agrees to hire a shaman to treat one of his favored field hands for what he believes to be merely a psychosomatic illness, encounters subsequent supernatural occurrences that he cannot explain.

For both the frontier humorists and Simms, the effect of the box narrative is threefold (Blair 91–92). First, it invokes an aura of realism by literally introducing both the gentlemanly speaker and the narrator of the second tale to the reader and by rationally establishing the situation of the inner narrative. Simms lends reality to the character of the second narrator in "The Two Camps" when he writes in the frame: "There are probably some old persons still living upon the upper dividing line between North and South Carolina, who still remember the form and features of the venerable Daniel Nelson. The old man was still living so late as 1817. At that period he removed to Mississippi, where, we believe, he died in less than three months after his change of residence" (40). In addition, Simms lends credibility to Nelson's tale when he notes that Daniel "has been heard to relate it a thousand times in his old age, at a period of life when, with one foot in his grave, to suppose him guilty of falsehood, or of telling that which he did not himself fervently believe, would be, among all those who knew him, to suppose the most impossible and extravagant thing in the world" (42). Likewise, as the source for the ghost story "Grayling," Simms introduces his own grandmother who, he says, "succeeded, at the time, in making me believe every word of it; perhaps, for the simple reason that she convinced me she believed every word of it herself" (2). Simms also establishes realistic narrative authority in "The Lazy Crow" by providing footnotes in explanation and support of the elements of voodoo and superstitious beliefs in the story.

The second effect of the box narrative is that it contrasts the time and setting of the original yarn with the current setting established by the narrator of the framing story. For example, in the outer narrative of "Caloya," Simms nostalgically recalls the Catawba Indian practice of making an annual springtime migration to the low country near Charleston for the purpose of making pottery to trade in the white settlements for supplies. This Catawba practice of a bygone era provides the exposition for the interior narrative and sets up the arrival of Caloya and Enefisto on the Ashley River plantation of Colonel Gillison, where Mingo is the driver.

Simms manipulates the nostalgic description of times past to full effect in "Grayling," in which he develops in the frame a semiautobiographical account contrasting his grandmother's belief in the supernatural with his father's rational explanations of visionary events. In addition, Simms compares his own response as a child listening to his grandmother's credible account of the ghost story and his father's opposing, rationalized version of the same events with his mature perspective as an author of romances in a world that, he complains, has "become monstrous matter-of-fact in latter days" (1). Simms uses the plot of the story—in which James Grayling's successful apprehension of the murderer depends upon several upper-level members of society's belief in Grayling's supernatural vision—to establish a criticism of his own society and its rejection of fanciful forms of literature. Simms asserts: "That cold-blooded demon called Science has taken the place of all the other demons. . . . Whether we are the better for his intervention is another question. There is reason to apprehend that in disturbing our human faith in shadows, we have lost some of those wholesome moral restraints which might have kept many of us virtuous, where the laws could not" (1).

The third effect of the box narrative is that it provides a vivid contrast between the grammatical, highly sophisticated language of the first narrator and the ungrammatical, homespun dialect of the second. The most striking example of this contrast in *The Wigwam and the Cabin* occurs in "The Two Camps" when the narrations of the exterior and interior tales overlap, and each narrator describes the same events in his own characteristic manner. The narrator of the exterior frame describes the actions of the backwoodsman Daniel Nelson at the beginning of his tale as he takes precautions against an Indian uprising. Simms writes:

> As soon as supper was over, [Daniel] resumed his rifle, thrust his *couteau de chasse* into his belt, and, taking his horn about his neck, and calling up his trusty dog, Clinch, he proceeded to scour the woods immediately around his habitation. This task, performed with the stealthy caution of the hunter, occupied some time, and, as the night was clear, a bright starlight, the weather moderate, and his own mood restless, he determined to strike through the forest to the settlement of Jacob Ransom, about four miles off, in order to prompt him, and, through him, others of the neighborhood, to the continued exercise of a caution which he now thought necessary. (42)

But when Daniel himself takes up the thread of the story in the interior narrative, he describes the same events in a different manner. Daniel says: "Well, my friends, seeing that the night was cl'ar, and there was no wind, and feeling as how I didn't want for sleep, I called to Clinch and took the path for Jake Ransom's. I knew that Jake was a sleepy sort of chap, and if the redskins caught any body napping, he'd, most likely, be the man" (43).

The contrast between the dialects of the educated and uneducated speakers is also evident in "The Lazy Crow," a story in which the narrator of the outer frame and the plantation owner participate as observers in the events of the inner tale.[8] The story revolves around the African American slave Scipio, who finds himself closely followed by a persistent and slow-moving crow after having angered the local shaman Gullah Sam by laughing at Sam when he fell into a pond. In an early scene, the plantation owner, Mr. Carrington, discusses the arrival of the enchanted crow with Scipio. Mr. Carrington states, "Why, you seem angry about it, Scipio; this crow must be one of the most impudent of his tribe, and a distinguished character" (334), to which remark Scipio replies: "He no feared of me 't all. When I stan' and look 'pon him, he stan' and look 'pon me. I tak' up dirt and stick, and trow at um, but he no scare. When I chase um, he fly dis way, he fly dat, but he nebber gone so far, but he can turn round and cock he tail at me, jist when he see me 'top. He's a mos' cussed sassy crow, as ebber walk in a cornfield" (334).

The abrupt conjunction of different levels of language often produces a hilarious incongruity, as in the following passage from "Caloya," in which the narrator describes the drunken ravings of Enefisto, or Richard Knuckles. The narrator says: "The savage grew gradually eloquent on the subject of woman's worthlessness, weakness, folly, &c.; and as the vocabulary of broken and imperfect English which he possessed was any thing but copious, his resort to the Catawba was natural and ready to give due expression to his resentment and suspicions" (420). Next, we have Enefisto's speech in his own words: "Huh! woman is fool—Injin man spit 'pon woman— ehketee—boozamogettee!—d--n,—d--n,—damn! tree d--n for woman!— he make for cuss. Caloya Ganchacha!—he dog,—he wuss dan dog— romonda!—tree time dog! anaporee, toos-wa-ne-dah! Injin man say to woman, go! fill you mout' wid grass,—woman is dog for cuss!" (420). After Enefisto's ravings, the narrator dryly concludes: "The English portion of this blackguardism is amply sufficient to show the spirit of the speaker, without making necessary any translation of that part of the speech, which, in his own dialect, conceals matter far more atrocious" (420).

Indeed, it is in the language (the diction and syntax, imagery and dialect) of these stories, "Grayling," "The Two Camps," "The Lazy Crow," and "Caloya," in which Simms reveals his closest affinity with the frontier humorists. M. Thomas Inge writes that the humorists' tales, which were derived from the "frontier pastime of telling stories," contained many "conventions of oral repetition—digressions, surprise endings, dialogue, and leisurely pace" (2). Furthermore, Cohen and Dillingham describe the

"backwoods language" as "[r]ich in similes and metaphors," "characterized
by concreteness, freshness, and color," "accompanied by unrestrained exaggeration," and combining "the wild imagination of the frontiersman with
the concreteness of poetry" (xvii–xviii).

Within these tales, Simms proves himself to be a master of dialect:
the backwoodsman, the African American, the hardy pioneer, the Native
American, and the aristocratic planter—each is assigned his own realistic
dialect and mannerisms of speech. For instance, James Grayling, after seeing his ghostly vision, describes his family's reaction to his decision to
search for the presumed murderer of his friend Major Spencer: "Mother
was mighty sad, and begged me not to go, but Uncle Sparkman was mighty
sulky, and kept calling me fool upon fool, until I was almost angry enough
to forget that we were of blood kin. But all his talking did not stop me, and
I reckon I was five miles on my way before he had his team in traces for a
start" (21).

The characteristic speech patterns of the Native American Enefisto and
the African American Scipio are evidenced in the passages quoted above;
but the most distinctive and comic language in these tales is found in the
speeches of Daniel Nelson and Mingo Gillison.

In "The Two Camps," Daniel Nelson's account contains many similarities to those of the frontier humorists—including digressions, inventive
metaphors, and vivid images. Nelson even uses expressions that are clichés
of frontier humor. For instance, he calls his daughter the "very flower of
the forest" and likens his own combined emotions of fear and rage at the
prospect of an Indian attack to feeling "wolfish, as if the hair was turned in
and rubbing agin the very heart within me" (70, 43). Nelson also gives
expression to his own homespun wisdom, as when he explains why he did
not press the injured Lenatewà to disclose who had wounded him and left
him for dead. Nelson says, "I didn't push him to know, for I was pretty
sure the head of the truth will be sure to come some time or other, if you
once have it by the tail, provided you don't jerk it off by straining too hard
upon it" (50).

Like the frontier humorists' tales, which Cohen and Dillingham note
were marked for their "lack of respect for delicate sensibilities," Nelson's
narration also contains stark, realistic details and gory descriptions that are
presented matter-of-factly (Cohen and Dillingham xiv). For instance, when
Nelson discovers the injured Lenatewà, he says, "The head was clammy
with blood, so that my fingers stuck, and when I attempted to turn it, to

look at the face, the groan was deeper than ever; but 'twarn't a time to suck one's fingers" (*Wigwam* 49). Nelson's narration also contains a liberal sprinkling of humor, such as when he and his dog Clinch are suddenly surprised by the appearance of the mysterious and ghostly Indian campfire. He says, "When I saw this I stopt and looked at Clinch, and he stopped and looked at me, but neither of us had any thing to say" (44). Nelson's story also exhibits characteristics common to the orally transmitted tale, such as digressiveness and a leisurely pace. For example, in the following passage, Nelson interrupts the narrative story line for an interpolated, suspense-building explanation. Nelson says, "I bolted on the road to the fire. I say road, but there was no road; but the trees warn't over-thick, and the land was too poor for undergrowth; so we got on pretty well, considering" (44).

In contrast to the simple backwoods character of Daniel Nelson, the character of Mingo in "Caloya" reveals a remarkable blend of stock comic conventions. An exceptionally handsome man, Mingo is also self-absorbed, conceited, and blindly egotistical, and his puffed-up vanity continually amuses the reader. Although he is a slave, Mingo takes on the characteristics of the rip-roaring braggart from frontier humor as he proudly boasts of his own power and generosity. Mingo brags with characteristic hyperbole, "I makes the law for this plantation—all round about, so far as you can see from the top of the tallest of them 'ere pine trees, I'm the master!" (376). By far the most amusing of Mingo's linguistic mannerisms are the numerous malapropisms that invade his speech whenever he attempts to wax eloquent. For instance, in an attempt to beguile Caloya, who will not speak to him, with his generosity and largess, Mingo makes the following speech to Caloya's husband, Enefisto: "if that 'ere gal was my wife instead of your'n, Knuckles, do you think I'd let her extricate herself here in a br'iling sun, working her fingers off, and I lying down here in the grass a-doing nothing and only looking on? No! I'd turn in and give her good resistance; 'cause why, Knuckles? . . . My women I redulges—I never pushes 'em—I favors them all that I kin, and it goes agin me mightily, I tell you, when it's a needcessity to give 'em the lash" (384).

Like the ring-tailed roarers of frontier humor, Mingo's most humorous boasts concern fights and physical prowess. After his brief scuffle with Enefisto has been interrupted by the intervention of Caloya, Mingo tells Enefisto: "the butt of my whip would have flattened you, until your best friend couldn't ha' said where to look for your nose. You'd ha' been all face after that, smooth as bottom land, without e'er a snag or a stump; and you'd have passed among old acquaintance for any body sooner than yourself" (376). Later in the tale, when angry with the sullen Enefisto, Mingo threatens: "Ef I was to take you in my arms and give you one good hug, Lor' ha' massy 'pon you! You'd neber feel yourself after that, and nothing would be lef of you for you wife to see, but a long greasy mark, most like a little old man, yer, 'pon my breast and thighs" (386).

By surveying the tales in *The Wigwam and the Cabin*, one can see that Simms employs numerous elements of Southwestern humor in tales other than his comic masterpieces, "Sharp Snaffles" and "Bald-Head Bill Bauldy." In the stories "Grayling," "The Two Camps," "The Lazy Crow," and "Caloya," Simms reveals, through his choice of topics, format, characterization, and diction, his affinity with other writers of Southern humor of his time. And in imagery, dialect, and narrative power, Simms proves himself, once again, to be a master storyteller. William Gilmore Simms's tales deserve to be known by scholars and studied in relation to other tales of Southwestern humor; but most of all, they deserve to be read and laughed over once more.

NOTES

1. In his article, Parks writes: "I do not understand the relative neglect by anthologies of William Gilmore Simms as a frontier humorist. . . . But even such authorities on Southern humor as Franklin J. Meine and Walter Blair have omitted Simms's masterly story, 'How Sharp Snaffles Got His Capital and Wife.' It has all the best characteristics of the genre" ("Three Streams of Southern Humor," 156).

2. In *William Gilmore Simms as Literary Critic* (9), Edd Winfield Parks declared that "Sharp Snaffles" is "one of the finest tall tales ever written by a Southern humorist." For additional recent critical commentary, see James B. Meriwether, "Simms' 'Sharp Snaffles' and 'Bald-Head Bill Bauldy'"; Ian Marshall, "The American Dream of Sam Snaffles"; Mary Ann Wimsatt, "The Evolution of Simms's Backwoods Humor"; and Wimsatt's *The Major Fiction of William Gilmore Simms*.

3. Although M. Thomas Inge cautions repeatedly against "the dangers of generalization" concerning the frontier humorists or their tales in his introduction to the collection of essays *The Frontier Humorists*, critical generalizations abound and have limited the definition of *frontier humor* to only those tales containing "raucous, ribald, and extravagant" humor. This fact, combined with the ready availability of modern anthologies that contain stories and passages of only certain types and the

comparable inaccessibility of the full range of original tales, has generated regrettable misconceptions concerning the frontier humorists and their works and has resulted in the neglect of some fine comic tales—including Simms's.

4. In *Humor of the Old Southwest: An Annotated Bibliography of Primary and Secondary Sources*, Nancy Snell Griffith, comp., limits the frontier humorists to nine authors: Baldwin, David Crockett, Harris, Hooper, Lewis, Longstreet, Charles F. M. Noland ("Pete Whetstone"), Thompson, and Thorpe.

5. For a discussion of Simms's comments on contemporary humor writers see Edd Winfield Parks, *William Gilmore Simms as Literary Critic*, 138 n. 26; and Mary Ann Wimsatt, *The Major Fiction*, 117–19.

6. For a thorough analysis of the panic and its effect on Simms (including his loss of income, his shift toward alternative publications, and his subsequent pursuit of political office) see Wimsatt, *The Major Fiction*, 136–45.

7. These twenty subjects are expanded in Cohen and Dillingham's text from the list of ten offered by Franklin J. Meine, ed., in *Tall Tales of the Southwest*.

8. Of Simms's comic tales, "The Lazy Crow" was selected by William E. Burton for publication in the fine two-volume *Cyclopedia of Wit and Humor* (1:169–77), which included an extensive selection by frontier humorists such as Longstreet, Thompson, Tensas, Thorpe, and Smith, along with works by Irving, Poe, Hawthorne, and numerous other popular writers of the era.

WORKS CITED

Blair, Walter. *Native American Humor.* New York: American Book Company, 1937. San Francisco: Chandler Publishing, 1960.

Burton, William E. *Cyclopedia of Wit and Humor of America, Ireland, Scotland, and England.* 2 vols. New York: D. Appleton and Co., 1858.

Cohen, Hennig, and William B. Dillingham, eds. *Humor of the Old Southwest.* Boston: Houghton Mifflin, 1964. Athens: University of Georgia Press, 1976.

Griffith, Nancy Snell, comp. *Humor of the Old Southwest: An Annotated Bibliography of Primary and Secondary Sources.* Westport: Greenwood, 1989.

Guilds, John C., ed. *"Long Years of Neglect": The Work and Reputation of William Gilmore Simms.* Fayetteville: University of Arkansas Press, 1988.

Holman, C. Hugh. "Detached Laughter in the South." *Comic Relief: Humor in Contemporary American Literature.* Ed. Sarah Blancher Cohen. Urbana: University of Illinois Press, 1978. 87–104.

Inge, M. Thomas, ed. *The Frontier Humorists: Critical Views.* Hamden: Archon, 1975.

Marshall, Ian. "The American Dream of Sam Snaffles." *Southern Literary Journal* 18, no. 2 (spring 1985): 9–107.

Meine, Franklin J. "Tall Tales of the Southwest." *The Frontier Humorists: Critical Views.* Ed. M. Thomas Inge. Hamden: Archon, 1975. 15–31.

———, ed. *Tall Tales of the Southwest: An Anthology of Southern and Southwestern Humor 1830–1860.* New York: Knopf, 1930.

Meriwether, James B. "Simms' 'Sharp Snaffles' and 'Bald-Head Bill Bauldy': Two Views of Men—And of Women." *South Carolina Review* 16, no. 2 (spring 1984): 66–71.

Parks, Edd Winfield. "The Intent of Ante-bellum Southern Humorists." *Mississippi Quarterly* 13 (1960): 163–68.

———. "Three Streams of Southern Humor." *Georgia Review* 9, no. 2 (1955): 147–59.

———. *William Gilmore Simms as Literary Critic.* Athens: University of Georgia Press, 1961.

Rubin, Louis D., Jr., ed. *The Comic Imagination in American Literature.* New Brunswick: Rutgers University Press, 1973.

Shelley, Philip Anderson. "Annuals and Gift Books." In *Benet's Reader's Encyclopedia of American Literature.* Ed. George Perkins et al. New York: HarperCollins, 1991. 49–50.

Simms, William Gilmore. *The Letters of William Gilmore Simms.* 5 vols. Ed. Mary C. Simms Oliphant, Alfred Taylor Odell, and T. C. Duncan Eaves. Columbia: University of South Carolina Press, 1952–1956. (A sixth volume, *The Letters of William Gilmore Simms: Supplement [1834–1870],* ed. Oliphant and Eaves, was published by the University of South Carolina Press in 1982.)

———. *Views and Reviews in American Literature, History and Fiction.* Second series. New York: Wiley and Putnam, 1845. Cambridge: Belknap, 1962.

———. *The Wigwam and the Cabin.* New York: Wiley and Putnam, 1845. New York: AMS Press, 1970 (rpt. from the 1885 edition).

Wimsatt, Mary Ann. "The Evolution of Simms's Backwoods Humor." In *"Long Years of Neglect": The Work and Reputation of William Gilmore Simms.* Ed. John Caldwell Guilds. Fayetteville: University of Arkansas Press, 1988. 148–65.

———. *The Major Fiction of William Gilmore Simms: Cultural Tradition and Literary Form.* Baton Rouge: Louisiana State University Press, 1989.

Facing the Monster:
William Gilmore Simms and
Henry Clay Lewis

W illiam Gilmore Simms's appreciation of and contribution to
the genre of frontier humor has been well documented. Mary Ann Wimsatt, for example, calls Simms "one of the major creators of comedy in the
era" and further notes, "His humor springs from a raucous, unbridled
streak in his personality, and it was encouraged by his experiences in the
same parts of the South that nourished the talents of the antebellum humorists: the Gulf South or Old Southwest of the 1820s and early 1830s
and the Piedmont or Mountain South throughout the antebellum period"
("Evolution," 148). As a literary critic, Simms was, as John Caldwell Guilds
puts it, "a noted champion of national and sectional literature . . . committed to a policy of encouraging writers on native themes. . . . Simms could
(and did) encourage authors of national themes even when he conscien-
tiously could not (and did not) praise them" (*Literary Life*, 346–47).
Among those humorists Simms did praise were such contemporary figures
as A. B. Longstreet (whom he considered the best of the lot), Johnson Jones
Hooper, Joseph Glover Baldwin, and Thomas Bangs Thorpe.

One, however, of whom Simms did not approve was Henry Clay Lewis,
or, to use his pseudonym, "Madison Tensas," author of *Odd Leaves from
the Life of a Louisiana "Swamp Doctor,"* a collection of largely interrelated
sketches published by A. Hart in 1850.[1] Simms's brief notice (from the July
1850 issue of the *Southern Quarterly Review*) is worth quoting in full:

> One of a class to which we do not seriously incline. Our Swamp
> Doctor affords us sundry scenes sufficiently ludicrous; and, where he
> fails to provoke merriment, our excellent artist, [Felix O. C.] Darley,
> is at hand to produce the effect in which the author lacks. Some of
> these "pictures to match" are very diverting, truly; and what a genius
> must the artist be who can thus endow the conceptions of the author

with a life which he himself so completely fails to impart! Of our Swamp Doctor's humour, the less we say the better. "Purge us of that, Doctor," will suffice; and must not be taken so much as an acknowledgement of his ability, as in the nature of an exhortation that, from this day forth, he ceases to make use of it. (537)

Any review that finds more to praise in the artist's sketches than in the text they illustrate goes beyond simple dismissal. It reminds one of Simms's better-known review of *Moby Dick* for the *Southern Quarterly Review* (1852), in which he wrote, "In all the scenes where the whale is the performer or the sufferer, the delineation and action are highly vivid and exciting. In all other respects, the book is sad stuff, dull and dreary, or ridiculous." Ludicrous Lewis; ridiculous, or worse, insane Melville: these are strong denunciations.[2]

Although Simms's antagonism toward Melville and his book can be explained—Guilds notes that Simms was certainly not alone at the time in questioning Melville's sanity (*Literary Life* 346)—his attitude toward Lewis seems unduly harsh. Mary Ann Wimsatt proposes that Simms "preferred comedy that was genteel, realistic, and believable to that which was extravagant, exaggerated, or grotesque" (*Major Fiction* 152). But Simms's own humor could be all of the above, and his more obviously "realistic" fiction of the frontier could also be graphic, sensational, brutal, and even vulgar.[3] Moreover, there are a number of reasons, it seems to me, why Simms should have been more sympathetic to Lewis and what Lewis was attempting to do in his small book of sketches, for Lewis was traveling a path Simms himself had earlier trod and was employing many of the locales, character types, themes, and concerns that Simms had also examined.

The sketches in *Odd Leaves* are held together by an autobiographical framework, starting (after a brief prologue comparing the swamp doctor to his counterpart, the city physician) with an extended story, "My Early Life." As John Q. Anderson, the scholar who brought to light most of what we know about Lewis, has shown, Lewis wrote the autobiographical material largely for the publication of the book.[4] Although I think it important to distinguish between the author Lewis and his fictional protagonist "Madison Tensas" (something Anderson does not always do), it is true that many of Tensas's experiences can be traced to events in Lewis's own life. Simms, reading the book, should have been struck by certain obvious similarities between Tensas's life and his own. For example, both men (Simms and Lewis) were native Charlestonians, Simms born in 1806, Lewis in 1825. Lewis's father was a merchant in Charleston but moved his family to Cincinnati around 1829. Lewis's mother died in 1831 when Lewis was six, and his father then moved to New Orleans, leaving the child with an older married brother, Alexander. Lewis never saw his father again; the elder Lewis died of yellow fever in 1839, and, as Anderson writes, "Henry evidently felt no deep attachment to his father as he did to his mother" (5). In 1835 Henry ran away from his brother's home and, after a year of working riverboats, located in Yazoo City (then called Manchester), Mississippi, where another brother, Joseph, lived. Joseph was a well-to-do businessman and promised his younger brother a fine education, but the Depression of 1837 wiped out his wealth and Henry spent the next five years working in nearby cotton fields. In 1842 his fortunes again changed; he became medical apprentice to Dr. Washington Dorsey for the summer, and in August of that year his first sketch, "Cupping on the Sternum," was published in *Spirit of the Times*. Returning to medical school in the fall, Lewis received his M.D. in March 1846, at the age of twenty. Although Dr. Dorsey had died during his absence, Lewis was unable to assume his mentor's practice and soon moved into the wilds of Louisiana, where he established an office on the Tensas River and, in Anderson's words, "adopted the clothing, manners, and customs of the 'swampers'" (41). He worked in the swamp from 1846 to early 1849. During that time he published several other sketches in the *Spirit* but, more significantly, began to develop the literary persona of Madison Tensas, the figure who would give focus to the more ambitious concept of interrelated tales found in *Odd Leaves*. Lewis left the wilderness and moved to Richmond, Louisiana, the parish seat of Madison County, in 1849. In March of 1850, his book was published. It was reviewed by Simms in July. The next month, Lewis, returning from a call, drowned while attempting to cross a river near Richmond. He was twenty-five.

Even this brief review of Lewis's life should bring to mind similarities with Simms—the Charleston background; the lost, mourned mother; the absent father; the sense of alienation, of being an outsider (in Lewis's case no doubt exacerbated by his Jewish heritage) and of needing to prove himself to a perceived unfriendly (and unfair) society. Lewis wrote, "Those only who have lived in similar circumstances can appreciate my situation; censured for errors and never praised for my industry, the scapegoat of the family and general errand-boy of the concern. . . . This condition of things continued until I had passed my tenth year, when, grown old by drudgery

and wounded feelings, I determined to put into effect a long-cherished
plan, to run away and seek my fortune wheresoever chance might lead or
destiny determine" (27). Compare to Simms, who wrote, "My mind was
of a very uncompromising sort, my temper exceedingly earnest & impassioned, and my pride, springing, perhaps, something from the feeling
of isolation in which I found myself at an early age—without father or
mother, brother or indeed, kindred of any kind—was always on the look
out for opposition and hostility" (*Letters* 1:164).

In addition, both men were later inspired by the same setting—the Yazoo territory of Mississippi and the swamplands of Louisiana—in their
writing. Simms, we know, traveled in the same general region where Lewis
came to live. "I have just returned from a journey on horseback, of seventeen days into the Yazoo purchase, over and through swamps and creeks
and bayous, half the time swimming and wading through mud and water
waist deep," Simms wrote in 1831, during his third trip to the Southwest
frontier (*Letters* 1:37). In such works as *Border Beagles* and *Helen Halsey*, he
recreated this swamp world, turning it into a land of deception and mystery
and treachery, a place where outlaws laid ambushes and then disappeared,
leaving no signs. For Simms, the swamp naturally illustrated the dangers of
(and, in some cases, the scary attractions of) the untamed and unstructured
and uncivilized. But in Simms it was a wilderness that nevertheless awaited
the stabilizing order and justice of society. In other words, the swamp was
not the whole world, and a decent and upright man like Harry Vernon in
Border Beagles, a "'stand-in' for Simms," according to Wimsatt (*Major Fiction* 128), could come from the outside, bringing with him standards of
proper behavior, of right action, and impose these standards on the wilderness and its rough inhabitants.

Vernon comes into the swamps on a mission of justice, to apprehend
a thief. However, as a young and adventurous man, Vernon finds a definite delight in the dangerous undertaking. As Simms writes, "To one like
Vernon . . . bold, and governed by a temperament that gloried in a dash of
romance, the occasional perils of such a course were lost altogether in the
novelty of the circumstances; and he dashed through the creek with a confident spur, without stopping like more wary adventurers to probe his footing with a pole, then drive his horse through the stream, while he 'cooned
a log' above it" (*Border Beagles* 96).

Compare the above description to a similar one in Lewis's story "Valerian and the Panther." In it, Tensas is working the summer as apprentice

to the doctor in Yazoo City. Summoned in the doctor's absence on an emergency call into the swamp, Tensas makes preparation:

> The horse I intended to ride was a favourite one of the old doctor's, but one which, accomplished equestrian as he was, he dare not back, except when the visit lay over some old beaten road; and as for riding him through the devious path of the swamp . . . wading the backwater, jumping logs, swimming in the dark and sullen slough, or with feet raised to the pommel to clear the cypress-knees, which on every side, as the path would cross a brake, obtruded their keen points, ready to impale the luckless wight who there might chance to lose his seat; to ride "Chaos" midst such paths as these, the old doctor, I have said, would never have dreamed of doing, and, most assuredly, had he been at home, would not have allowed me to undertake; but such a ride, with its break-neck peril, chimed well with my youthful feelings. (91)

Both Tensas and Vernon act with abandon and, while, certainly, Vernon's impetuosity does get him in a great deal of trouble, he is, for the most part, level-headed, composed, and prepared. Tensas, on the other hand, pays dearly for his rashness. The horse he rides into the swamp is, appropriately, named "Chaos," and the story, which begins as dark comedy (he has been called to treat a young boy whose fingers have been almost bitten off by his father when the boy attempts to snatch the sleeping man's quid of tobacco from his mouth) devolves into hysterical nightmare when Tensas becomes lost on his way home and is pursued by a ravenous panther attracted to the stick of valerian Tensas carries in his pocket. Like Ichabod Crane fleeing the Headless Horseman, Tensas anticipates reaching the safety of civilization—"I imagined I could almost see the lights in the windows—but this I knew could not be." For Tensas, there is no safety in civilization, in God or anywhere else, to be had. "I strove to breathe a prayer; but my parched tongue clove to the roof of my mouth, and what I uttered served but to add to the damning chorus of hellish sounds. I tore the neck of my poor horse with my teeth, to incite him to greater speed; but my time had come." At the last minute, Tensas cuts the carotid artery in Chaos's neck, thinking "may not the panther be satisfied with his blood, and allow me to escape?" After this attempt fails, he decides to commit suicide by drinking from a vial of prussic acid he has with him, "when, as if by inspiration, came the blessed thought, that when the panther seized me, to pour the instantaneous poison down his throat," which he does (100, 101).

It is easy to see from this example why Simms could denounce Lewis's work, for this is pretty overheated and disturbing stuff, especially if the reader is expecting humor, no matter how rough-and-tumble. And I suspect that this is a problem readers besides Simms might have with Lewis. But Lewis, to my mind, was not primarily a humorist. His work is dark, cruel, psychologically complex.[5] The young Lewis's persona, for example, is self-described as an old man, a bewigged bachelor, alone and worn with care. His one attempt at romance is detailed in the gruesome sketch "Stealing a Baby," in which, as a young medical student, he lifts the corpse of a Negro baby from the morgue (taking it from beside its dead mother) and carries it away under his cloak with the intention of practicing dissection on it in the privacy of his room, "whilst I was waiting for my meals— something to wile away my tedious hours with" (134). On the way he meets his sweetheart Lucy, whom he is seeing against her father's wishes. When the father is subsequently sighted, Tensas and Lucy try to hide in a doorway but slip and fall on the icy sidewalk: "My cloak flew open as I fell, and the force of the fall bursting its envelope, out, in all its hideous realities, rolled the infernal imp of darkness upon the gaze of the laughing, but now horrified spectators," Tensas recalls. "Picking up my baby, I explained the whole to a constable who was on the point of arresting me for child-murder. . . . I have never seen Lucy since, and my haggard features and buttonless coat testify that the swamp doctor is still a bachelor" (137).

"[L]aughing, but now horrified"—this is the effect Lewis often has on his readers. His works are confessional in exactly such horrible ways—giving birth to an "infernal imp of darkness," to "my baby" in public. The stories in *Odd Leaves* abound with such macabre images of violent revelation and purgation. In "Valerian and the Panther," for example, Lewis describes the hideous death of the horse Chaos: "Giving a terrible spring, the hot blood gushing all over me, he ran as none but a noble horse, in the agonies of death, can run, and then, with a low, reproachful moan, fell dead; whilst I, disengaging myself, at a full run strove to make my escape" (101). However, a similar description of a mule, set on fire by Tensas and his fellow drunken revellers to disrupt a camp meeting in "The Day of Judgment," strongly suggests that ultimate escape, even that of final salvation, is never attained: "The stream was nearly reached; with ecstasy the poor brute beheld the glistening waters; he sped on with accelerated steps—one more spring, and he would find surcease of anguish 'neath their cooling waves. But he was destined never to reach them; he fell exhausted on the brink, vainly endeavouring, with extended neck, to allay his fiery thirst; as the flame, now bereft of fuel, sent up its last flickering ray, the poor mule, with a low reproachful moan, expired" (64). Clearly, Tensas's tales are motivated not only by guilt and self-loathing (note, for example, the repetition of "a low reproachful moan" in both passages), but also by a need for mortification and penance, a need to face the monster within himself.

What first brought me to this topic was, in Simms's *Border Beagles*, the character of Richard Stillyards, the humpbacked dwarf Tom Horsey encounters in the swamp. Simms describes him as follows:

> His arms were long like those of an ape; his ears of corresponding dimensions; his lips, pursed into a point like two bits of shrivelled coonskin, were covered with a thick furze, not unlike that of the hair upon the same animal. . . . He seemed almost entirely without flesh. The lower limbs were not merely short and deformed, but slender to a degree, which made the spectator apprehensive that they might snap as readily as pipestems under the swollen and dropsical bulk of body which they carried. But this show was deceptive. The urchin had an elasticity of muscle, a capacity of stretch and endurance in his sinews, and a share of positive strength in his excessive breadth of shoulders, which made him little inferior in conflict to most ordinary men, and in speed he could have outwinded the best. (303–4)

Although Stillyards is a fascinating creation (Simms's complete catalogue of his deformities extends to two pages), his ultimate role in the book is driven by plot more than by character and there is, finally, little sense of true horror at either his condition or his deeds. His actions are motivated, as Guilds has noted, primarily by "greed, lust, or revenge" (*Literary Life* 99), and he seems more a primitive caricature of Richard III than a true embodiment of evil. Indeed, to the roving actor Tom Horsey, Stillyards is largely a figure of fun, an absurd rather than tragic or appalling creature. Simms provides many titles to describe Stillyards—incubus, imp, ape, urchin—and Horsey that many more—"comical little fellow," "little apology for a man," "pretty little deformity," "youngest son of the little old gentleman in black," and "queer little coxcomb" among them (305–6), all indicative of Stillyards's bizarre but not particularly threatening appearance.

The last story in *Odd Leaves* is "A Struggle for Life," in which Tensas is led on a call into the swamp by a misshapen slave: "He was a negro dwarf of the most frightful appearance; his diminutive body was garnished with legs and arms of enormously disproportionate length; his face was hideous: a pair of tushes projected from either side of a double hare-lip; and taking him altogether, he was the nearest resemblance to the ourang outang mixed with the devil that human eyes ever dwelt upon. I could not look upon him without feeling disgust" (192–93).

Although both creatures share similar physical deformities, Lewis's dwarf, in keeping with the darker tone of his work, is much more disturbing and resonant. He serves, in fact, as the book's final embodiment of horror, bringing together disparate dark images from earlier tales in the collection. The Negro slave's small stature is anticipated by the black baby in "Stealing a Baby." His face is foreshadowed in "The Curious Widow," in which Tensas, playing a trick on a nosey landlady, slices away the face from the corpse of a Negro murderer and hides it for the woman to find in her snooping: "Every feature was deformed and unnatural; a horrible hare-lip, the cleft extending half way up his nose externally, and pair of tushes projecting from his upper jaw, completed his bill of horrors" (76–77). "I endeavored tó sleep," he writes, "but that hideous face, which we had locked securely in a trunk, kept staring at me through its many envelopes" (77),[6] recalling the "envelope" of Tensas's cloak holding the dead baby inside next to his own body.

At night, in the swamp, Tensas gives the dwarf a drink of brandy, which renders him drunk, another recurring image in the tales, wherein intoxication inevitably provokes violence and obscene cruelty.[7] When the dwarf demands more, and the doctor refuses, the dwarf threatens him. Tensas at first reacts much as Tom Horsey: "The idea of such a diminutive object destroying without weapons a man of my size, presented something ludicrous, and I laughingly awaited his attack, ready to tie his hands before he could bite or scratch me." However, "Woefully I underrated his powers!" (199). The dwarf carries Tensas to the ground, his teeth in the doctor's throat:

> I did not pray. I did not commend my soul to God. I had not a fear of death. But oh! awful were my thoughts at dying in such a way— suffocated by a hellish negro in the midst of the noisome swamp, my flesh to be devoured by the carrion crow, my bones to whiten where they lay for long years, and then startle the settler, when civilization had strode into the wilderness, and the cane that would conceal my bones would be falling before the knife of the cane-cutter. I ceased to

breathe. I was dead . . . but I still retained the sentient principle within my corpse. (200)

When Tensas regains movement, he finds the dwarf burned to death in the flames of the campfire into which he has drunkenly cast himself. "Great God!" Tensas exclaims in true horror, "can that disfigured half-consumed mass be my evil genius?" (202). The dwarf's fiery death echoes the terrible demise of the sacrificed mule, set aflame in a moment of drunken revelry, and, significantly, Tensas is led from the swamp to safety by the dwarf's own mule. The bones of the dwarf, however, are left "to bleach where they lay. I would not for the universe have looked again upon the place" (203).

Border Beagles ends in triumph, confirmation, and union. The outlaws are routed and captured (Stillyards himself subdues the chief outlaw, Saxon, by dropping upon him from the rafters and digging his fingernails, "which had been suffered to grow to an inordinate length—entirely into the ears of his late leader" [482]); the heroes marry their ladies in a triple wedding ceremony; a rough justice wins out (the outlaws are summarily hanged by a mob); and a new day dawns. *Odd Leaves* ends bleakly, pessimistically, in the death (at least figuratively) of the protagonist and of his "evil genius," the dwarf's bones substituting for Tensas's own in the middle of the "noisome" swamp awaiting the coming of civilization. The ending represents the ultimate purgation for the swamp doctor, but what remains is a lonely, solitary figure.[8] Tensas refers to his "single bed, buttonless shirts, premature wigdom, and haggard old-bachelor looks" in recounting "My Early Life" (28), and he acknowledges that, instead of a wife, he has "wedded his books and calling—rather a frigid bride" (179).

I suspect that Simms, like many readers, found Lewis's book uncomfortably dark, violent, and unhealthy, especially since it presented itself as a humorous work. Denied a serious, even tragic base, the tales do appear overwrought, fervid, perhaps even "ludicrous." Guilds has remarked on Simms's "need, almost an obsession, to be in charge . . . to take control of situations through his ability to explain, interpret, clarify, or make plausible to others, who looked to him for leadership" (*Literary Life* 332). I imagine Simms simply disliked the emotional tenor of the work, the consternating *lack* of control and of narrative distance, and the personal weaknesses he perceived they suggested.

Alan Rose further argues that Lewis, as a Jew and thus as an essential outsider in the society of the antebellum South, was less inhibited about depicting certain "regional taboos" in his work, chief among them the "expression of the Negro." "Lewis was one of the few Southern humorists to treat the black man in his fiction extensively and often without stereotype," Rose maintains (26). Although these judgments are open to question, it is true that Lewis's image of the Negro is, in general, quite different from that found in Simms. With some notable exceptions, Simms's Negroes, from Hector in *The Yemassee* (1935) to Tom in *Woodcraft* (1854) and beyond, are loyal and loving supporters of the system of slavery, bound to their white masters even to the point of death. There is little fear of black insurrection in Simms's fiction, for there is no rational basis acknowledged for such revolt, from the viewpoint of either white or Negro. To have admitted it would have been to question the institution itself, and thus the society it supported.[9]

Lewis's tales, however, do confront the specter of racial violence. As already noted, Lewis embodies his guilt and fears in animals (the horse, mule, panther, and so on) and then in blacks (the baby, the executed murderer, the dwarf). "D--n you, white man, I will kill you ef you don't give me more brandy!" the dwarf screams just before attacking Tensas (198); and outside of "Benito Cereno," which Melville published in 1856, it is hard to think of a more brutal representation of racial rebellion from the prewar era.

Simms, through his commanding narrative voice and his dauntless protagonists, brought rationality and order to the wild and unlawful and chaotic in his fiction. Lewis, like Melville, saw a different world, one in which man seemed ruled by fate or even madness, not by will or intent (see notes 2 and 6). Lewis's world was defined by treachery, deception, violation, and overriding guilt. Madison Tensas flees hysterically through the uncharted swamp, haunted and pursued by creatures of the land and of the mind. Both Simms and Lewis recognized there were monsters in the world. For Simms, the monsters were mostly external, and could be faced and vanquished by the confident and determined hero. But for Lewis, the monster's face, ultimately and insidiously, was his own.

NOTES

1. *Odd Leaves* was reissued at least six times during the nineteenth century and achieved wide popularity. However, its last verifiable printing was in 1881 (see the entry for "Henry Clay Lewis" in Griffith, *Humor of the Old Southwest*, 129). After

years of relative obscurity, Lewis was brought back into print by John Q. Anderson, who edited *Louisiana Swamp Doctor: The Life and Writings of Henry Clay Lewis* in 1962. Anderson rearranged the original sketches in *Odd Leaves* "chronologically according to subject matter so that the Swamp Doctor's story has continuity." He also added other sketches printed in *Spirit of the Times* but not included in the book, edited Lewis's punctuation, and modernized spelling (vi–vii). A facsimile reproduction of the original text was published by Literature House–Gregg Press in 1969.

2. Simms further wrote of Melville: "his mad Captain, who pursues his personal revenges against the fish who has taken off his leg, at the expense of ship, crew, and owners, is a monstrous bore, whom Mr. Melville has no way helped, by enveloping him in a sort of mystery. His ravings, and the ravings of some of the tributary characters, and the ravings of Mr. Melville himself, meant for eloquent declamation, are such as would justify a writ de lunatico against all the parties" (Rev. of *Moby Dick*). Lewis (a year earlier than Melville) presented a character anticipating Ahab in the woodsman Mik-hoo-tah, the title personage of his story "The Indefatigable Bear Hunter," who prides himself on being the "bear-hunter of Ameriky." When Mik loses his leg to an unusually ferocious grizzly, the Swamp Doctor replaces it with a wooden one. Unable to hunt, Mik wastes away until he decides to make one last stand against a bear, which he ultimately beats to death with the artificial leg (*Odd Leaves* 164–75). A later critic, Alan Henry Rose, would bring similar charges of madness against Lewis himself. "Lewis's lack of self-control sometimes may have reached dimensions resembling schizophrenia," he writes. "Violence in his fiction attains monumental proportions. Moreover, again and again Lewis's darker autobiographical tales give evidence of a blurring of primary psychological distinctions, momentary failures of the capacity to demarcate the boundaries of the self. . . . The form of Lewis's tales may also have been influenced by the disorder of his personality, since it does not share the stability customary in Southwestern humor" (26–27).

3. Guilds provides a thoughtful discussion of Simms's use of sometimes graphic violence in his quest for realism. See *Literary Life* 338–42.

4. Three sketches included in *Odd Leaves* had first appeared in *Spirit of the Times*—"A Tight Race Considerin'," "Valerian and the Panther," and "A Rattlesnake on a Steamboat." See Anderson's "The Life of Henry Clay Lewis" in *Louisiana Swamp Doctor* 3–70.

5. As Charles Israel has put it, "The world of Lewis's sketches is largely one of chaos, alienation, injustice, and imminent despair." See Israel, "Henry Clay Lewis's *Odd Leaves*" 62. Alan Henry Rose has also convincingly discussed the explosively unstable world of Lewis's fiction (25–38).

6. Compare the following passage from Herman Melville's *White Jacket* (published in March 1850, the same month and year as *Odd Leaves*), which describes the sadistic fleet surgeon Dr. Cadwallader Cuticle:

In particular, the department of Morbid Anatomy was his peculiar love; and in his stateroom below he had a most unsightly collection of Parisian casts, in plaster and wax, representing all imaginable malformations of the human members, both organic and induced by disease. Chief among these was a cast, often to be met with in the Anatomical Museums of Europe, and no doubt an unexaggerated copy of a genuine original; it was the head of an elderly woman, with an aspect singularly gentle and meek, but at the same time wonderfully expressive of a gnawing sorrow, never to be relieved. You would almost have thought it the face of some abbess, for some unspeakable crime voluntarily sequestered from human society, and leading a life of agonized penitence without hope; so marvelously sad and tearfully pitiable was this head. But when you first beheld it, no such emotions ever crossed your mind. All your eyes and all your horrified soul were fast fascinated and frozen by the sight of a hideous, crumpled horn, like that of a ram, downward growing out from the forehead, and partly shadowing the face; but as you gazed, the freezing fascination of its horribleness gradually waned, and then your whole heart burst with sorrow, as you contemplated those aged features, ashy pale and wan. The horn seemed the mark of a curse for some mysterious sin, conceived and committed before the spirit had entered the flesh. Yet that sin seemed something imposed, and not voluntarily sought; some sin growing out of the heartless necessities of the predestination of things; some sin under which the sinner sank in sinless woe. (248–49)

Cuticle, however, is not affected by this face, as the guilty Swamp Doctor is by his.

7. One of the first of such images is the drunken Choctaw Indian Tubba in "Getting Acquainted with the Medicines" (Lewis 36–42). The young apprentice Tensas considers testing the effects of arsenic on Tubba, thinking, "but this Indian, he is of no earthly account or use to any one; no one would miss him, even were he to take an overdose" (37). He later discovers that the doctor keeps his whiskey in the jar marked "Solution of Arsenic," and the connection between liquor and poison is clearly made. Simms, describing his visit to Mobile on March 1, 1826, stated, "The Choctaw Indians, or those mixed stragglers, who are not tolerated in the nation, throng in immense numbers to this city, lying almost in a state of nudity in every angle or turn; a public nuisance and offending forever the eye of delicacy" (Kibler 89).

8. Anderson admitted that when he began his research, "I never imagined that I was on the trail of a lusty young man rather than an elderly physician, so deceptive was the pose that 'Tensas' maintained in his sketches" (v). Anderson, however, sees the elder Tensas in a happier light than I do: "From the detachment of age and experience, [Tensas] looks back on the follies of youth and is amused, even a little nostalgic, chuckling over the amusing episodes he remembers" (63). I find both the tales and the teller motivated by much darker concerns.

9. Rose maintains that Simms shifted these fears from the Negro to the Indian: "By focusing his full complement of racial anxieties upon the red man, and then brutally eliminating him, the Southern writer was able to effect at least a momentary catharsis" (41).

WORKS CITED

Anderson, John Q. *Louisiana Swamp Doctor: The Life and Writings of Henry Clay Lewis.* Baton Rouge: Louisiana State University Press, 1962.

Griffith, Nancy Snell, comp. *Humor of the Old Southwest: An Annotated Bibliography of Primary and Secondary Sources.* Westport: Greenwood, 1989.

Guilds, John Caldwell. *Simms: A Literary Life.* Fayetteville: University of Arkansas Press, 1992.

———, ed. *"Long Years of Neglect": The Work and Reputation of William Gilmore Simms.* Fayetteville: University of Arkansas Press, 1988.

Israel, Charles. "Henry Clay Lewis's *Odd Leaves:* Studies in the Surreal and Grotesque." *Mississippi Quarterly* 28 (winter 1974–75): 61–69.

Kibler, James E. "The First Simms Letters: 'Letters from the West' (1826)." *Southern Literary Journal* 19, no. 2 (1987): 81–91.

Lewis, Henry Clay. *Odd Leaves from the Life of a Louisiana "Swamp Doctor."* Philadelphia: A. Hart, 1850.

Melville, Herman. *White-Jacket or The World on a Man-of-War.* Evanston and Chicago: Northwestern University Press and the Newberry Library, 1970.

Rose, Alan Henry. *Demonic Vision: Racial Fantasy and Southern Fiction.* Hamden: Archon, 1976.

Simms, William Gilmore. *Border Beagles: A Tale of Mississippi.* 2 vols. Philadelphia: Carey and Hart, 1840. New and rev. ed. New York: Redfield, 1855.

———. *The Letters of William Gilmore Simms.* Ed. Mary C. Simms Oliphant, Alfred Taylor Odell, and T. C. Duncan Eaves. Vol. 1. Columbia: University of South Carolina Press, 1952.

———. Rev. of *Moby Dick. Southern Quarterly Review* 5 (January 1852): 262.

———. Rev. of *Odd Leaves. Southern Quarterly Review* 17 (July 1850): 537.

Wimsatt, Mary Ann. "The Evolution of Simms's Backwoods Humor." *"Long Years of Neglect": The Work and Reputation of William Gilmore Simms.* Ed. John Caldwell Guilds. Fayetteville: University of Arkansas Press, 1988. 148–65.

———. *The Major Fiction of William Gilmore Simms: Cultural Tradition and Literary Form.* Baton Rouge: Louisiana State University Press, 1989.

Irish Folklore Influences on Simms's "Sharp Snaffles" and "Bald-Head Bill Bauldy"

In order to judge Simms's achievement in the two tall tales "How Sharp Snaffles Got His Capital and Wife" and "Bald-Head Bill Bauldy," it is useful to examine briefly the state of literature in Ireland thirty years after his death and one hundred years after the elder Simms left Ulster for America.

In 1888, recognizing the need to document folklore and to present it in literary form to an English-reading public, the poet William Butler Yeats assembled Irish tales from printed sources in a collection entitled *Fairy and Folk Tales of the Irish Peasantry*. The period was a crucial one for Irish literature and politics: Ireland, a country of two languages, was developing under Yeats a tentative national literature whose language was inspired by the syntax of formal English and the music of the native Gaelic, as spoken by storytellers who rarely wrote anything down. Yeats had read the results of earlier folklore anthologists who had refused to view the Irish as anything but amusing, illiterate characters who told a good tale: "The impulse of the Irish literature of their time came from a class that did not—mainly for political reasons—take the populace seriously, and imagined the country as a humorist's Arcadia: its passion, its gloom, its tragedy, they knew nothing of. What they did was not wholly false; they merely magnified an irresponsible type, found oftenest among boatmen, car men and gentlemen's servants, into the type of whole nation, and created the stage Irishman" (qtd. in Kiely 12).

The offenders were writers who wrote stylized versions of folk tales, robbing them of their simplicity and force. Elliott Gose cites a tale translated from the Irish by Nicholas O'Kearney in 1855 as an example of an "Elaborate style that is the opposite of the simple, direct language of indigenous tales. Like others of his time . . . O'Kearney presumably felt obliged to elevate the language of the peasant who told it" (xviii). Yeats believed that people such as folklorist Crofton Croker, who had gathered and published folk tales, embellishing them with an Anglo-Irish sensibility, had committed the "great sin against art—the sin of rationalism. He tried to take away from his stories the impossibility that makes them dear to us" (Kiely 11). As Gose points out, however, many of the stories Yeats chose for his collection were "literary versions, sometimes even couched in stage Irish" (xviii).

A late-nineteenth-century surge in Irish nationalism had awakened interest in neglected Gaelic folklore, leading to Joseph Curtin's highly regarded *Myths and Folk Tales of Ireland* (1890) and *Hero Tales of Ireland* (1894). Curtin, an American, had learned Gaelic for the purpose of making a close translation to the English of village folk tales. Yeats was particularly pleased with Douglas Hyde's contribution to *Fairy and Folk Tales* and referred to the latter's collection *Beside the Fire*, published shortly before Yeats's, as "a book written in the beautiful English of Connaught, which is Gaelic in idiom and Tudor in vocabulary . . . the first book to use it in the expression of emotion and romance . . . the uncritical folk-genius, as no Irish or Englishman has ever had it, writing out of imitative sympathy" (*Autobiography* 146). Yeats mourned the dissipation of Hyde's genius in the face of Gaelic purists who insisted that literature would have to conform to the polarizing realities of politics: "It must be either English or Irish" (147). Thus, the literature of Ireland conformed to the principles of a country heading for civil war: a country torn between Irish tradition and the English language, not yet ready to permit its creative translators the freedom to transpose tradition. As the playwright John Millington Synge, Yeats's associate, noted in his "The Irish Literary Movement," published in *L'European* (May 31, 1902): "This period has been fruitful . . . since it has seen the birth, or at any rate the flowering of three highly significant movements: the Gaelic League, an association for the preservation of the Irish language; a movement for the development of agriculture and stockbreeding; and, finally, a new intellectual movement, which is now creating a literature for us" (*The Aran Islands*, 361).

The reference to a "new" intellectual movement relates to the fact that Irish had petered out as a written literary language by the end of the seventeenth century. Synge, in the same essay, noted that "all the intellectual traditions of the country vanished with it." Nothing distinctly Irish came into the literary canon until William Carleton (born 1798) published his

Traits and Stories of the Irish Peasantry, which Synge believed marked "the beginning of modern Irish literature" (361). However, little of real value came from this modern Irish literature until Yeats's new movement sought to combine the best of both traditions. Synge noted approvingly: "With the broadening of culture, patriotic sentiments are no longer an obsession" (362).

Yeats, despite his eclecticism, was not immune to the impulse to refine the literature of the common people for the more literate: "We had in Ireland imaginative stories, which the uneducated classes knew and even sang, and might we not make those stories current among the educated classes" (*Autobiography* 131). His Irish Literary Society was an attempt to unite the country with the help of "the applied arts of literature . . . to deepen the political passion of the nation" (131). Synge observed how Yeats's friend, Lady Gregory, arrived at her translations. While discussing her published version of the epic tales of Cuchulain, *Cuchulain of Muirthemne,* he echoed Yeats's wish for an Ireland united by a single language: "The peasants of the west of Ireland speak an almost Elizabethan dialect, and in the lyrical episodes it is hard to say when Lady Gregory is thinking of the talk of the peasants and when she is thinking of some passage in the Old Testament . . . and in her intercourse with the peasants of the west [she] has learned to use this vocabulary in a new way, while she carries with her plaintive Gaelic constructions that makes her language . . . a language of Ireland" (368).

Synge noted another difficulty facing Gregory and other translators: the arrangement of ancient stories was often chaotic. Although formed as a cycle in the seventh to ninth centuries, they were preserved in scattered manuscripts, and the tales often overlapped; therefore, "in order to construct a literary version, arrangement of a somewhat elaborate kind was needful" (368–69).

To sum up, the problem facing the new Irish literary movement was at once simple and irredeemably complex: how to translate the sometimes chaotic nature of the ancient Irish oral tale into a literary version acceptable, in style and politics, to the average contemporary reader, while remaining faithful to the storytelling tradition and the rustic simplicity of its language.

Simms's great achievement in "Sharp Snaffles" and "Bald-Head Bill Bauldy" is that he reproduces accurately the oral style of American frontiersmen in the postbellum South. He does not reinvent the diction of the illiterate for an audience of heightened sensibility, and so preserves the pe-

culiar dynamics of the tall tale that might have been lost in formal rework-
ing. He gives us the realism that Yeats and Synge sought a hundred years
later in another country.

The setting of both narratives—a hunters' fireside gathering—shows a
storyteller in action as he attempts to construct a skillful and entertaining
falsehood for his alert companions. In any tall tale, the storyteller must
arrange artistically a series of inflated episodes based on a kernel of truth
with "the amount of exaggeration fluctuated so skillfully that the [reader]
is uncertain what to believe and what to disbelieve" (Guilds 804). Simms
faithfully reports the Sharp Snaffles and Bald-Head Bill narratives in all
their comic absurdity and without literary veneer. We are left with the
dictions, gestures, and mock seriousness that are hallmarks of the tall tale
in the oral tradition. As Padraic Colum writes in his introduction to *A Treasury of Irish Folklore*, such an awareness of culture "creates and fosters that
which is most distinctive . . . the oral, the thing said rather than written,
the colorful, the extravagant, the dramatic" (xvi). Given the relative tur-
moil that similar exercises caused in Ireland, we can be thankful that Simms
was not one to subject his fiction to politically correct editorializing. Sam
Snaffles and Bald-Head Bill Bauldy are no stage Southerners.

It is not my intention to list every instance of similarity between the
Simms and Irish tales: such an exercise is better suited to a folklorist. Nor,
indeed, is Irish folklore the only influence at work in Simms's two frontier
stories. The magically reappearing wig sequence between Bald-Head Bill
and the Seminole Indian could be a variation of the trickster tale of the self-
returning robe, common among Plains Indian tribes, in which the Indian
protagonist steals either a robe or a moccasin that immediately returns to
its owner, much to the consternation of the thief. The Sharp Snaffles flight
sequence could have an origin in the Central Woodland Indian tale of the
trickster Manabozho, who dives under a lake and ties the legs of swimming
ducks together; the ducks carry him into the air until the string breaks. As
a final example, the magical hunt theme is present in the Irish Cuchulain,
Welsh Mabinogian, and German heroic sagas. Of course, Irish folklore itself contains foreign influences. Colum states: "The formative power of
the fireside gathering is strong: books read or stories picked up are turned
into familiar patterns. . . . That stories from bookish sources enter the Irish
storyteller's repertoire cannot be gainsaid. A listener to a recital, a reader
of a collection, often comes on a story out of Arabian Nights or The
Bible" (xv).

The Simms stories do share specific syntactical and thematic elements

with Irish folklore. I summarize them as follows: The Gaelic Run; Rivalry/
Audience Checking the Storyteller; Being Physically Carried Off/Search
for Capital; and The *Geis*. I then address specific elements in the stories
that suggest a familiarity with the Ulster oral tradition on the younger
Simms's part.

The Gaelic Run is described by Stith Thompson as "a recurring prose
pattern conventionally used to describe some series of events in a tale, such
as the fights of the hero with various adversaries. When the storyteller gets
to these points he changes his style of speech and recites the rigmarole as
fast as he can speak" (458). In "Bald-Head Bill Bauldy," the reader comes
across passages where the oral narrative style, as written, modulates into
breathless descriptions of flight and fight. While recounting the bear sequence, Bald-Head Bill reports: "Soon as he sees me coming at him with
two blazing stars in my mouth, he begins to back again; snorting free, as ef
he was still feeling the fire! He went on, waddling backward, tail foremost,
clumsy enough and cur'ous to see; and I a'ter him, puffing my cigars hairder
than ever" ("Bill Bauldy" 478). This is more than an accomplished prose
writer creating a syntax that echoes the heat of the moment: the quoted
section is a conscious decision about pacing in a tightly structured narrative. We can include the speech style of the famous African Cudjo in the
Gaelic Run category. Cudjo's language blends two cultures; it reflects and
responds to—instantly and without any mental reservation—the fear of
the moment he describes. While explaining how he tried to cross a river,
Cudjo utters a sentence of ninety words: "Yer we is now, jis a 'turning and
a twisting all about; we can't git across and we can't git back; de water takes
us one way; de win' takes us anoder way" (470).

It is interesting to note here how the Irish philosopher Arland Ussher
described the language in the plays of John Millington Synge: "As for the
expressiveness of the Gaelic folk-idioms, only the 'Irish-English' of Synge's
plays can give strangers some idea of it; it is a language . . . of a race which
has 'tired the sun with talking,' a language of quips, hyperbole, cajo-
leries . . . lamentations, blessings, curses, tirades—and all very often in the
same breath" (qtd. in Colum xiv).

Cudjo, however, seems remarkably restrained when answering McCord's
questions on alligator navigation. He repeats the refrain "You hab no
sense" before answering the major's bemused inquiries, each of which begins with an incremental refrain, "But, suppose that . . ." (471). A similar
sequence of a question-and-answer refrain exists in the classic Irish tale *The*

Destruction of Da Derga's Hostel, in which Fer Rogain begins each of his answers to Ingcäl's nineteen questions with a formulaic "Not difficult that" (Gantz 80–102). Another such sequence may be found in the Ulster story *The Intoxication of the Ulaid,* when Cromm Derùil asks a riddle of Medb that starts with "Outside and to the east of the fort." She begins each answer with an incremental refrain, such as "Regal the description," and "Regal and dignified that description" (204–10).

While addressing the concept of rivalry in the Irish oral tradition, Thompson notes that "The sense of rivalry is strong with these *shana-chies.* . . . Often these storytellers meet and have what is essentially a competition. . . . When the rumor goes about a village that one of them is in action a crowd of interested listeners will always gather . . . they love to hear [the tale] repeated . . . each man delivers his story with his own characteristic manner of voice, gesture, and literary style" (454–55).

This description corresponds to the setting of "Sharp Snaffles" and "Bald-Head Bill Bauldy." In the latter tale, the rivalry becomes intense when Major Henry finishes his anecdote, and Bald-Head accuses him of stealing: "I'll be dod-derned, Major, but you've got hold of a leetle piece of my history of the campaign I had in Goodwyn's Rigimint in the Flurriday war" (472). Major Henry apologizes and professes that this is news to him, which, of course, is all an excuse to get Bald-Head started on his story. Bald-Head's interruption is an aside introduced by way of a protest. The interruption from the listener creates a need to tell another story. Through rivalry, listeners become storytellers, and storytellers, listeners.

Bald-Head's interruption is only one aspect of interaction between teller and listener. Thompson notes that in Ireland, "The actual material of the tale alone remains intact, and this is carefully checked by the presence of many who have heard it from others" (455). Gose cites an example from the Aran Islands at the turn of the century: a shanachie would be interrupted and corrected if he confused incidents in a tale (4). This checking procedure can briefly alter the shape of the story in midstream, as in the opening sections of "Sharp Snaffles," when Sam tests the response level of his fireside audience by playing with numbers. After having stated that the wild geese descended on the lake—"Millions upon millions, till I was sartin there waur pretty nigh on to forty thousand in the lake" (439)—he later qualifies his estimate: "Well, thar they waur, forty thousand, we'll say, with, it mout be, a few millions and hundreds over" (440). He measures the lake's boundaries meticulously to help bolster his inflation of numbers and thus delights his listeners with such plausible detail and very obvious untruth. When he recounts wringing the necks of the geese, he puts the number at twenty-seven hundred—"many hed got away"—and is instantly challenged by the hunters. "Why, Yaou, whenever you telled of this thing before you always counted them at 3150" (448). All of this is really a parody of the maintenance of perfection, a reflection of the need to preserve spoken material in the face of altering Zeitgeist. Although Simms is writing fiction, he has recognized and adapted this subtle technique because it restrains the use of "a certain realm of fiction, the ingenuities of which are made to compensate for the exaggerations" ("Sharp Snaffles" 424).

The theme of being physically carried off is strong even to this day in Irish folklore and seems to be paralleled by Sharp Snaffles and Bald-Head Bill's respective journeys to self-worth. Kevin Danaher tells the story of James Maloney, a farmer, who sat one evening on his old wooden plough and watched the sunset, when all of a sudden a horde of fairies descended on him. The wheels of the plough turned to ponies and "The old wooden plough took off like a Jet Clipper. . . . after a bumpy crossing of the Bay of Biscay and bad icing conditions above the Cantabrian mountains, where should James find himself but in Spain, wooden plough and all" (Danaher 90).

In "Sharp Snaffles," flight or travel is closely related to gain and capital. The flock of birds, the bear, and the alligators all provide transportation beyond impossible obstructions; they represent a rich crop of nature ready to be harvested and transformed into capital; a perfectly disciplined, mindless nature that assembles itself in one convenient place so that a single man might hitch a ride into the realm of capital, a man who will be transformed as a result of what he takes from them. Sharp Snaffles, holding plow-lines, is carried into the air by geese "screaming and flouncing, meaning, I reckon, to take the back track to Canniday" (440). Nature behaves oddly when our unlikely heroes are around: the alligators, nature's oldest predators, march in lines alongside man (Bald-Head Bill), the wilderness's newest inhabitant, in a parody of civilization. The birds behave by conveniently growing tired of hauling Sharp, despite their number.

Cuchulain, the Ulster hero of ancient Irish mythology, had a particular dislike for birds, and destroyed them at every opportunity. As recounted in a story called "The Wasting Sickness of Cú Chulaind,"[1] Cuchulain and the court of Ulster are celebrating Samain (Halloween) when they spy a flock of birds hovering over a lake. The birds are so beautiful that the warriors' wives wish for them; Cuchulain brings down the whole flock and distributes them among the women. Afterward, a pair of birds flies across the lake, linked by a chain of red gold. Cuchulain pursues them, although his charioteer warns him that birds linked by a chain signal otherworldly transformation. He falls into a deep sleep and receives the vision of a beautiful woman (Gantz 156–57). Both Sharp's net, which will link the birds together and transform him into a wealthy man, and the chain of red gold, a symbol of transformation, are analogous to the hero Cuchulain's trapping a flock of birds over a lake in order to acquire capital. In Irish folklore, Samain, or Halloween, is a time when the supernatural changes the fate of man. New kings replace old kings. As Gantz writes in *Early Irish Myths and Sagas*, "The mythic subtext harbours the remains of a ritual killing story" (188). The Sharp Snaffles tale is set in the period of Samain (early winter, October), and Sam Snaffles removes Hopson from his position of power with supernatural help and gains the keys to his kingdom.

The *geis*, or taboo, figures in all major Irish cycles. A geis informs a person of the danger of reneging on his word. The geis becomes a challenge to heroic action inasmuch as it prevents a character from taking the easy way out of a difficult situation. By having Merry Ann curse Grimstead, Sam Snaffles is, in effect, trapping her with her own word, and thus puts her in danger of being thrown out by her father. Sam's insistence that she curse Grimstead becomes the modus operandi. She cannot marry a man she has cursed.

The oral tale lives on in Ireland. Thompson writes, "It was the writer's privilege several years ago [in western Ireland] to hear some of the best of these shanachies. . . . The best of these old men could tell fifty to a hundred full-length fairy tales, any one of which takes at least a half hour for the telling" (454). Simms's tale of Bald-Head Bill rivals the longest of the Irish tales: its twenty-five thousand words would require a skillful raconteur indeed. In Ireland, the shanachies were the central figures in rural entertainment. They received respect and admiration, and the fireside was their throne in thatched cottages all over the Irish countryside. Padraic Colum notes that "The Irish have remained an oral rather than literate people. . . . It should be noted, however, that culture does not depend upon reading and writing: the present editor knew an old man, technically an illiterate, who delighted in repeating an Irish translation of the *Iliad*" (xiv). Simms's two hunters are really professional shanachies, probably illiterate and, therefore, capable of prodigious feats of memory. The gathering by the fireside, the attentive listeners, and the art of the yarn are all found in the Irish oral tradition. Jim Fisher, as the judge of the "Big Lie," embodies the "right to interrupt" on the part of the audience, which in turn creates an enduring bond between the professional and the amateur. Simms takes note of the power of listenership.

What are the characteristics of these Irish tales? Elliott Gose prefers the term *Irish wonder tale*. He outlines four elements that differentiate the wonder tale from the European fairy tale: first, the Irish wonder tale was not intended for children, but was recited late at night, to an adult audience, as part of an active oral tradition; second, the wonder tale was usually told by men, and had ordinary peasant men as heroes; third, the storyteller was usually illiterate, and his audience illiterate peasants; and fourth, the wonder tale was not subject to literary revision (xiii–xiv).

The art of storytelling has preserved a certain integrity of subject matter, shape, tone, and style through the centuries. In the context of studying the oral rendition of folk tales, Thompson argues that if texts are not recorded exactly as heard, any analysis of the tale is of little value for stylistic purposes: "One cannot be too insistent upon accuracy of the text if one is to study the form of the folktale. . . . Best of all, of course, is phonographic recording . . . voice modulations and arrangements of words are thus preserved with absolute accuracy" (450).

The oral tradition was very strong in the Ulster that Simms's father left in the last years of the eighteenth century. Most of the native Irish were illiterate hunters and farmers, denied a solid education by occupying forces that had effectively banned the native language. The Irish storytelling landscape mirrored closely the societal microcosm portrayed in "Sharp Snaffles": a close-knit group of regional folk, sharing a dialect and a way of life far from "what the conceited world calls civilization" ("Sharp Snaffles" 421).

Since Simms's father has been described as an avid storyteller, one can reasonably assume that he had heard of two of Ireland's then most renowned poets and storytellers, both Ulstermen: Peadar O'Doirnin, who died in 1769, and Art MacCooey, whose death is put at 1773 by a major scholar of Irish history, Cardinal Tomas O'Fiaich (60). Both O'Doirnin and MacCooey were active in South Armagh, a region approximately forty miles from Larne. MacCooey's South Armagh and Simms's Larne shared strong political ties in the years preceding the Irish rebellion of 1793. The Lappin brothers of Mullaghbawn, South Armagh, made the bayonets used in the rebellion in the McQuilly Forge. The bayonets were ferried secretly to the Larne area, which was a center of rebel activity. There can be no doubt that MacCooey's nationalist songs were known to all storytellers in Larne.

Simms may have based the character of Sharp Snaffles in part on Art MacCooey, who wrote one of his most famous pieces, "Urchill an Chreagain," about his banishment by a parish because he had wished to marry his own cousin. MacCooey, with no capital or wife, did not have the money to make himself worthy of a dispensation from the Catholic Church. When he did marry in a Protestant church, he was excommunicated by his priestly nemesis and ostracized by his neighbors. After working as a gardener in Dublin, MacCooey was finally granted permission to marry his cousin in a Catholic church. He composed songs that detailed his treatment at the hands of what Cardinal O'Fiaich calls "[t]he snobbery and respectability of the (new) classes who were aping the ways of the gentry and had little time for native cultural values" (62)—people like Squire Hopson. The fact that this story of MacCooey being the banished suitor was widespread in Ulster in the late eighteenth century and is famous to this day suggests that Simms's father knew the story well and may have passed it on to his son through his own recitations of it. Not a page of MacCooey's work survives. Most of the manuscripts were used as packaging material in a shop in Mounthill during the nineteenth century (O'Fiaich 65).

Simms's father may also have passed on the style of telling a tale, since the oral tradition was very active in Larne when he lived there. During my research for this essay, I located a tape recording of a living Irish shanachie that shows how remarkably similar are the eighteenth-century Larne and nineteenth-century W. G. Simms styles. In my search for a recording, I had two requirements: first, the shanachie, although speaking in English, would be fluent in Gaelic; second, he would come from the Ulster tradition, be active in the general area of Larne, and tell stories typical of the Ulster tradition.

One tape satisfied all three requirements: *On the Hip of Sliabh Gullion* (Stories of South Armagh), as told by storyteller John Campbell, recorded in 1989 before live audiences in County Down and Belfast. (The tape was provided to me by Galway writer Michael Carragher, who also made invaluable observations concerning the similarity in styles.) During my interview with Carragher, he made reference to two of the tales on the tape, "Peter-Go-Slap" and "Paddy the Creel and Con the Dandy," which mirror

Simms's tales in key stylistic respects: the set-up of the nickname, the explanation of the nickname, the throwaway detail, and the hook and parallel.

What we encounter first and foremost in "Sharp Snaffles" is the traditional oral setting. The hunters are gathered around the campfire, the American frontier equivalent of the Irish cottage's fireside. Jim Fisher, having been installed as the "Big Lie," announces his choice of raconteur with a single word: "Yaou!" "Yaou was the *nom de nique* of one of the hunters, whose proper name was Sam Snaffles, but who, from his special smartness, had obtained the farther sobriquet of Sharp Snaffles. Columbus Mills whispered to me that he was called 'Yaou' from his frequent use of that word, which, in the Choctaw dialect, simply means 'Yes'" (424).

The Irish style makes frequent use of the name set-up and nickname explanation at the beginning of a narrative. In the following segment of John Campbell's tale "Peter-Go-Slap" we hear a description of how Peter got his name:[2] "She come one year to cut the seed spuds for the farmers and where did she end up cuttin' seed spuds only for an ole fella called Peter-Go-Slap that lived over at the foot of the mountain. That was a nickname. His proper name was Peter Murphy, but the poor fella had a big foot and then he had a bigger one and when he went down the road the bigger one used to go Slap in the potholes. And they called him Peter-Go-Slap."

Note the parallels. First comes the nickname: in Simms, "Yaou was the *nom de nique* of one of the hunters"; in Campbell, "and where did she end up cuttin' seed spuds only for an ole fella called Peter-Go-Slap. . . . That was the nick-name."

Next comes the description of how the name was earned: in Simms, "Yaou . . . whose proper name was Sam Snaffles, but who, from his special smartness, had obtained the farther sobriquet of Sharp Snaffles"; in Campbell, "[h]is proper name was Peter Murphy, but the poor fellow had a big foot and then he had a bigger one and when he went down the road the bigger one used to go *Slap* in the potholes. And they called him Peter-Go-Slap."

What we hear in this segment, then, are the syntactical parallels of the name set-up and the nickname explanation. This form of tagging places the character firmly in the minds of listeners and is indispensable to the storyteller, who often tells long tales to an audience that must keep complex characters and plots straight.

The next similarity between Simms's story and the Irish oral tradition lies in the use of the hook and parallel, as illustrated in Campbell's story,

"Paddy the Creel and Con the Dandy." Campbell begins the fourteen-minute tale by recounting how a laborer called Paddy the Creel gets a job in an old schoolhouse. Campbell develops a seemingly irrelevant episode in the exposition: "He started in good time in the morning with mortar and stones, and he was smoking a Ben Nevis Cutty: that's a long-shank clay pipe with a wee tit on the head of it. He was smoking War Horse tobacco, and the fumes of smoke went up and down and under the door and through the cracks in the window, and the ole schoolmaster was up at the blackboard, and he smelt the tobacco, and he started clapping his pockets and lookin' and searchin' for his own pipe."

The schoolmaster realizes that he has left his pipe at home; he finds Paddy and asks him for a few pulls of his pipe:

> "Certainly, master," says Paddy, and he handed him the pipe. And when the ole schoolmaster got the pipe he put his hand into his pocket and he took out a great big handkerchief and he started to rub and rub and rerub at the mouthpiece of the pipe, and when he had it very well rubbed, he put it in his mouth and he smoked it for a while. And he was finished smoking it, he gave it back to Paddy and he thanked him. Paddy took the pipe off him, put it up on the pier, took the trowel and cut an inch-an-a-half off the end of the shank and stuck it in his mouth. I'm only telling you that part of the story to let you see that, although Paddy was a very humble man, he was very particular about what he put into his own mouth.

Note the reference to the Ben Nevis pipe, which Campbell takes pains to describe. When Campbell says, "I'm only telling you that now," he is essentially treating the pipe as a throwaway detail; however, as a feature of the Irish oral tradition, the aside will eventually come back to haunt the story; in this case, the pipe is really a hook on which Campbell will hang an ironic parallel, but only after the hook has been implanted in the minds of the listeners.

Six minutes of ancillary storytelling pass. Nothing is mentioned of the pipe. Campbell then tells us that Paddy found another job: "But one of the jobs Paddy got was driving a Clydesdale horse and a swing plough for a man called Con the Dandy that lived in the townland of Cashel: will you remember that?" Campbell asks the audience to remember the horse; this request is a signal that the horse will play a pivotal role in the development of the hook into a parallel. Paddy and Con both worked a horse and plough

in a very stony field. One day, the horse stopped and wouldn't move. Paddy
saw that the horse's eyes were turned upside down in his head. The vet was
called, who inserted a rubber hose "under the horse's tail," and blew until
the horse's eyes reverted to their normal position. However, next day, when
Paddy and Con were working the horse and plough, the horse stopped
again. Con told Paddy to fetch a sprayer from the farmhouse. The story
ends as told by Campbell:

> Up come the sprayer and out comes the penknife from his pocket
> and he cut the hose off the sprayer. "Hold him tight now," says he,
> and he went back with the hose, tryin' to hold the tail and put in the
> hose . . . and after a lot of kicking and sputtering he got the hose
> in. . . . "Now," says he, "I'm going to blow, and you be ready with your
> hand," says he, and he started to blow. . . . "I'll tell you what," says he,
> "I'll hold the horse and you come back and blow, for you're a pipe
> smoker and there'll be more wind in you than what's in me." Paddy
> went back, and the first thing he done when he went back, he pulled
> the hose out and he turned it round and started puttin' the other end
> of it in.
> "Damn your skin," says Con, "What are you at with that flamin'
> hose after the trouble I had puttin' it in?"
> "Damn your soul," says Paddy, "you don't think I'm going to put
> the same end in my mouth that you had stuck in your rotten mouth?"

The hook has come full circle to a parallel. The pipe, placed in the mind
of the listener as an aside at the beginning, by way of explaining Paddy's
preoccupation with hygiene, is reintroduced as a rubber hose, and sets up
the punch line. There are less obvious parallels: Paddy's cutting of the pipe
at the beginning of the story is matched by the cutting of the hose sprayer
at the end, and Con makes a reference to Paddy's pipe-smoking as a
reminder of the set-up. Finally, we come to the episode of inserting a
hose—i.e., pipe—in the mouth. The storyteller must draw to the listener's
memory all the elements necessary for that final irony to work.

Simms uses the same techniques of hook and parallel in "Sharp Snaffles,"
chiefly through placement of the words *obzarve* and *capital*. When Sam informs Hopson of his wish to marry Merry Ann, the squire "knocks all the
fire out of his pipe on the chimney . . . and he says 'Git up, Sam Snaffles.
Git up, ef you please'" (430) and leads Sam by the collar to the large, ornate
mirror. In an oral tale, the tension created by the silence of this procedure

would be palpable. In fiction, it lasts a second or two. Simms takes great pains to describe the mirror: "Now that looking-glass, Jedge, was about the biggest I ever did see! It was a'most three feet high . . . it had a bright, broad frame . . . with a heap of leetle figgers worked all round it" (430). Simms is preparing his hook—the mirror—that will support the ironic parallel to come later.

Hopson speaks: "'Look good,' says he, *'obzarve* well,'" and presently "'Now *obzarve*. . . . Jest now answer me, from your honest conscience, a'ter all you've seed, ef you honestly thinks you're the sort of pusson to hev my da'ter!'" (431).

Obzarve is repeated nine times in this scene; *Capital,* ten times. Toward the end of the story, Sam enters the squire's house. In a gesture to the preliterate society that gave birth to the tale, Simms relates that Hopson is "smoking his pipe and reading the newspaper. He looked at me through his specs over the newspaper" (454). The order of the steps to full closure is precise in Simms's skillful hand. Hopson's "What the old Harry's that to you?" is a new hook that will become a parallel presently, when Sam will use it against Hopson. Next, Hopson will smash his pipe on the chimney, paralleling a similar action when he was in a position of power. Sam then recounts that he "tuk him quiet by the collar of his coat, with my thumb and forefinger, and I said 'Git up Squaire, for a bit.'" Hopson stands before the mirror. Sam asks him to tell "what he *obzarves*" (461). The word has come full circle.

NOTES

1. One of a number of spellings that exist for this Irish hero's name—e.g., Cuchullan, Cuchulain, Cúchulainn, and Gantz's Old Irish version of the name.
2. I have attempted to render faithfully the spoken English.

WORKS CITED

Campbell, John. "Paddy the Creel and Con the Dandy." Rec. October 31, 1989. *On the Hip of Sliabh Gullion.* Spring Records, CSP 1020, 1990.
———. "Peter-Go-Slap." Rec. November 1989. *On the Hip of Sliabh Gullion.* Spring Records, CSP 1020, 1990.
Carragher, Michael. Personal interview. April 4, 1992.

Colum, Padraic, ed. *A Treasury of Irish Folklore*. New York: Crown, 1954.

Danaher, Kevin. *Gentle Places and Simple Things*. Dublin: Mercier, 1984.

Gantz, Jeffrey, ed. *Early Irish Myths and Sagas*. London: Penguin, 1988.

Gose, Elliott B. *The World of the Irish Wonder Tale*. Toronto: University of Toronto Press, 1985.

Guilds, John Caldwell. "Bald-Head Bill Bauldy"—Explanatory Notes. *The Writings of William Gilmore Simms: Centennial Edition*. Volume 5: *Stories and Tales*. Columbia: University of South Carolina Press, 1974. 803–5.

Kiely, Benedict. *Yeats' Ireland: An Illustrated Anthology*. London: Aurum, 1989.

O'Fiaich, Tomas. "Poets and Scholars of Creggan Parish." *Creggan: Journal of the Creggan Local History Society* 6 (1992): 55–67.

Simms, William Gilmore. "Bald-Head Bill Bauldy." *Stories and Tales*. Ed. John Caldwell Guilds. Columbia: University of South Carolina Press, 1974. 466–521.

———. "How Sharp Snaffles Got His Capital and Wife." *Stories and Tales*. Ed. John Caldwell Guilds. Columbia: University of South Carolina Press, 1974. 421–66.

Synge, John Millington. *The Aran Islands and Other Writings*. Ed. Robert Tracy. New York: Vintage, 1962.

Thompson, Stith. *The Folktale*. Berkeley: University of California Press, 1977.

Yeats, W. B. *The Autobiography of William Butler Yeats*. 1924. New York: Collier, 1978.

Simms and the Changing Frontier

JAMES E. KIBLER

Stewardship and *Patria* in Simms's Frontier Poetry

Culture preserves the map and the records of past journeys so that no generation will permanently destroy the route. The more local and settled the culture, the better it stays put, the less the damage. It is the foreigner whose road of excess leads to a desert.

—WENDELL BERRY, "Damage"

The two versions of "The Traveller's Rest" (1842 and 1849) are both narrative poems but differ greatly in their narrative forms.[1] The 1842 version has only one speaker—a young man traveling across the prairies of Alabama. He has us, his listeners, for companions. We are tired and have no water. There are no trees, and the noonday sun is baking us. But he says in the opening lines, "Don't faint; in a short while we'll be in a cool wooded area where there's a spring, and we'll rest." It is the year 1832. He tells us he was here five years ago as a thoughtless, wandering boy, as wild as the Muscoghee Indians who just that short while back were "masters of these plains" and in so brief a time are now vanished.

Though the red race is gone, he remarks how unchanged nature is. All the natural landmarks are here, including the blaze marks on certain pines that will guide us to the spring. These blazes are the kind work of old woodsmen who made them to guide "less experienced . . . less fortunate brothers" like us.

We reach the spring, drink our fill, rest with the great "arabesque" ceiling of interlaced limbs and vines above us, celebrate the fertility and variety of nature, reflect on the melancholy fate of the red man, and speak soberly of mutability in good Romantic fashion. At this point, the narrator shifts his focus from nature and the red race to the white man. He says: "If such swift change can sweep away the whole Indian nation, what are we who muse on their fate to say of ourselves? Might we not, if not mindful, pass from the scene as completely?" The narrator becomes even more specific and asks himself what moral monuments he has left behind "to compel his memory after death." He sees himself as an "unperformer," while

> Those gray usurpers, Death and Change, have been
> Familiar in his household, and he stands,
> Of all that grew around his homely hearth,
> Alone,—the last!—and this hath made him now,
> An exile, better pleased with woods and streams,
> Than the city's porch.

Like the red man, he has become a wanderer, leaving no moral monuments, and thus also invites extinction. Past these melancholy reflections, the poem ends with a song of thanks for the water and shade, the song of birds, the cooling breeze of late evening:

> gratitude, o'er all
> To God in the highest! He it is who guides
> The erring footsteps; prompts the woodman's heart
> To kindly office; shelters from the sun:
> Withholds the storm; and with his leaves and flowers,
> Sweet freshening streams, and ministry of birds,
> Sustains . . . and invigorates;—
> To Him the praise and homage,—Him, o'er all!

The Creator thus becomes our great guide in the woodcraft of life, leading erring footsteps, guiding the woodsman's heart to mark the path for less experienced travelers. In this way, we all become metaphorical frontiersmen. It is through God's mercy that the storm is withheld, that these leaves, flowers, and waters refresh us with their "ministry." And *ministry* is probably the single most important word in the 1842 version, though its implications are not made clear and are yet to be developed. We leave the poem in proper state of mind, with a right spirit of reverence and thankfulness, and with a kind of benediction, a peace that passeth all understanding.

This is the early poem of 1842, set a decade before, when Simms was twenty-six years old, and possibly originally penned at that time. It is clearly autobiographical. The narrator had passed this way five years ago as a boy, that is, in the 1820s. As we know, so had Simms. By 1832, Simms had lost his wife and father—hence "Those gray usurpers, Death and Change," familiar in his household, and he is now the last of his lonely hearth, and an "exile" better pleased with woods than the city's porch.

Simms had to make some of the biggest decisions of his life in 1832. He still could have migrated west as his father had desired. He also contemplated moving north and in 1832 even did so; but love of home brought him back. He gives his reasons clearly and movingly in his poetry. The exile returns to the hearth and his native soil. Certain decisions have been made.

He will not go west to get rich quick. Simms wrote his essay *The Social Principle* in 1842, the same year of publication of the first version of "The Traveller's Rest." In the essay he says that the rootlessness caused by western migration erodes the stability, ties, and traditions necessary to the forming of high culture. Art must have a settled traditional base to generate and support it. If lasting moral monuments are to be created, man simply cannot be a nomad. He has to stay put and learn to value and make the best of what is at his own doorstep, the place he knows best, and the soil and its traditions from which he grew, its memories and associations—in other words, what the poet Virgil called the *patria* in his *Georgics;* the *patria*, that little postage stamp of land called home, not the national or even regional *palatia Romana*, as Willa Cather, Thomas Hardy, and William Faulkner also so clearly came to understand.

In Simms's mind, in refusing to move west he was choosing art over certain and easy wealth. To take his decision in favor of literature a second step further, he removed briefly to the North because of seemingly better literary opportunities. He could be nearer his new publishers and the emerging center of the American literary scene. In less than a year he came home, however, making the choice in favor of his *patria*, owing to homesickness and the knowledge that his own native place and its traditions were the wellspring of his art. Just as importantly, he disapproved of the North's growing materialism, commercialism, and industrialism. His essay "The Philosophy of the Omnibus" was written in 1834, appropriately just after his return. In it, he calls the Northern tendency a "mercantile and money-loving condition of things . . . Yankee all over" (403–4). Money is more important than place. And place, as a result, is abused. The Northern spirit of the age, as Simms saw it in 1834, was motion, utility, equality, and "levellism," where great art would eventually suffer and be destroyed at the hands of an industrial and mercantile way of life that was breaking the folk-chain of memory and human association essential to the creation of a great and lasting literature. Again, in *The Social Principle* of 1842, he writes: "The powers of steam . . . railroads—the capacity to overcome time and space, are wonderful things—but they are not virtues, nor duties, nor laws, nor affections. I do not believe that all the steam power in the world can bring happiness to one poor human heart. Still less can I believe that all the rail-roads in the world can carry one poor soul to heaven" (53).[2]

Anticipating by nearly a century such writers as Ezra Pound and the Agrarians of *I'll Take My Stand,* Simms states that the concerns of the shop and marketplace are threatening to subvert the arts, education, and community. Therefore, by 1842, the year he was writing both *The Social Principle* and the first version of "The Traveller's Rest," he was solidifying his choice of place, and for clearly stated reasons: choosing the South over the Southwest owing to a commitment to art rather than getting rich quick, and the South over the North, because he saw the traditional South as the place where the sustaining values of Western civilization were likely to have a better chance of survival—if indeed they were to survive anywhere. At any rate, it would be in the South that they would make their last stand.[3]

So what changes does Simms make to his second version of "The Traveller's Rest"? The most striking difference is that in the 1849 version, Simms creates a second narrator and thus forms a frame story, the kind popular in the backwoods humor tale of the day. There are now two named travelers, a young man and an elderly traveling companion, the latter perhaps modeled after Simms's dead father or a relative such as his Uncle James. The setting is still around 1832; and the vanished red man, forest, and spring are still primary symbols. Yet Simms now takes what was a minor image in the first version and makes it his chief and controlling metaphor. This is the mentor or guide metaphor. The older traveler is now himself the boy's mentor, passing wisdom to him in the manner of traditional societies, through an oral narrative. To set up the frame, Simms creates an entirely new opening for the poem:

> For hours we wandered o'er the beaten track,
> A dreary stretch of sand, that, in the blaze
> Of noonday, seemed to launch sharp arrows back,
> As fiery as the sun's. Our weary steeds
> Falter'd, with drooping heads, along the plain,
> Looking from side to side most wistfully,
> For shade and water. We could feel them,
> Having like thirst; and, in a desperate mood,
> Gloomy with toil, and parching with the heat,
> I had thrown down my burden by the way,
> And slept, as man may never sleep but once,
> Yielding without a sigh,—so utterly

> Had the strong will, beneath the oppressive care,
> Failed of the needed energy for life,—
> When, with a smile, the traveller by my side,
> A veteran of the forest and true friend,
> Whose memory I recall with many a tear,
> Laid his rough hand most gently on mine own,
> And said, in accents still encouraging:—
> "Faint not,—a little farther we shall rest."

With "Faint not," the 1842 version had begun, ostensibly in the poet's own words. Now, most of the poem is recast to be in the second speaker's words, thus creating the frame narrative.

This allows for much complexity. The young narrator can interrupt:

> Boy as I was, and speaking still through books—
> Not speaking from myself—I said: "Alas!
> For this love's spring-time—quite unlike the woods,
> It never knows but one; and, following close,
> The long, long years of autumn, with her robes
> Of yellow mourning, and her faded wreath
> Of blighted flowers, that, taken from her heart,
> She flings upon the grave-heap where it rots!

At which the experienced narrator disagrees. "This is false!" he says:

> Love hath its thousand spring-times like the flowers,
> If we are dutiful to our own hearts,
> And nurse the truths of life, and not its dreams.
> But not in hours like this, with such a show
> Around us, of earth's treasures, to despond,
> To sink in weariness, and to brood on death.

In his wisdom, he is saying, "So you have lost your first love and feel you can never love again. Don't be so egocentric. Look around you: love has its many springtimes like the flowers." The older counselor teaches him renewal and rebirth, himself using the guide of nature's seasons, God given.

In the early version, the youth leaves us with the gloomy conclusion that no love can replace a first love. In the new version—written after Simms's marriage to Chevillette—he can now have a wiser narrator tell him that he will indeed be able to love again.

In a sense, then, we have an older, wiser Simms speaking from experience to a young Simms still looking at life through the histrionic, romantic views of books. This creates in the poem a dramatic tension—or dialectic. The older and wiser traveler can tell his young friend from experience, not books, that

> A thousand times, when I was near exhausted as yourself
> That gash upon the pine-tree strengthen'd me,
> As showing where the waters might be found.

He thanks the rough old woodsman whose frank and generous heart had counseled him, like the patriarchs of old,

> To make provision for the stranger's need.
> His axe . . .
> Was in that office consecrate . . . [and]
> Holier than knife, in hands of bearded priest.

But the old narrator knows the destructiveness of the frontiersman, as well, and thus provides a further dialectic. In his own western home, there had once been great trees more majestic than the famed Cedars of Lebanon, "sung by Princes to the music of high harps." There had been great forests over which "hung brooding the countenance of God, when beneath his creative word, / They freshened into green, . . . memorials of His presence." Virgin forests are thus imaged here as monuments or memorials of God's presence—a very fine image. Now the older man sees these memorials reduced to smoking stumps, and then replaced by worn-out, barren fields. He notes of the traveler's rest itself:

> Alas! the forward vision! a few years
> Will see these shafts o'erthrown. The profligate hands
> Of avarice and of ignorance will despoil
> The woods of their old glories; and the earth,
> Uncherish'd, will grow barren, even as the fields, . . .
> Which in my own loved home, half desolate,
> Attest the locust rule,—the waste, the shame,
> . . . which still robs
> The earth of its warm garment and denies
> Fit succour, which might recompense the soil,
> Whose inexhaustible bounty, fitly kept,
> Was meant to fill the granaries of man,
> Through all earth's countless ages.

Although part of this passage had been present in the 1842 version as a prediction, it is expanded and sharpened in the 1849 as a certainty. As a wise planter properly valuing the soil as his lifeblood, Simms now added the lines about its proper stewardship. He thus revised his poem to strengthen the environmental issues. Simms is able to do so because his new narrator has seen a longer span of destruction and, because he is speaking from experience, is thus more credible—especially when standing next to the bookish youth.

The abiding and unchanging nature of the frontier that stands in contrast to the vanished red man in the 1842 version has in the new poem yielded to the specter of a despoiled natural landscape. Verdant nature surrounding this spring can be celebrated, but only set against the certain vision of cut trees and sterile, worn-out soil, a situation that the old narrator states is certain to follow for even this very charmed and sacred place where they rest. In the future, woodsman's blazes, trees, cool spring and shade, and all their association and remembrance will be swept away. No longer will there be guidance from either God the Creator or the woodsman's heart, which God has informed with the lesson of benevolence. Instead, the monotony of blazing prairies will spread out in all directions, with no respite from the burning sun—not even a shadow from a red rock. This will be no less a wasteland than Eliot's.

Now, the old narrator (whether Simms's father, uncle, or someone else) can at the end of the 1849 version berate himself for running to the West and regret not having left "moral monuments" of his own. He has, in his own nomadic way, built nothing lasting to benefit those to follow. And as Simms writes in 1842 in *The Social Principle,* "A wandering people is more or less a barbarous one." The young narrator of the 1849 version apparently learns the lesson well. The poem itself is the proof. Unlike his companion, he does not become an exile from his *patria,* and as a planter, he becomes a practical, good steward of that *patria*'s soil, with his feet in that soil. He also devotes his life to creating (in the poem's image of God the Creator of trees) those moral monuments that stand as lasting guides for mankind.

Thus, the poet, in his *ministry* to man, is like the benign old woodsman who blazed the path to the spring, to sustain the weary traveler in a parched and desolate landscape. The old woodsman did this out of feeling for those he would never see—his "brother travellers," as Simms put it. And in like way, so does the poet. The spring is of course archetype for the source of life (as, for example, in Frost's poem "The Pasture," where the poet-speaker again leads the listener to a spring and for like symbolic reason). As artist, Simms saw himself as minister to man, one of the pillars and props to sustain him. How? By guiding him, in mentor fashion, to a way of seeing; by opening up possibilities, not restricting them; by showing the wellspring of life, which is not material or utilitarian, but spiritual, after all. Questions and mysteries are more important to him than empirical answers. In this way, Simms is the quintessential Southern author.[4] There is no single *ism* or *ology* to explain life; and he knows there never will be. Like Poe, he knows transcendentalism certainly will not do it. Neither will naturalism, nor realism, nor yet even romanticism. All these would indeed be restrictions and limitations. I suppose that is why, to his credit, we never can place Simms comfortably in any particular school or pigeonhole him in any easy category.

For Simms, the greatest limitation of man would of course be empiricism or utilitarianism; and on these two false gods of the age he focused his strongest dislike. His affirmation and demonstration of a fuller way of seeing pervade so many of his poems, stories, novels, and essays as to constitute, for me at least, *the* major theme of his canon, and by far his greatest contribution to literature—a truth relevant to men of all ages and places. Understanding that theme can allow us to see Simms as a whole, and until we understand it, I wonder if we can ever fully appreciate his genius.

In the 1849 version the blazes of a benevolent pilgrim, with the aid of a kindly guide, lead the novitiate to a spring that sustains him on his journey in a burning dry landscape. Simms, as a poet, will do the same. His blaze or mark is the poem that we read. It is his "moral monument" created out of rootedness in a tradition that adamantly rejects the material and utilitarian view of life. The complex 1849 poem now presents us with four guides: first, God, the Creator of nature, which itself acts as teacher; second, the old narrator, father surrogate and priestlike; third, the old patriarch woodsman who leaves the blazes; and, finally, the poet, ministering through his poem, in a world that has thus become essentially sacramental. With all these guides, the mystery is not of how one finds his sure way, but of how one could get lost. And yet Simms knows that man still does, and constantly.

As mentor and guide, Simms the poet shows the healing power of nature—of nature as the source of man's life. A right attitude toward nature is celebrated here and in his poetry in general. The contrasting wrong attitude is also damned severely in no uncertain terms: this wrong response grows out of greed, narcissism, egocentrism, empiricism, hedonism, insensitivity, waste, profligacy, and alienation. All these set about destroying a sense of place, traditions, continuities, harmonies, ties, memories, associations, community, family, reverential and sacramental attitudes, and finally man's very humanity itself. These traits are thus self-destructive for the individual and cataclysmic for physical nature itself. They make stewardship impossible.

All this long litany of pejorative adjectives sounds very contemporary. It describes the language of the modern wasteland that we know so well. Simms as poet-seer envisioned our age. As poet-prophet, he predicted it. And as with most prophets, few listened, or listen today. Our failure to understand Simms is not Simms's failure, I suspect, but the failure of our society to understand itself.

His message is often especially lost on us literary critics, who, in trailing clouds of glory, come from academia, which is our home—academia, where we are trained as "professionals" to go where the job is, and without much consideration of a *patria*.

Simms above all advocates an inspired way of seeing, not bounded by the utilitarian or empirical but, rather, open to the deepened mystery of the world around. Certainly not the reduced and impoverished materialist's way of seeing the world as real estate or resources to exploit for profit. As modern agrarian poet and environmentalist Wendell Berry has phrased it: when you stop living in the *Price* and start living in the *Place*, then you are indeed in a different line of succession (68). When that place is redolent of family associations over a long span of time, it is a particularly rich and valuable place, to be treasured, protected, and defended with all the force of one's being.

Simms knew this; and as an artist who recognized the true value of place, he was one of our first environmentalists, his view of stewardship supported by a remarkably complete vision of society. And literally hundreds of his poems and essays, written long before Thoreau, prove it. His 1836 poem "The Western Emigrants" provides a final good example. Here, Simms encounters a Carolina family on their way west. It is a fine descriptive poem, visually brilliant, a realistic vignette, but at the same time so much more; an affirmation of the centrality of place and that which is gained by devotion to it or lost by desertion of it:

An aged man, whose head some seventy years
Had snow'd on freely, led the caravan:—
His sons and sons' sons, and their families,
Tall youths and sunny maidens—a glad group,
That glow'd in generous blood and had no care,
And little thought of the future—follow'd him;—
Some perch'd on gallant steeds, others, more slow,
The infants and the matrons of the flock,
In coach and jersey,—but all moving on
To the new land of promise, full of dreams
Of western riches, Mississippi-mad!
Then came the hands, some forty-five or more,
Their moderate wealth united—some in carts
Laden with mattresses;—on ponies some;
Others, more sturdy, following close afoot,
Chattering like jays, and keeping, as they went,
Good time to Juba's creaking violin.
I met and spoke them. The old patriarch,
The grandsire of the goodly family,
Told me his story, and a few brief words
Unfolded that of thousands. Discontent,
With a vague yearning for a better clime,
And richer fields than thine, old Carolina,
Led him to roam . . .
. . . His are sparkling dreams,
As fond as those of boyhood. Golden stores
They promise him in Mississippian vales,
Outshining all the past, compensating—
So thinks he idly—for the home he leaves,
The grave he should have chosen, and the walks,
And well-known fitness of his ancient woods.
Self-exiled, in his age he hath gone forth
To the abodes of strangers,—seeking wealth—
Not wealth, but money! What affections sweet—
What dear abodes—what blessing, happy joys—
What hopes, what hearts, what affluence, what ties,
In a mad barter where we lose our all,
For that which an old trunk, a few feet square,
May compass like our coffin! That old man

Can take no root again! He hath snapp'd off
The ancient tendrils, and in foreign clay
His branches will all wither. Yet he goes,
Falsely persuaded that a bloated purse
Is an affection—is a life— . . .
I could weep for him,
Thus banish'd by that madness of the mind,
. . . Let him go.

(*Poems* 2 : 163–65)

The trunks of western settlers imaged as coffins. A once sturdy old tree uprooted and unable to produce leaves from a withered branch. This is the stuff of Simms's poetic genius; and Simms is the genuine poet: mentor, prophet, seer, minister to man, and, as well, a careful and consummate craftsman.

His poems are the moral monuments of the spirit's making that he intended them to be. They come out of old America to speak most pertinently to a present whose problems often arise from a wholesale disregard and violation of place; in other words, from the same rootlessness, alienation, and empiricism that can finally only lead to extinction, and of which our mentor-poet forewarned us in a work like "The Traveller's Rest."

NOTES

1. The 1842 version is in *Magnolia* ns 1 (November 1842): 285–88. The 1849 version appeared in Simms's *The Cassique of Accabee* 53–69; and in Simms's *Poems* 2: 22–35. It is reprinted in Kibler, *Selected Poems of William Gilmore Simms* 155–65.

2. Simms's *The Social Principle* was delivered as a speech at the University of Alabama in 1842 and published as a pamphlet in Tuscaloosa in 1843. In the last sentence, note the similarity to Hawthorne's "Celestial Railroad" (1843).

3. This is, in fact, a major unifying theme of *I'll Take My Stand*.

4. As expressed in Richard Weaver's *The Southern Essays of Richard Weaver* 50–73.

WORKS CITED

Berry, Wendell. *The Wild Birds.* San Francisco: North Point, 1986.
Kibler, James E., ed. *Selected Poems of William Gilmore Simms.* Athens: University of Georgia Press, 1990.

Simms, William Gilmore. *The Cassique of Accabee.* Charleston: John Russell, 1849.
———. "The Philosophy of the Omnibus." *Southern Literary Journal* 4 (December 1838): 401–10.
———. *Poems.* Vol. 2. Charleston: John Russell, 1853.
———. *The Social Principle.* Tuscaloosa: The Erosophic Society of the University of Alabama, 1843.
———. "The Traveller's Rest." *Magnolia* ns 1 (November 1842): 285–88.
Weaver, Richard. *The Southern Essays of Richard Weaver.* Indianapolis: Liberty, 1987.

The Cub of the Panther:
A New Frontier

It is probable that *The Cub of the Panther* is the least read of all Simms's books; one reason, of course, is that its only publication is the serialization in *The Old Guard* in 1869.[1] W. P. Trent may have read the book; he said it "deserves only one comment. It shows plainly that Simms was beginning to realize that the day of the romancer was over, and that that of the realist was dawning" (315).[2] Charles Watson has read it and pointed out that Simms's plot and theme are adapted from George Eliot's *Adam Bede* to fit the detailed notes taken on his mountain trip, composing as Watson claims "a full-fledged local-color novel" (30). Mary Ann Wimsatt devotes several pages of her book to *The Cub*, emphasizing its realistic setting, its legendary events, the mountain dialect, "the conflict of social groups," and the main plot of "a rural girl's love for a rich outsider who brings her only infamy and suffering" as typical of local color (241–42).[3] Guilds's biography dwells mainly on the composition of *The Cub* and its real-life genesis in a hunting trip to Polk and Buncombe Counties, North Carolina, in 1847 (*Simms* 314–16).[4]

Postbellum life was very difficult for Simms. The plantation had suffered alternating drought and monsoons for years. Living in Charleston in 1868 and overseeing the rebuilding of his home at Woodlands from the burned ruins left by Union Army stragglers in 1865, Simms had now rebuilt four rooms and was seeking secondhand furnishings. His grown family scattered in several locations, he tried to secure medicines for his grandchildren, and he himself had a motherless child of six. Friends of his, and widows of friends, were destitute. The local blacks, now free and often homeless, marauded the countryside, picking up anything they could, worrying Simms about violence,[5] and now Simms had to come up with material for monthly installments of another novel.

Antebellum life rested on slavery, and postbellum experience was short, painful, and to Simms probably not very interesting as literary material. With only three years' experience of Southern life without possessions or slaves, Simms no doubt cast around for a subject. He found a new frontier when he attempted through his fiction to understand and accept the new postwar social order. Hence, as he had looked to the Revolutionary War backwoods for *Joscelyn* in 1867 and to the 1820s North Carolina mountains for *Voltmeier* in 1868, he turned to the contemporary backwoods for *The Cub of the Panther* in 1868–1869.

Simms must have worried that his postwar audience, even the pro-Southern audience of a "Copperhead" publication, would find slavery unacceptable even if used only as a social symbol. Therefore, in defining characters he had to rely less on the way they treated slaves (as he had done in earlier stories), and more on their attitudes toward work and hired servants, a class of people not previously used extensively in Simms books. And so, slavery being no longer an appropriate paradigm for identifying social relationships, he moved his setting from low-country South Carolina to western North Carolina, where historically there were few slaves and a hardy yeoman class.

Setting this story in the North Carolina mountains did three things for Simms. 1) It took the germ of the narrative, along with the scenery and folklore, from the notes ready-made in his journal and from several previous nonfiction usages.[6] 2) Realistically, it gave him a historically accurate setting essentially without slaves.[7] 3) Most important, when divorced by geography and social norms from the antebellum low country, Simms was left to face the fact of postwar life, not only devoid of slaves but also devoid of all those other class distinctions that accompanied slavery in the Old South.[8] As Simms said, this was "out of the beaten path."

Simms's selection of mountain material for four of his five last-written fictions represents not merely a geographical and historical frontier, but also a psychological one.[9] Somewhat like Rip Van Winkle, whose pre–Revolutionary War coping tactics are not always appropriate when he wakes up to a new order, Simms must try to portray Southern life before the Civil War in a way that will be both truthful—his first criterion for fiction—and acceptable to a postwar Northern audience.[10] And so Simms's new frontier is a new order of domestic society where distinctions between common sense and pretense and between class and crass cannot be so easily symbolized merely by the possession of happy and occasionally outspoken

Negro servants. In spite of its supposed legendary theme, Simms devoted at least half the novel to the domestic drama of manners, as he already had done in scores of books; but to portray servitude and class in 1868 he had to find a mode for examining and understanding the values and social mores appropriate to the reconstructed new nation.

The Cub of the Panther is really two stories. The first (comprising eight installments) is the courtship and betrayal of Rose Carter. Mike Baynam, a professional hunter, courts Rose, a poor but educated and pretentious neighbor. Both Baynam's sister Mattie Fuller and Rose's aunt Betsy Moore recognize that Rose's flirtations and Mike's social awkwardness make the match difficult, but they encourage the relationship as a sensible one for Rose. The rich and haughty Widow Fairleigh "hires" Rose as her companion, leading not only to economic and social exploitation, but ultimately to her seduction and pregnancy by the widow's dissolute son Edward. When Rose flees into a snowstorm and dies giving birth to the Cub, the babe is rescued and adopted by Mike Baynam. The second story (comprising the last four installments) is a hunting tale and resolves the conflict between Baynam and Fairleigh when the teenaged Cub, now an accomplished hunter, kills his natural father in self-defense. The Widow Fairleigh dies, Edward's estranged wife inherits the estate, and the Cub and his adopted family continue their simple life.

Determining the historical context for this book may be more important than for any other Simms wrote. The narration was virtually contemporary with its composition, that is, around 1867, but its story begins twenty years earlier—Simms's only book spanning the Civil War. In chapter 10, the writer cites several folk games that "existed, for a century, and within the last thirty years," games about which he had "notes made on the spot about a quarter of a century ago," meaning 1847, when Simms made the mountain hunting trip. A main character, Sam Fuller "had been, at fifteen, a pupil of [Jim] Fisher at sixty" (198).[11] Therefore, the courtship of Rose Carter must have occurred around 1847, the Cub of the Panther would have been born around 1850, and the culminating event of his father's death on the boy's seventeenth birthday must have occurred in 1867. The Civil War stands as a significant cultural and psychological divide between these two important fictional events.[12]

Simms's primary mode of examining postwar values was to adapt an old method. He set up contrasting pairs of characters, overlapped the pairs, and teased out parallel scenes. The most obvious pairs of characters are the two professional hunters, brothers-in-law Sam Fuller and Mike Baynam and their sons Mike Baynam Fuller and the orphaned adopted child, the Cub of the Panther. Another pair are the inept hunters whom Simms calls the squirearchy—hard-drinking, womanizing college friends Bulkley and Fairleigh, the latter also contrasted to Mike Baynam, his rival for Rose Carter's attentions. And implicitly Simms contrasts Rose and the woman who eventually marries young Fairleigh.

Simms's development and use of these pairings can be best summarized in the dialectic between the plain, commonsensical, and outspoken Aunt Betsy Moore and her social-climbing and pretentious sister, the Widow Jane Carter. Simms refers to them as "Doric and Corinthian in the same Building" (262). The Widow Carter insists that her daughter Rose "is worthy of any gentleman. . . . I should prefer that she should marry a gentleman of one or other of the professions. She has a right to enter the best society, and to associate with fashionable people . . . and need not fling herself away upon any man living in obscurity" (24). To this her sensible sister Betsy Moore just quips, "That's very well, Jane, but you might have said it in fewer words" (24). When the Widow Carter opines that "Hunters are generally rude men, of bad manners, rough, uncourtly, not knowing how to behave well in company, and society refuses to recognize them accordingly" (22), Aunt Betsy's terse humor makes her the clear spokesman for the "correct" point of view. She chastises, "what's the use of talking generally about hunters, when here's the particular pusson before us, and we all know that he aint none of your common hunters, and is a gentleman by natur. And natur kin make a gentleman, sister Carter, quite as well as society. It's born in a man" (22).

But each of these good ladies is also reflected: Aunt Betsy is mirrored by Mattie Fuller, the sister of hunter Mike Baynam, the wife of the yeoman farmer and hunter Sam Fuller, and the woman who becomes the surrogate mother of the Cub. Both speak in the vernacular, and Mattie is said to have "a good deal of low humor, and [she] possessed a coarse talent for mimicry, which, in dealing with the stately Lady Carter, she put to the most mischievous uses. . . . and her imitations of the big dictionary language of the widow were quite . . . ludicrous" (194). Mattie's opinion of the Widow Carter is fully as low as the widow's opinion of Mattie's brother Mike: she's a "cantankerous, redickilous, rheumatic, old head-twisted woman" (194).

If the Widow Carter suffers from "conceits and vanities" and would be "finished . . . and polished . . . ef only the money was not wanting" (194), she is mirrored by Widow Flora Fairleigh. When the Widow Fairleigh calls at Rosedale Cottage, she "proposed to take the Widow Carter by storm," but, listening to Widow Carter attempt to counterimpress her with Rose's accomplishments and education, "Mrs. Fairleigh was fairly overcome, overwhelmed! Mrs. Carter had beaten her at her own weapons. Mrs. Fairleigh gasped for breath. But Mrs. Carter, even at the close of her speech, betrayed no symptoms of exhaustion" (336–37). This verbal sparring is designed by Widow Carter to encourage a match between young Fairleigh and Rose and by Widow Fairleigh to seduce Rose into becoming her "companion." This false and pretentious conversation foreshadows Widow Fairleigh's deception about Rose's companionship, which deteriorates into servanthood, a fraudulent marriage, and finally a midnight flight.

Mirror images also occur within the three pairs of men—the yeoman hunters, the foppish squirearchy, and the youths. But the pairs confront each other, and hence their value schemes, when hunters and fops cross paths first in the courtship of Rose Carter in 1847 and again on the hunting field in 1867. In the courting (or stalking) of Rose Carter, young Fairleigh, seconded by Bulkley, is educated, pretentious, flashy, selfish, aggressive, and savvy, while Mike Baynam, seconded by Fuller, is uneducated, socially backward, indecisive, and ultimately melancholy. Rose is seduced by the glamour of being companion to Widow Fairleigh and her son Edward on the summer social circuit to New York and New England, only to be abandoned by the son after a secret marriage performed by a fake priest. The melodramatic ending to Rose's story is not unexpected since she and her mother had the benefits of a protective suitor and of Aunt Betsy's common sense. Rose chose the false values.

The hunting motif, culminating with two hunts at the end of the novel, shifts from the contrast between the suitors of Rose Carter in 1847 to the contrast between the father, Squire Fairleigh, and his natural son, the Cub of the Panther, around 1867. The Cub and his adopted father Baynam have amply demonstrated their skill as professional hunters and their generosity in supplying meat to neighbors, while the natural father Fairleigh and his postwar cronies have displayed gross incompetence in both bear and deer hunting. It is no surprise, then, that in the first hunt the drunken Fairleigh botches a bear kill; the Cub "puts in" with his knife to split the bear's heart, saving his father's life and in the melee stabbing Fairleigh's thigh. This so enrages the squire that, when he returns to the lodge, he strikes his wife Gabriella in the mouth and then slaps her. The contrast is obvious between the debauched destroyer and wastrel Fairleigh and his altruistic son, who has saved a stranger's life.

On the second hunt—the occasion of the Cub's seventeenth birthday—the Oedipal theme is concluded. The unlearned youth unwittingly violates the rules of *venerie* when he shoots a deer in territory staked out by Fairleigh's party. "Inflamed with passion and strong drink, Fairleigh . . . vent[s] the bitterest curses upon the youth" and then strikes him with his horsewhip (897). Shocked, the Cub drives "his knife deep into the body of his assailant." Fairleigh is transported home, where he dies, learning in his mortal suffering of the kinship between them (898). All this sounds familiar; it is Simms doing what he has done before: exploring the class, social, economic, and educational differences—false and true—in domestic relations.

The war had put Simms in a dilemma that he solved by choosing a politically neutral setting. Yet, social commentary in the scenes between these two important hunts provides additional insight into Simms's own struggle to realign his thinking to the new order. Conduct that may have been foolish, yet condoned, in the old order can no longer be assumed automatically to be appropriate; Simms now lacks the ready clichés, such as dueling, that were available to him in earlier fiction. Fairleigh's act of striking his wife is, naturally, condemned by the narrator, the Widow Fairleigh, and her houseguests. Despite previous representations of Gabriella as the haughty Englishwoman, in this scene "the contrast between her noble presence and that of her lord, he bloated, obese, and somewhat infirm from frequent debauchery, made itself felt to all spectators" (814). In 1867, after Gabriella flees the lodge with her Irish maid under escort by Bulkley on the seventeenth anniversary of Rose's midwinter flight, one Major Todd approaches Fairleigh to entreat him to duel his old college friend Bulkley as a matter of honor.[13] Although the convention of dueling seems anachronistic, its use in this scene evokes antipathy toward the practice, and hence toward the social class that would condone it.

Simms does not risk the reader's mistaking Major Todd for an honorable man, nor Fairleigh for an imperceptive fool. First, for example, the major, as spokesman for an anachronistic code of honor, refers to Gabriella's flight under Bulkley's escort as having "dishonored [Fairleigh's] name forever." He believes that, "according to the custom of the country, Fairleigh should either challenge Bulkley or shoot him down upon the highway," and Todd offers to be Fairleigh's second (817). The erroneous "opinion of Major Todd, as that of everybody besides, regarded the flight of Mrs. Fairleigh as only the crowning act" of a long and treacherous liaison between herself and Bulkley, and Todd insists that Fairleigh has suffered a "mortal disgrace" (818). Second, and in contrast, Fairleigh is perceptive enough to know that Bulkley will fight and therefore wants nothing to do with a challenge. In fact, Fairleigh proclaims his gratitude at being relieved of "a most burdensome charge, of a great annoyance" by Bulkley's apparent elopement with Gabriella. Fairleigh recognizes that Todd is merely a "d--d fire-eater, who is for getting everybody into a fight to gratify his own vanity" (819). Finally, the narrator, who uses rhetoric associated with the highly charged political acrimony preceding the Civil War, condemns a class whose honor needs defending by a duel. According to the narrator, "Major Todd was a fire eater" (817). After Fairleigh drunkenly decries public opinion and declares that money, good food, and liquor are the only requisites for companionship, the narrator says he suffers from "imbecility,"[14] and his circle of acquaintance is "obtuse . . . and greedy" (819). In short, Fairleigh "had declined . . . upon a lower range of companions, that class to whom the phraseology of the present day has given the name of 'scallawags'" (819).

Simms was in good control of several structural elements, including parallel scenes, that advance his themes. Fairleigh's English wife Gabriella, suffering under his violence and fraud, learns (unlike Rose) to moderate her supposed superiority, and, like Rose, she also flees on a winter night to the protection of a benefactor. But, unlike the mountain girl who languishes in 1850 in childbirth in the snow, when the Cub kills Fairleigh in 1867, Gabriella inherits Fairleigh Lodge, despite having already initiated divorce proceedings. Gabriella is able to inherit because her mother-in-law, hearing of her son's injuries, predeceases him by five hours. The Widow Fairleigh's dying of shock upon hearing of the mortal wound of her child is itself a repetition of the Widow Carter's sudden death in 1850 upon hearing that the unmarried Rose had given birth and was dying in Mattie Fuller's cabin.

Other paired episodes and themes could be examined: two charivaris (the wedding party and the chinquapin hunt), bear and deer hunts precursive to the climactic ones mentioned above, the midnight flights from Fairleigh Lodge, and so on. As they mature the youths learn to respect that young Fuller is bookish and undextrous, while the Cub is stealthy but unacademic.

Toward the end of the novel the unschooled master hunter Baynam validates education by sending his nephew Fuller to high school in Spartanburg
and to further study to become a successful clergyman.

The last point about Simms's new frontier concerns the servants in *The
Cub of the Panther*. For the first time Simms finds black slaves politically
incorrect and is unwilling to give them speaking parts. It will be well to
recall a scene that, though typical in the prewar fiction, was no longer available to Simms. In *Woodcraft* (1854) Captain Porgy attempts to free his faithful slave Tom, whose reply is well known: "No! no! maussa. . . . I kain't t'ink
ob letting you off dis way. . . . You hab for keep dis nigger long as he lib;
and him for keep you. You hab for fin' he dinner, and Tom hab for cook
'em. Free nigger no hab any body for fin' 'em he bittle [victuals]. . . . I no
guine to be free no way you kin fix it; so, maussa, don't you bodder me wid
dis nonsense t'ing 'bout free paper any more. . . . You b'longs to me Tom,
jes' as much as me Tom b'long to you; and you nebber guine git you free
paper from me long as you lib" (528).[15]

Instead, in the postbellum novel Simms features only white females as
servants, depicting them as exploited yet fully capable, in some cases, of
being mean-spirited exploiters themselves. In spite of some comfort and
much pretension in the antebellum Rosedale Cottage, Aunt Betsy apparently does, or at least supervises, all the work there: "I'm a doing all the
work from sun up to sun down; I puts the house to rights every day; sees to
the garden; I milks the keows; scours the floor hafe the time; washes up the
plates and dishes, and cups and sassers; makes the coffee; makes the beds;
and when any comp'ny comes, who cooks the dinner ef 'taint me?" (314).
The Carter family is assisted, in 1847, by a young share-farmer named
Jupe, a Negress who is cook and washerwoman, and a twelve-year-old Negro girl. Nothing more is said of them. In contrast, Widow Fairleigh boasts
that she owns "twenty thousand acres of the best lands in North Carolina,
two hundred slaves, seven hundred head of cattle, and all things of the plantation," and she rides in a carriage with a driver. Still she needs Rose to
entertain her by reading, singing, and playing the piano (341), a role never
before required of white women in a Simms novel.

When she attempts to secure an unpaid traveling companion in Rose Carter, Widow Fairleigh suggests that she will "pay all expenses of Rose. . . .
[and] a liberal allowance—a salary." Her mother declares, however, that
Rose "can take no salary, . . . only another name for wages" (341). Widow

Fairleigh proclaims that her use of the word "salary" was "a mere inadvertence." Thus, the greed and mean spirit of the Widow Fairleigh and the vanity and conceit of the Widow Carter conspire to make a virtual slave of Rose Carter, leading to her betrayal and death. The narrator states, in fact, that the Widow Fairleigh "contemplated the acquisition of a servant" (339), and Simms is no doubt being ironic when the narrator refers to Rose as an "inmate of Fairleigh Lodge" (342).

In 1847 a Miss Hall has been companion to the Widow Fairleigh for five years, and she had, to quote the narrator, "made the poor girl a slave; giving her small compensation and exacting all manner of service, which left her but little repose or leisure. From this bondage Miss Hall was about to escape. She was about to marry" (333). Had the Widow Carter been more humble and less talkative, she would have realized, when she insisted that "Rose Carter can take no salary. . . . She is no hireling, no servant, no housekeeper, no governess" (341), that she was merely giving her child up into slavery. Simms did not do this inadvertently: he was completely aware of his point that the hireling was nothing more than a wage slave, and one of the points he drove home is that bad mistresses oppress slaves and servants alike.[16]

Sweetzer, the third servant, is the housekeeper and treacherous confidante of Widow Fairleigh, apparently responsible for keeping her fully informed about all the other servants, including Rose Carter. It is this old lady who discovers Rose's fake wedding ring and her pregnancy. Sweetzer searches Rose's clothing while the poor girl sleeps, but she is unable to find the fraudulent marriage certificate sewn into the skirt. Sweetzer has more luck intercepting the black mail boy with Rose's letter to her supposed husband, young Edward Fairleigh. Upon this revelation, Rose produces the certificate, which the Widow Fairleigh snatches and destroys. That night Rose runs away and is dead the next morning. To the widow's credit, she does send Tom and Boston, presumably two Negro slaves, into the night looking for Rose. No other servants appear in the episodes set in 1847–1850.

In the postwar story several servants are mentioned, including Gabriella's Irish maid. Yet only one servant is identified as being a Negro, Fairleigh's "body servant, Jared," whose main duties consist of carrying Fairleigh's "capacious valise, . . . bountifully supplied with . . . an ample store of mountain rye, and the inevitable peach and honey" (812). He returns to the lodge for clothing and dressings after Fairleigh is wounded in the thigh, and while on this errand apprises "the household, high and low" of Fairleigh's drunken mishap. This servant may hold some opinions disapproving of his employer's actions, but—unlike Hector or Tom—he has no opportunity to say so.

The point here is that manual work is done by the plain characters both before and after the war and is apparently valued by Simms. Yet Simms is ambivalent about whether work should be done by educated or upper-class characters. Certainly Simms had known hard work all his life and in 1868 was attempting to perform subsistence farming with only family members to do the labor. Yet the duties required of Rose by Widow Fairleigh—in addition to musical performance they include domestic services, such as reading aloud, sewing, knitting, and "doing up of the muslins" (411), and clerk's duties, such as writing to tenants, bookkeeping, accounting, and "other business matters" (418)—are chores inappropriate in the author's mind for a young woman of Rose's education, accomplishments, and aspirations. Widow Fairleigh's thinking of Rose as a possession surely denotes in Simms's scheme that Rose has become enslaved by her own vanity. Miss Hall is pitied by the narrator for having been made "a slave" from which "bondage" she "escapes" through marriage. Those who have slaves are depicted as overbearing and materialistic—a far cry from most slaveholders in Simms's earlier works. Finally, Sweetzer is analogous to the heartless overseer, a character often depicted in antebellum fiction, yet she "oversees" white governesses instead of field slaves. Only the Irish maid Bridget, who accompanies her mistress on her flight in the postwar episode, is well treated by the now-redeemed Gabriella.

The Cub of the Panther may be a more important book than we have heretofore recognized. Simms was approaching a new frontier, not only in technique and setting, but also in structure, characterization, theme, and personal acceptance of a different "world order." But like his Revolutionary War fiction, particularly *Woodcraft* and *Katharine Walton*, this novel of the North Carolina mountains is a vehicle for contemplating the change from the old order to the new. It had been a wrenching change in Simms's homeland, in his social order, in the economic order, and in the moral order, as Simms himself was learning. Simms was struggling with these changes; but he had his vocation to help him understand them. He was not fully successful, and maybe he would have abandoned the attempt, for he intended to go back to the American Revolution in his next project—the study of

George Washington. Yet under the adverse conditions he suffered in 1868–1869, the novel looks forward, not only to realism and local color, but to a new postbellum South with revitalized social structures, values, economics, and even popular education.

NOTES

1. *The Old Guard* 7 (January–December 1869): 11–26, 91–102, 183–200, 255–68, 331–45, 411–23, 491–504, 571–83, 651–65, 731–48, 811–26, 891–99. Hereinafter cited within the text by page numbers.

2. According to Trent, Simms "did his best in the early chapters, and indeed throughout the story, to give a plain description of the life of a peculiar mountain people. He did not succeed."

3. Wimsatt points out that this is the first novel in which the rustic characters represent Simms's values.

4. Guilds tracks the composition and concludes that the "story lacks unity and balance, . . . [and] suffers in comparison with Simms's better work" (*Simms* 315).

5. *Letters* 5:131, 136.

6. Simms, "Summer Travel." See Shillingsburg, "From Notes to Novel," and Shillingsburg, ed., "Idylls of the Apalachian" parts 1 and 2.

7. Simms's concurrent fictional accounts of the mountain material include *Voltmeier* in *The Illuminated Western World* and "How Sharp Snaffles Got His Capital and Wife" in *Harper's Magazine*.

8. Shillingsburg, "Simms's Last Novel," describes the character distinctions: the rustic hero Baynam "is never pompous in his language, but he is correct, characterized by neither the country idiom, mispronunciation, nor incorrect grammar. The widows, Rose Carter, and the 'nabobs' of Fairleigh Lodge are usually pretentious in their language, while the simple hunters and farmers and Aunt Betsy employ highly picturesque figures of speech, dialectic pronunciations, and any number of 'vulgar' terms" (117).

9. The apparently last-written story is set in New York City, a place not unknown in Simms's works but seldom used in his fiction.

10. In speaking of the moral of this novel, Simms wrote toward its end that the moral "is always present in the perfect truth, which is, however paradoxical it may seem, the true secret in all perfect fiction" (815).

11. See Shillingsburg, "An Edition of William Gilmore Simms's *The Cub of the Panther*" 39–40. This would date Fuller's tutelage around 1837, for, from Simms's notebook, we know that the real-life hunter Jim Fisher was about seventy years old when Simms had met him in 1847 on the hunting expedition, and Fuller is twenty-five years old in the novel's earliest episodes.

12. However, the fringes of the narration are very ragged. In the last paragraph it is discovered that the two hunters Baynam and Fuller were "when last heard from . . . seventy-five [and] seventy-two." This would mean that Fuller was born around 1795 (the approximate birth date of his tutor, the real-life Jim Fisher), and nearly thirty years would have transpired between the death of the Cub's father and the last paragraph. Moreover, Mattie Fuller is said to have "been long since gathered to her mothers, having left five stalwart sons, all hunters like their sire"; yet her son Mike Baynam Fuller (who became an Episcopal clergyman) was apparently an only child for seventeen years, hunting with his supposed cousin, the Cub. Clearly, somebody got confused in tying up the last paragraph.

13. Simms was well acquainted with Southern dueling: his marriage to Chevillette Roach may have been delayed because of the death in 1836 of her only sibling, the result of a duel in 1833. Moreover, Simms himself apparently was challenged to a duel in 1846 over a review he had written; because of intervention by a mutual friend, the duel never took place. (See *Letters* 1:90 n; 2:201–3, 258–61; and Guilds, *Simms* 246.)

14. See Shillingsburg, "Simms's Failed Lecture Tour of 1856." *Imbecile* was a key word in Charles Sumner's speech on Kansas, in which he maligned South Carolina and Senator Butler in 1856, and in Simms's refutation in 1857 of Sumner's misrepresentations.

15. An equally familiar passage occurs in *The Yemassee*, when Hector thrice refuses his freedom, at last explaining:

"I d--n to h-ll, maussa, ef I guine to be free!" roared the adhesive black, in a tone of unrestrainable determination. "I can't loss you company, and who de debble Dugdale guine let feed him like Hector? 'Tis onpossible, maussa, and dere's no use for talk 'bout it. De ting ain't right; and enty I know wha' kind of ting freedom is wid black man? Ha! you make Hector free, he turn wuss more nor poor buckrah—he tief out of de shop—he get drunk and lie in de ditch—den, if sick come, he roll, he toss in de wet grass of de stable. You come in de morning, Hector dead—and who know, he no take physic, he no hab parson—who know, I say, maussa, but de debble fine 'em 'fore anybody else? No, maussa—you and Dugdale berry good company for Hector. I tank God he so good—I no' want better." (437–38)

16. A more sophisticated fictional presentation of the dialectic over slavery occurs in the story "Oakatibbe, or the Choctaw Sampson" concerning whether the Indian, reared in white society, will revert to his native state upon leaving the society. A surrogate for the debate on the benefits and burdens of slavery, Simms's narrator concludes that only nations—not individuals—can be raised from savagery to civilization, such as with the Hebrews and the Saxons of ancient times. Such experiments have been successful only when "under the full control of an already

civilized people" (*Wigwam* 184). Although black slaves are prominent in "Oaka-tibbe," and although the Indian "will defer even to the negro who has been edu-cated by the white man" (189), the story is only implicitly a parable of the European and the African, though it cites the Texans and the Mexicans and other master-slave or conqueror-conquered pairs.

WORKS CITED

Guilds, John Caldwell. *Simms: A Literary Life.* Fayetteville: University of Arkansas Press, 1992.

———, ed. *"Long Years of Neglect": The Work and Reputation of William Gilmore Simms.* Fayetteville: University of Arkansas Press, 1988.

Shillingsburg, Miriam J. "An Edition of William Gilmore Simms's *The Cub of the Panther.*" Diss. University of South Carolina, 1969.

———. "From Notes to Novel: William Gilmore Simms's Creative Method." *Southern Literary Journal* 5, no. 1 (1972): 89–107.

———. "Simms's Failed Lecture Tour of 1856: The Mind of the North." *"Long Years of Neglect": The Work and Reputation of William Gilmore Simms.* Ed. John Caldwell Guilds. Fayetteville: University of Arkansas Press, 1988. 183–201.

———. "Simms's Last Novel, *The Cub of the Panther.*" *Southern Literary Journal* 17, no. 2 (1985): 108–19.

———, ed. "Idylls of the Apalachian" parts 1 and 2. *Appalachian Journal* 1 (1972–1973): 2–11, 146–60.

Simms, William Gilmore. *The Cub of the Panther.* Printed in installments in *The Old Guard* 7 (January–December 1869): 11–26, 91–102, 183–200, 255–68, 331–45, 411–23, 491–504, 571–83, 651–65, 731–48, 811–26, 891–99. Manuscript chapters in Charles Carroll Simms Collection, South Caroliniana Library, Columbia, South Carolina.

———. "How Sharp Snaffles Got His Capital and Wife." *Harper's Magazine* 41 (October 1870): 667–87.

———. *The Letters of William Gilmore Simms.* 5 vols. Ed. Mary C. Simms Oliphant, Alfred Taylor Odell, and T. C. Duncan Eaves. Columbia: University of South Carolina Press, 1952–1956. (A sixth volume, *The Letters of William Gilmore Simms: Supplement [1834–1870],* ed. Oliphant and Eaves, was published by the University of South Carolina Press in 1982.)

———. "Summer Travel in the South." *Southern Quarterly Review* 17 (September 1850): 24–65.

———. *Voltmeier.* Columbia: University of South Carolina Press, 1969.

———. *The Wigwam and the Cabin.* New York: Wiley and Putnam, 1845.

———. *Woodcraft; or, Hawks About the Dovecote.* New York: Redfield, 1854.

———. *The Yemassee*. New and rev. ed. New York: Redfield, 1853.
Trent, William Peterfield. *William Gilmore Simms*. Ed. Charles Dudley Warner. American Men of Letters Series. Boston: Houghton Mifflin, 1892.
Watson, Charles S. "Simms and the Beginnings of Local Color." *Mississippi Quarterly* 35 (1981–1982): 25–39.
Wimsatt, Mary Ann. *The Major Fiction of William Gilmore Simms: Cultural Traditions and Literary Form*. Baton Rouge: Louisiana State University Press, 1989.

Literary Legacies:
Simms and Other Writers

DIANNE C. LUCE

John A. Murrell and the Imaginations
of Simms and Faulkner

Although John Murrell is relatively unknown today, his exploits
as a bandit on the Natchez Trace, as well as his attempt to establish in
the South a criminal organization of unparalleled scale and to maintain it
through his knowledge of the law, have earned him a place in the history
of the Tennessee and Mississippi frontiers. But his only worthwhile accomplishment is having ignited the imaginations of such Southern fiction writers as William Gilmore Simms, in Murrell's lifetime, and William Faulkner a century later. There is no doubt that Simms knew of John Murrell
before he began writing *Richard Hurdis* (1838) and *Border Beagles* (1840).
Simms's two novels were written soon after the public excitement over
Murrell's design to organize a simultaneous insurrection of slaves throughout the South with the help of hundreds of secret, often socially respectable
members of his "Mystic Confederacy." The detection of this plan led to
the publication of the two nineteenth-century accounts that best document
Murrell's career and that serve as the primary foundation for twentieth-
century accounts.

The first, a pamphlet of fewer than eighty pages published in late February 1835 under the name of Augustus Q. Walton in Cincinnati, addresses
Murrell's initial detection and capture almost exclusively, recounting the
adventures of a young Tennessean named Virgil Stewart. In January 1834,
Stewart set out in pursuit of Murrell, hoping to recover some stolen slaves,
but when Murrell unexpectedly overtook Stewart on the road and gradually
revealed the workings of his outlaw gang, including plans to incite a slave
insurrection on Christmas 1835, Stewart's goal became to rescue society
from murder and mayhem. Stewart left the outlaw camp and returned to
Tennessee with his story. Murrell was arrested and tried for stealing Negroes in July 1834. According to Stewart, Murrell's allies attempted to discredit his testimony and plotted against his life: on his way to Lexington,
Kentucky, he was accosted by assassins and was wounded. Several weeks

later, fearing he would die, he gave his papers to Walton, who oversaw the publication of the narrative.[1]

The second account of Stewart's dealings with Murrell, published in New York in 1836 or very early 1837 under the name of H. R. Howard, preserves the earlier version almost in its entirety, though revising and expanding it. It seems that this later account was prompted by Stewart's fear that Murrell, with accomplices in esteemed positions within the border communities, would succeed not only in evading justice but in destroying the reputation of the man who had dared to testify against him (two of Murrell's associates had published a pamphlet of their own in his defense). Almost every addition in the Howard version corroborates Stewart's story, vindicates his actions, or defends his honor and public spirit. Early portions of the narrative are interspersed with numerous documents attesting to Stewart's character and verifying his account. A major addition is "a full history of the insurrectionary movements among the negroes in the southern country during the summer of 1835" (vi), including evidence that the proposed slave uprising would have occurred on the Fourth of July, 1835, if the alerted citizens had not summarily prevented it by hanging suspected conspirators. Such allegations were apparently intended to confirm that Stewart's warning published the previous February had been valid.[2] For this reason, the Howard account also includes evidence gathered after the fact against those who had targeted Stewart for retribution.

In both the first and revised editions of *Richard Hurdis*, Simms directly refers to one or the other of these accounts when he identifies the Mystic Confederacy as "a fraternity, upon the borders of the new states, the history of which, already in part given to the public, is a dreadful chronicle of desperate crime, and insolent incendiarism" (221; see also 1838 ed. 2:63). Though the novels include no verbal echoes of either the Walton or the Howard narratives except for the argot of the Murrell outlaws (the "Mystic Confederacy," "clan" or "brotherhood," "mystic signs," the "Grand Council," "strikers," and his use of the names Nawls and Yarbers, both mentioned, though not prominently, in Stewart's accounts [Howard 117; Walton 61]), it is likely that Simms read at least the Howard narrative.[3]

The reader of Simms will easily recognize the material that he derived from Stewart. The existence of an extensive confederacy of outlaws throughout the Southern states, a secret anti-society with its own laws, customs, power structure, and systems of reward and punishment, whose members infiltrate and prey upon the legitimate social order and are dedicated to its overthrow, is a seminal concept behind the plots of both *Richard Hurdis* and

Border Beagles. In each novel, the hero is motivated by his loyalty to individuals to defend the larger cause of the emerging frontier society from the internal threat posed by the confederacy of the respectable but ruthless— and their tools, the poor and disaffected. Although the role of Murrell is reproduced in Simms's novels in the characters of Foster and Saxon, and that of Stewart in Richard Hurdis and Harry Vernon, Simms was less concerned with the historical personalities of the clan's leader or his captor than with the nature and workings of the confederacy itself, and he follows Stewart very closely for these details without constraining himself to historical realism in the depiction of his heroes and villains. For *Richard Hurdis,* Simms drew primarily on the plot of detection that is the focus of Walton's account, while the plot of *Border Beagles* owes more to the chronicles added in Howard's version of the clan's attempts to kill or discredit Stewart and of the frontier government's efforts to squelch the outlaws. Simms borrows from Stewart's experiences the device of the trickster tricked, as Richard Hurdis, like Stewart, draws the outlaw leader to reveal his secrets and the location of his headquarters at the very time that Foster thinks he is drawing Hurdis into the confederacy. In *Border Beagles,* this plot element undergoes comic transmutation as the actor Tom Horsey unwittingly infiltrates the outlaws' camp in the swamp. A related borrowing is the theme of the double hypocrisy in *Richard Hurdis*—the outlaw who pretends to be a parson, the good citizen who pretends to be corrupt—and its comic subordination in the acting and disguise material centered on Tom Horsey in *Border Beagles.*

Like Stewart's accounts, Simms's novels of the frontier are at least partly meant as a depiction and perhaps a warning of the present danger to the social fabric of the emerging border communities. Though in his "Advertisement" to the revised edition of *Richard Hurdis* Simms claims to have "exercised the artist's privilege of . . . suppressing the merely loathsome" (11), his outlaws are no lightweights. They condone, order, and commit murders at will. They steal horses, Negroes, and unwary travelers' money. Simms's graphic description of the murder of William Carrington is a composite of several accounts Murrell gave Stewart of murdering travelers who naively revealed that they were returning from markets or setting off to buy Choctaw lands with ample supplies of cash. As in Murrell's organization, Foster and his council delegate to an underclass of outlaws those crimes they do not wish to implicate themselves in, a practice Simms indicts as cowardly.[4] And Simms's outlaws outdo Murrell's in using blackmail to recruit new members, as in the cases of Pickett and John Hurdis.[5]

What, then, did Simms suppress? Most importantly, he makes no direct mention in either novel of the plot for a large-scale slave rebellion, the prevention of which was the prime motivation, according to Stewart, for all of his actions after leaving Murrell in the swamp. Rather, in *Richard Hurdis* Simms alludes to the insurrection so delicately that only the reader who knew one of Stewart's accounts, or lived in the border states affected, would understand him. When Richard Hurdis meets with Foster in the Sipsy swamp and is shown letters that "develop the large extent of the single confederacy," Richard observes that "Some of the plans contained in these letters were of no less startling character. One . . . was a simultaneous robbery of all the banks" (329). Murrell had told Stewart that a corollary to the slaves' murdering the plantation owners and torching their houses was to be the robbing of the banks in the ensuing confusion. In the next paragraph, Richard says Foster outlined a plan "infinitely more profitable, but far more dangerous." Richard finds this scheme, "the atrociousness of which curdled my blood to read," so appalling that he almost forgets himself: " 'But you will hardly act upon this—it is too—' I was about to say horrible—it was well I did not. Foster fortunately finished the sentence for me in a different manner.

'Too dangerous you would say! It would be to a blunderer. But we should be off the moment it was over. Having made use of the torch, we should only stay long enough to take what was valuable from the house, and not wait until it had tumbled upon us' " (329–30). Only those familiar with Stewart's accounts will infer that Foster speaks of the house as a metaphor for society and will recognize Murrell's plan for a slave insurrection. In *Border Beagles*, Simms refers once to slave rebellion when Edward Mabry accuses his rival John Yarbers of "talking insurrection stuff among the niggers" (218). But Mabry's motives for making this charge are complicated by his competition with Yarbers for the love of Mary Clayton; and there is no hint that Yarbers is part of a wider conspiracy for a nationwide insurrection.

Simms's reasons for suppressing this "loathsomeness" may have been both social and aesthetic ones. First was the simple problem of credibility. Stewart claimed that he had hesitated to disclose the plan for a slave insurrection until he could gather corroborating evidence. When Murrell was arraigned in February 1834,

> In his testimony . . . Mr. Stewart confined himself to such facts as related to the abduction and subsequent disposition of Mr. Henning's

negroes. The deep-laid and sanguinary plot which Murrell had confessed to him was in progress against the southern community, he
deemed it both imprudent and unsafe to disclose at a period so early,
and when the public mind . . . was so little prepared to receive and
credit it. He foresaw the great difficulty of bringing his fellow-citizens
to believe, upon his simple assurance, a narrative, in itself so unnatural
and startling; and revealing a scheme of villany so dark in its conception, so extensive in its operations, as the one which he felt himself
charged with making known to the public. (Howard 123–24)

Stewart's accusations were in fact doubted by many who were readier to
believe counteraccusations that Stewart was maligning an honest citizen.

Even if Simms's art could have conquered the aesthetic problem of plau-
sibility, his sense of social responsibility may have made him reluctant to
present an outline for such a "loathsome" scheme to be read by criminals—
or by abolitionists, some of whom were already recommending insurrection as a "desperate remedy" to the problem of slavery.[6]

Finally, Simms probably found the element of the slave rebellion too
sensational for the purposes of his novels. Its inclusion might have mud-
died his plot and obscured the thematic concerns at the center of his border novels. Rather than focusing on a particular historical assault against
Southern social and economic structure, which would have introduced the
debate over slavery and abolition, he chose to present a more generalized
warning of the danger to his society from within that is especially close to
breaking through in border areas where the institutions of civilization, especially law and justice and education, are weak.

In his depictions of Foster and Saxon, Simms departs from Stewart's accounts of Murrell's background and temperament wherever it suits his purposes, and the characters of the outlaw leaders in *Richard Hurdis* and *Border Beagles* are no more identical than their names. Perhaps because in
Guy Rivers he had already created a lapsed lawyer-villain, in *Richard Hurdis*
Simms suppresses the information that Murrell was learned in law in favor
of the other profession Murrell had historically affected for his criminal
purposes, that of a Methodist preacher.

The most profound difference between Foster and Saxon lies in their
contrasting attitudes about romantic love and women (symbols for Simms
of the civilizing influence in human life, or of civilization itself). In these
areas, Saxon is much closer to John Murrell than is Foster. In his youth,
Murrell had become a "libertine," frequenting the brothels in New Orleans

and Natchez. Though the crimes he confessed to Stewart involved the abduction of slaves rather than women, this licentiousness in Murrell's character, meshed with material already explored in *Guy Rivers*, became the germ for Simms's subplot concerning Florence Marbois's ruin and Saxon's callousness toward her.[7] Saxon exhibits none of the mercy that allows Clement Foster to sympathize with Eberly's tender passion for Julia Grafton while still condemning his allowing it to compromise his allegiance to the clan.[8] Indeed, in *Border Beagles* Murrell's rapaciousness is reflected primarily in Saxon's ruining of Florence and abduction of Virginia Maitland, actions that have no parallel in *Richard Hurdis* except in the ineffectual impulses of Eberly and John Hurdis toward Julia Grafton and Mary Easterby. There Simms shifts some of Murrell's more atrocious characteristics to Matthew Webber while attributing to Foster those traits that allowed Murrell to maintain his leadership of the outlaws.[9]

To one who has read Stewart's accounts of Murrell, Simms's analogue Clement Foster seems a genial villain. But with this fictional splitting out of Murrell's vicious tendencies, Simms was able to keep the cowardly John Hurdis properly at the center of his revenge plot, here again reducing the sensationalism of his sources to avoid distracting attention from his exploration of the tendencies within the social family that endanger it. In *Border Beagles*, however, we find a plot of action centered on the expulsion of the lawless by agents of law and order represented in the stern figures of Harry Vernon and the Mississippi governor; here Saxon's character represents the very principle of the anti-society that recognizes no societal or human contract.

It is certain that even before meeting Stewart or reading his work, Simms had heard of the exploits of Murrell and other frontier outlaws. John Guilds has pointed out that the activities of Murrell were recounted in tall tales by Simms's father and others when Simms visited him in Mississippi in 1824– 1825 and 1831 (83). *Guy Rivers* displays Simms's early recognition that the raw life of the border communities was fertile ground for his imagination and that their frail connections with Southern institutions made them a perfect backdrop against which to play out conflicting impulses toward civilization and anarchy in Southern society. Just as Saxon is adumbrated in Rivers, so Simms's Mystic Confederacy is adumbrated in the Pony Club. But it is no accident that after the publication of Stewart's accounts, Simms found a new energy to fuel the production of two border novels that, while reusing certain situations in *Guy Rivers*, introduce a wealth of new material drawn from the contest of wits and wills between Stewart and Murrell, as well as a new focus on the potential of the frontier to spawn a "society" antithetical to the civilized South. It may be that this new energy contributed significantly to the very genesis of Simms's border series—a series that parallels his Revolutionary War series and also depicts, from another perspective, the victorious emergence of a stable society.

Almost exactly one hundred years later, in the postlapsarian South of the middle 1930s, William Faulkner began writing novels that grew out of his thinking about Mississippi's frontier and antebellum past. Before the publication of *Absalom, Absalom!* he had written a few short stories about the Indians of the Choctaw nation ("Red Leaves" and "A Justice," collected in *These 13*, 1931) and about the end of the Civil War ("Mountain Victory," collected in *Doctor Martino and Other Stories*, 1934). All of Faulkner's novels, however, including the early drafts of material that would eventually become his Snopes trilogy, were set primarily in the post-Reconstruction or contemporary South, in the years spanned by his own and his parents' lifetimes. In novels, his foray into the Mississippi frontier and Civil War days began and in important ways culminated with *Absalom, Absalom!* (1936) and *The Unvanquished* (1938), though he continued to evoke Mississippi's frontier past in his books and essays of the 1950s: in the "Notes on a Horsethief" episode of *A Fable* (1950), in the section of *Requiem for a Nun* (1951) entitled "The Courthouse (A Name for the City)," in "Mississippi" (1954), and in the introduction to *Big Woods* (1955). In these works of the 1950s, the focus of Faulkner's evocation of frontier times in Mississippi is almost always historical, and each includes references to John A. Murrell, usually in conjunction with the earlier bandits of the Natchez Trace, Mason, Hare, and the Harpes.

One of Faulkner's sources of information about the Natchez Trace, though not his most important one, is the 1938 WPA-compiled *Mississippi: A Guide to the Magnolia State*. The *Guide*'s description of the Trace offers a concise overview of its significance in Mississippi's past and concludes: "It was for 300 miles a wilderness road, yet all who passed that way carried with them much or all of their fortune. . . . To fasten on this stream of wealth came the outlaws who formerly infested the river: the Harpes, Mason, Hare, and the Murrell gang. Together they branded the early nineteenth century as the 'outlaw years'" (84).

It is quite certain that most of Faulkner's knowledge of these men came from Robert M. Coates's *The Outlaw Years: The History of the Land Pirates of the Natchez Trace* (1930), a readable compilation of several mostly nineteenth-century accounts of the Trace and its outlaws: those typically named together by Faulkner. For the chapters on Murrell (spelled *Murrel* by Coates, and sometimes by Faulkner), Coates draws heavily on the Walton and Howard versions of Stewart's adventures, supplementing these with other sources for the earlier and later portions of Murrell's life.

Faulkner owned a copy of *The Outlaw Years* at least by October 1935, when, according to Joseph Blotner, he returned to Oxford from New York with several volumes to add to his home library (*Faulkner* 903).[10] He had clearly read Coates and was using him at least by 1950 (and probably as early as 1934, as I show). In his study of *Requiem for a Nun*, Noel Polk has demonstrated that Faulkner drew specifically on Coates's account of the historical mail rider, John L. Swaney, for his depiction of Pettigrew, and that Coates provided the germ of Faulkner's story of the Jefferson militia's jailing of outlaws reputed to be of the Harpes' gang.

The Harpes' arrest and jailbreak occurred near Knoxville in the 1790s, and interestingly, Faulkner takes pains to accommodate his story of Jefferson's beginnings to historical fact. He writes: "twenty-five years later legend would begin to affirm, and a hundred years later would still be at it, that two of the bandits were the Harpes themselves. . . . Which—that they were the Harpes—was impossible, since the Harpes and even the last of Mason's ruffians were dead or scattered by this time, and the robbers would have had to belong to John Murrel's organization—if they needed to belong to any at all other than the simple fraternity of rapine" (5). The "hundred years later," at which time the legend is still going strong, would, of course, be approximately the 1930s or '40s—about the time that Faulkner was reading Coates, and it may be that *The Outlaw Years* corrected Mississippi legend that Faulkner had heard all his life.[11]

Requiem for a Nun contains other reflections of *The Outlaw Years* and the accounts by Stewart that lie behind it, in addition to the two pointed out by Polk. In Murrell's pragmatic decision to catch slaveholders off guard by staging his slave insurrection on the Fourth of July, when slaves would be released from their normal duties in house or field, and in the description of the vigilantism just before Independence Day deriving from Stewart's warnings and resulting in the lynching of accused conspirators, Faulkner seems to have found the ironies of his setting the creation of Jefferson in the context of a Fourth of July militia muster and barbecue-turned-drunken-brawl, with the lines of distinction among outlaws, militia men, and civilians wryly blurred (5–6).

In Faulkner's sergeant of militia, who according to some is an exconfederate of the bandits, we see reflected the controversy over Stewart's motives and credibility. More importantly, this borrowing makes it clear that drawing from closely related historical materials, Faulkner and Simms made very different choices, ones that reflect their contrasting views of the natures of man and civilization. When Simms suppressed the "loathsomeness" of Murrell's brutal plan for slave insurrection, he also downplayed another very prominent feature of Stewart's accounts—the ambiguity of each citizen's moral nature—by creating unimpeachable main characters as representatives of law and order, heroes who may be maligned by outlaws but whose moral stature remains unambiguous for the narrator. Where Simms's treatments of the frontier represent the vanquishing of the outlaw element by a community of honorable men, Faulkner, even in the relatively comic treatment of the frontier settlements offered in *Requiem*, internalizes the contest, and his uses of the Murrell material emphasize the conflicting impulses toward rapaciousness and civilization in every human heart.

Faulkner's treatment of the militia band is adumbrated in Coates's transformation of the materials related to vigilantism in the Howard version. Near the end of the Howard book is a chapter describing measures taken by Vicksburg citizens against the gamblers operating there. Howard writes, "It will be seen that the difficulty with the gamblers at that place was unconnected with the insurrection, except the high state of excitement that pervaded the whole southern country at that time, which had led the citizens to deal more rigorously with all offenders; and more especially those of an abandoned and dissolute character, as all professional gamblers are" (263). He proceeds in the same unironic vein to describe an assembly of the corps of Vicksburg Volunteers for a Fourth of July barbecue. At the celebration, a gambler named Cabler insulted one of the officers and struck a citizen. He was expelled, but the commandant prevented further punishment. Later Cabler was reported to be returning with vengeful intent, and he was arrested, found armed, and lynched (265). Coates retells this story, embellishing it with details of the bumbling of Cabler and the transparent expediency of frontier justice (277–78).

In this undercut story of Vicksburg's attempted expulsion of its gamblers, Faulkner found another specific source for his fictional inception of

Jefferson. As viewed in these instances by Coates and Faulkner, the outlaw is no more or less dangerous or effectual than the citizen, and the attempt to expel evil from society by singling out its individual avatars is shown to be futile and shortsighted. It should be stressed, though, that in Faulkner's novels, including *Requiem*, man's aspiration to contain his rapaciousness is celebrated even when the individual attempt proves comically or tragically ineffectual.

Coates's images of the Memphis mob boiling and ebbing as if it were a tide or part of the river on which it lived (278–79) may link *The Outlaw Years* to another of Faulkner's novels of the 1950s in which direct reference is made to John Murrell: *A Fable*. It has often been noted that the crowd in Faulkner's parable is described in tidal imagery, as are the mob in *Intruder in the Dust* (1948) and the flood of slaves surging toward "Jordan" in *The Unvanquished* (1938). A more significant borrowing is the use of Murrell himself in the "Notes on a Horsethief" section of *A Fable*, for here Faulkner uses a detail from history that he does not directly employ anywhere else. In this episode, Faulkner contrasts the federal deputy, who sees the abduction of the three-legged racehorse as an act of passion, with the cynical lawyer, who sees it as one of rapine. Daydreaming how he would defend the thieves if they were caught, the lawyer envisions himself

> a—perhaps the—figure in a pageant which in reality would be an historical commemoration, in fact, even more than that: the affirmation of a creed, . . . the postulation of an invincible way of life: the loud strong voice of America itself out of the westward roar of the tremendous and battered yet indomitably virgin continent, where nothing save the vast unmoral sky limited what a man could try to do, nor even the sky limit his success and the adulation of his fellow man; even the defence he would employ would be in the old fine strong American tradition of rapine, its working precedent having been already established in this very . . . land by an older and more successful thief than any English groom or Negro preacher: John Murrell himself, himself his own attorney: the rape was not a theft but merely a misdemeanor, since the placard offering the reward before the horse's demise had constituted a legal power of attorney authorising any man's hand to the body of the horse, and its violation had been a simple breach of trust, the burden of the proof of which lay with the pursuers since they would have to prove that the man had not been trying simply

to find the owner and restore him his property all the time. (*A Fable* 167–68)

The lawyer's defense strategy is indeed Murrell's own, and Faulkner's language is occasionally quite close to Coates's. Murrell explained to Virgil Stewart that he would coax Negroes to run away to his hiding place, and then he would wait for the owner to advertise for the lost slave: "Now, sir, that advertisement amounts to the same as a power of attorney, to take his property, the nigger, and hold it for him. And if a man chooses to make a breach of trust in this case, and instead of carrying the nigger to the owner converts him to his own use—why, that is not stealing, and the only way the owner can get at him is in a civil action" (Coates 185).

While it contains no direct reference to John Murrell, though set in Civil War and Reconstruction years and written more than a decade before *Requiem for a Nun* and *A Fable*, Faulkner's 1938 novel *The Unvanquished* is infused with the spirit of John Murrell and *The Outlaw Years*. Indeed, the characters of *The Unvanquished*—John Sartoris, his son Bayard, Bayard's grandmother Rosa Millard, and Grumby's "Independents"—all borrow wartime strategies from that old avatar of rapine, John Murrell, indicating that Faulkner perceived in the Mississippi of the Civil War and Reconstruction the reincarnation of her not-so-distant frontier past. Most obvious is Granny's scheme for requisitioning horses and mules from the federal government, selling them back to the Yankees at another encampment through the agency of Ab Snopes, requisitioning them again, and repeating the gambit until their odds of discovery become too risky. Murrell told Stewart of luring slaves away from their masters, selling and reselling them for profit. When the game became too troublesome or dangerous, the slaves were often murdered, disemboweled, and sunk in the river or swamp. Still like her model Murrell, Granny disposes of the animals, but in a much more humane way than Murrell disposed of his stolen slaves: she lends them to her countrymen so that they can make crops to feed their families.

There is also John Sartoris's vigilantism. After the war has ended but before any stability has been restored, his local militia enforces its own ideas of law and order not only against outlaw bands but also against carpetbaggers such as the Burdens, whom John kills at the polls. Like Murrell, he uses his knowledge of the law to accomplish his ruthless aims: he allows the Burdens to shoot first, and he insists on surrendering to the sheriff, confident that he will evade punishment. But his claim that he is "working for peace through law and order" (*Unvanquished* 239) after he has shot the Burdens aligns him also with the Vicksburg citizens who rationalized their lynching of Cabler though he had committed no crime. Later, John shoots a hill-country man who had been part of his regiment, "and we never to know if the man actually intended to rob Father or not because Father had shot too quick" (255). Like the frontiersman, John respects the idea of law but does not trust legal and governmental institutions as he finds them. Thus there is more than a little ambiguity and even insult in his last words to his son, whom he has encouraged to study law: "I have not needed you in my affairs so far, but from now on I shall," he says, explaining he had earlier "acted as the land and the time demanded" but had shielded Bayard from these activities. Now, however, the world had changed: "what will follow will be a matter of consolidation, of pettifogging and doubtless chicanery in which I would be a babe in arms but in which you, trained in the law, can hold your own—our own" (266). His advice to Bayard here ominously echoes Murrell's counsel for Stewart: "Let a man learn the use of the law, and nothing can touch him" (Coates 179).

John, in fact, has not shielded Bayard from the realities of "the time and the land." While still a boy of fifteen, when he and Ringo set out to avenge Grumby's murder of Granny, Bayard has taken law or justice into his own hands because there were no other hands to wield it. Virgil Stewart, too, was hardly more than a boy—twenty-two years old—when he undertook to pursue Murrell, and Faulkner seems to have based Bayard's dismal pursuit of Grumby from before Christmas until late February, through the north Mississippi environs of the old Natchez Trace, on Stewart's equally frightening and uncomfortable travels with Murrell through the sleet-frozen trails of west Tennessee and across the river to Murrell's camp in Arkansas, where there was "nothing but swamp and desolation, a long flat rain-stricken freezing stretch of cane-brake and swamp-willows" (Coates 250).

Some of the details Faulkner uses to delineate his outlaws may have been inspired by *The Outlaw Years* as well. Grumby, an unimaginative coward who murders Granny because her attempt to claim his stolen horses frightens him, is accompanied by a man with a black beard who is disgusted at Grumby's ineptitude and who finally delivers him up to Bayard's vengeance. When the bearded man first rides into their camp on a "good short-coupled sorrel mare," Bayard notices "his neat little fine made boots, and his linen shirt without any collar, and a coat that had been good, too, once, and a broad hat pulled down so that all we could see was his eyes and nose between the hat and his black beard" (*Unvanquished* 189–90). The description resembles Stewart's introduction to Murrell: "at last another man came riding, a handsome man with the glossiest beaver hat slanted over his insolent eyes, and a wide-skirted coat, fastidiously cut, well brushed and immaculate, buttoned tightly about his form. A brace of silver-mounted pistols showed at his saddle holsters. . . . [T]he gateman turned to Stewart. 'That's Murrel,' he said" (Coates 177–78).

Although Bayard's dandy is *not* Murrell, but only another avatar of the land pirate, his words to Grumby—"We had a good thing in this country. . . . And now we've got to pull out . . . because you lost your nerve and killed an old woman and then lost your nerve again and refused to cover the first mistake" (*Unvanquished* 206)—recall Murrell's remarks about a "squeamish" bandit who would not kill his victims: "that will never do for a robber; after I rob a man he will never give evidence against me. . . . There is but one safe way in this business . . . and that is to kill. If I could not afford to kill a man I would not rob" (Coates 224).

The profound influence of Coates's story of John Murrell on Faulkner's conception of *The Unvanquished,* together with certain other affinities that *The Unvanquished* shares with *Richard Hurdis,* raise the question of Simms's influence on Faulkner. The novels employ revenge plots of a similar type: in Southern states at times when social institutions of law and justice are weak or nonexistent, young men who have experienced the loss by murder of persons close to them undertake to track down and kill the murderers. In *The Unvanquished,* the situation occurs twice: once when Bayard and Ringo[12] kill Grumby and again, with significant variations, when Bayard confronts Redmond, his father's estranged business partner, who is maneuvered into shooting John when he assumes a dueling attitude unarmed. So extenuating are the circumstances in this second instance, and so changed are the land and time and Bayard himself in the five years since he killed Grumby, that he feels no desire to avenge this killing. But this is not so of the characters who have for years lionized John—lionized Bayard, too, for his act of vengeance that in their eyes most makes him "John Sartoris' boy" (*Unvanquished* 213). Chief among them is John's young widow Drusilla, whose first fiancé had been killed in the war, and who becomes a priestess of vengeance like Emmeline Walker, the fiancée of William Carrington in *Richard Hurdis.*

Pivotal scenes in both books depict the confrontation of each bereaved

woman with the young man she sees as the agent through whom her desire
for revenge is to be achieved. In *Richard Hurdis*, Emmeline articulates Richard's own sense of complicity in Carrington's death—his guilt at not having
protected his too-frank friend from men he distrusted. Richard struggles to
summon the courage to carry news of her fiancé's death to Emmeline and
is able to find the resolve only after he is counseled by Colonel Grafton: "Is
it not your duty to go back and declare the circumstances to all those who
are interested in the fate of your friend? It will be expected of you. To take
any other course will seem to show a consciousness of error with which you
can not reproach yourself" (198). When Richard reluctantly tells her the
circumstances of Carrington's death, Emmeline holds him accountable:

> She gazed on me for a few seconds with all the intensity of an ex-
> pression which was neither hate nor anger, but blind ferocity, and de-
> structive judgment; and then she spoke, in accents which would have
> been bitter enough to my heart, had I not well enough understood the
> maddening bitterness in hers.
> "And so he was murdered—and you led him on this expedition to
> be murdered! You were his friend—and while they pursued him . . .
> you lay quietly—without effort—having bonds, which a child— . . .
> which I would have broken at such a time—which you might have
> broken, had you been warmed with a proper spirit to help your friend!
> And he thought you a brave man, too—he told me you were so, and I
> believed it—I gave him in charge to you, and you suffered your villains
> to murder him! . . . You have neither shed the blood of his murderers,
> nor your own! . . . You are—ha! ha! ha! this is courage, is it?" (*Richard
> Hurdis*, 274–75)

Richard interprets this speech as a "moral requisition" (287), and he will-
ingly undertakes her charge of vengeance. It is a mission both of justice and
of atonement.

Like Richard, Bayard also seeks vengeance against his grandmother's
murderer partly out of a sense of complicity and a need for atonement.
Though he has been only passively involved in Granny and Ringo's horse-
stealing scheme, following their lead and not openly voicing any judgments
about its wisdom or honor, Bayard's passive support for their dangerous
activities ultimately leads him to a profound sense of guilt when his grandmother is killed; and his need for vengeance and atonement requires no
inciting from another. In the pursuit of Grumby, Ringo plays the second-

ary, supporting role (though Ringo is always a more willing and active participant in Bayard's fights than Bayard has been in the horse theft scam).

But when Redmond kills his father, Bayard feels no sense of guilt, aware as he is both of his father's complicity in goading Redmond and John's too-ready killing of men he distrusted. Unlike Richard's meeting with Emmeline, Bayard's confrontation with Drusilla represents the conflict within his society between the desire for peace and true justice and the old bloodlust, the reflexive vengeance that has become a habit of a people who have lived too long without stable institutions. Though less overtly deranged than Emmeline, Drusilla speaks for the madness within her postwar society that fosters a ritualistic and mindless violence as she holds out the dueling pistols and addresses Bayard:

> "Take them, Bayard," she said, in the same tone in which she had said "Kiss me" last summer, already pressing them into my hands, watching me with that passionate and voracious exaltation. . . . "Oh you will thank me, you will remember me who put into your hands what they say is an attribute only of God's, who took what belongs to heaven and gave it to you. Do you feel them? the long true barrels true as justice, the triggers . . . quick as retribution, the two of them slender and invincible and fatal as the physical shape of love?" (*Unvanquished* 273)

In the scene between Richard and Emmeline, after upbraiding him for failing to bring Carrington back safely and failing to avenge him, she falls into an hysteria-induced illness, in which she raves and finally dies. When Drusilla intuits that Bayard has no intention to kill Redmond, she upbraids Bayard, too, and must be led, hysterical, to her room.

Richard Hurdis meets his tests of courage by facing Emmeline with the truth and then by pursuing the outlaws who are responsible for Carrington's death. Bayard's tests of courage similarly involve his pursuit of Grumby and his facing Drusilla with a different kind of truth. But Faulkner's plot seems to engage in deliberate dialogue with Simms's when he sets up for Bayard a third test: his facing Redmond on his own terms, unarmed, risking death in order to postulate a different standard of justice for the world that will be more of his generation's making than his father's. Bayard postulates a different standard for courage as well: the courage to reject the norms of society when they conflict with one's moral sense: the courage not to do something just because, as Grafton tells Richard, "It will be

expected of you." Faulkner's novel suggests that a society moves from a
frontier state only as its individuals actively embrace the ideals its institutions have been created to incarnate. The struggle is not between outlaws
and citizens, but between man's contradictory impulses toward license
and responsibility. Bayard knows that his failure to take responsibility for
Granny's safety cannot be rationalized to his conscience; he knows there
were other choices he could have made had he been courageous enough.
When Drusilla, Ringo, and the men of his father's troop all make it clear
that they expect Bayard to avenge John's death, he invents a new response.
The acceptance of this new way by Wyatt, by the other men, and even by
Drusilla suggest that Bayard will hold his own in his time and land in ways
his father could not have imagined.

In his depiction of the women in his novel, too, Faulkner may be responding to *Richard Hurdis*. As Emmeline is wavering between life and
death, Richard questions whether she might not be better off dead and
imagines what her future life could be: "The heart was never destined to
know any other than the consciousness of sorrow. . . . The eyes might kin-
dle, and the lips might wear a smile, in after days, even as the tree which
the wanton axe of the woodman has wounded, will sometimes put forth a
few sickly buds and imperfect branches. But these do not speak for life always. The life of the soul is wanting. . . . The heart is eaten out and gone,
and when the tree falls, . . . men wonder of what disease it perished" (*Richard Hurdis*, 268).

Such is the fate of Julia Grafton, who lives only a year after Eberly's
departure. In a rather different way, Richard's musing foretells the fate of
Drusilla, who is left dead inside after the death of her fiancé Gavin Breck-
bridge. She decides that the hopes she had for her life were "stupid," and
she devotes herself to killing Yankees. Her forced marriage to John Sartoris
does not "speak for life"; and her demand for vengeance when John is killed
is merely a repetition of her never-appeased thirst for revenge for Gavin's
death.

But as if to dispute Simms's romantic convention of the necessity of dying for love, Faulkner creates a foil for Drusilla in Bayard's Aunt Jenny.
Bayard confronts Jenny as well as Drusilla when he returns home after his
father's death, and Jenny's influence—felt largely in her mere presence—is
a sane counterbalance, if Bayard needs one, to keep him from falling into
the romantic temptation to risk death for Drusilla. Jenny's loss of her young
husband has not robbed her of her inner life; she has not become her sor-

row. She keeps a garden, calls Bayard "Son," and readily accepts his decision not to kill Redmond.

We have no external evidence that Faulkner read *Richard Hurdis*, but the parallels between the women of *Richard Hurdis* and *The Unvanquished* and the roles they play in inciting the main characters to revenge, paired with the thoroughgoing treatments in both novels of the themes of courage, revenge, and justice in the context of plots that are strongly influenced by the Murrell legend, suggest that he did. I would guess that Faulkner read *Richard Hurdis* as a young man; perhaps he found it in one of the family libraries. But it seems plausible that as he began to write the stories that would comprise *The Unvanquished* from 1934 to 1936, his reading of *The Outlaw Years* and its stories of Murrell and the lawless days of the Mississippi frontier reminded him, consciously or unconsciously, of that older novel that had already given him parts of the story of Murrell. For Faulkner, as for Simms, the Murrell legend proved to be a fruitful influence, and it left its traces not only in those novels of the 1950s that invoke Murrell by name, but more substantially in *The Unvanquished*, which preceded them by fifteen years.

NOTES

1. Stewart's narrative of his adventures has always been suspect, partly because he and Murrell lived within five miles of each other but supposedly had never met, and partly because he was apparently engaged in some illegal business of his own before meeting Murrell. See James Lal Penick's *The Great Western Land Pirate* 175–81. However, I see no evidence in Simms's allusions to Stewart that he questioned his story.

2. Howard's account includes the signed confession of a Joshua Cotton, who wrote on July 4th, "from the exposure of our plans in said pamphlet [Walton's account], we expected the citizens would be on their guard at the time mentioned, being the 25th of December next; and we determined to take them by surprise, and try it on the night of the 4th of July, and it would have been tried to-night (and perhaps may yet), but for the detection of our plans" (243).

3. In the "Advertisement" to the revised edition of *Richard Hurdis*, Simms claims that he "knew Stuart, the captor of Murrell," and had "had several conversations with him, prior to the publication of his narrative" (11). If Simms knew Stewart as "the captor of Murrell," then the earliest possible date for their meeting would be February 8, 1834, when Murrell was first imprisoned on Stewart's testimony (Howard 126). Their latest possible date of meeting falls between mid-1836 and early

1837. The latest date mentioned in Howard's narrative is April 15, 1836, the date of
an affidavit printed very near the end of the book as the last pertaining to proceedings against those accused of inciting a slave rebellion. This may have been a late
addition, set in type just before the book was printed. Thus Howard's version was
published no earlier than May or June 1836, and it may have come out as late as
January or February 1837 and still carried its 1836 date. The range of possible
meeting dates is narrowed if Simms was referring to the Walton version, published
in February 1835.

We have no evidence that Simms was in the border states between 1834 and 1837
(Wimsatt 97–98), but that does not rule out the possibility that Simms met Stewart
elsewhere. For much of 1834 Stewart was on the road, sometimes in disguise, evading Murrell's strikers. He spent extended time only in Cincinnati, where he stayed
from November 1834 until spring 1835, recovering his health (Howard 184–204).
Even if Simms had been in the region during these years, he would not likely have
encountered Stewart. I suggest instead that they met when Simms was in New York
in the summer and fall of 1836 (Guilds 73). Stewart had been in Cincinnati while
the Walton pamphlet was in production there; it seems possible that he was enough
involved with the creation of the Howard version to oversee its publication in New
York by Harper (Simms's own publisher from 1832 until 1837). It also seems possible that "Walton" and "Howard" were pseudonyms Stewart assumed for reasons
of safety and seemliness.

4. "The clan are not all of the same grit; there are two classes. The first class
keep all their designs and the extent of their plans to themselves. For this reason, all
who would be willing to join us are not capable of managing our designs; and there
would be danger of their making disclosures which would lead to the destruction of
our designs before they were perfected. This class is what we call the grand council.
The second class are those whom we trust with nothing except that which they are
immediately concerned with. We have them to do what we are not willing to do
ourselves" (Howard 54; Walton 39–40).

5. In Walton's and Howard's accounts, blackmail is mentioned as a way of en-
suring a recruit's initial sincerity and continued loyalty to the confederacy: Murrell
tells Stewart, "There is no danger in any man, if you can ever get him once implicated or engaged in a matter. That is the way we employ our strikers in all things;
we have them implicated before we trust them from our sight" (Howard 58; Walton
41). Simms uses this in *Richard Hurdis* when Foster assigns Richard to murder
young Eberly. But with Pickett and John Hurdis, the recruiting itself is made possible by the clan's discovery that these men have committed a murder.

6. A long footnote in the Howard account, for instance, quotes from an "English
lecturer on slavery" whose arguments Murrell had used to solicit the cooperation
of the strikers to lead bands of black insurgents. The lecturer suggests that "if their
cities, with all the merchandise that is in the country, were destroyed, and their
banks plundered of all the specie, thousands of eastern capitalists would suffer great

loss, and would henceforth consider a slave country an unsafe place to make investments" (Howard 58–59).

In *Border Beagles*, Jamison's inclusion of "abolitionists, that haven't the fear of God in their eyes, and do large business with the devil" in his list of those that may learn a lesson by seeing Saxon's followers lynched in Lucchesa gathers more point in light of such abolitionists' recommendations, and this passage may be another very faint allusion to the Murrell clan's plot to incite a slave rebellion (445).

7. One passage that appears only in Howard's expanded version of Stewart's adventure seems especially pertinent to Harry Vernon's outrage at the abduction of Virginia: "viewing, as he did, the thickening clouds that hung in unseen but threatening terror over the defenseless heads of the fairer part of creation, charged with death, ravishment, and prostitution, in all their hideous, torturing, and humiliating forms . . . to appease the unholy vengeance and brutal ferocity of the unsympathizing and heartless assassin—made his [Stewart's] bosom swell with emotions 'too big for utterance,' and which have but imperfectly found vent in the details of his subsequent adventures" (Howard 73–74).

8. Richard accounts for Foster's humanity in the following manner: "There was something yet in his heart which partook of the holy nature of a childhood which, we may suppose, was even blessed with hopes and kindred, and which, however perverted now to the lessons and performances of hate, once knew what it was to do homage at the altar of confiding love" (345). But this seems to be contradicted earlier in the novel when Foster tells Richard that as a boy he "knew no parents, and had no friends" (312). As Floyd Deen has pointed out, Simms departs from the Murrell history when he makes Foster an orphan (407). But Deen overlooks the greater similarity of the passage about Foster's childhood, "blessed with hopes and kindred," to the passage in the Stewart accounts where Murrell describes his family: "My parents had not much property, but they were intelligent people; and my father was an honest man I expect, and tried to raise me honest, but I think none the better of him for that. My mother was of the pure grit; she learned me and all her children to steal as soon as we could walk, and would hide for us whenever she could" (Howard 63; Walton 45). Simms's inconsistency appears to be an oversight, and in neither passage does he attempt to reflect the precise details of Murrell's childhood.

9. Even Webber's name associates him more than Foster with Richard's metaphor for human rapacity: "Such is certainly a true picture of our social condition. Man is the prey of man—the weak of the strong—the unwary of the cunning. The more black, the more bloated the spider, the closer his web, and the greater the number and variety of victims" (314).

10. Faulkner signed and dated his copy of the book in 1935, and this is presumably the evidence on which Blotner dates his acquisition of the book (see *William Faulkner's Library* 23). It is, of course, possible that Faulkner acquired the book earlier than the date he inscribed in it.

11. Mark Twain had made similar use of the outlaw legend in *The Adventures of*

Tom Sawyer (1876), when Injun Joe's companion, the unkempt stranger, remarks that "'Twas always said that Murrel's gang used around here one summer" after he and Injun Joe find the box of gold in the haunted house (162; Seelye xxii). Historically, it is just as unlikely that Murrell "used" in Missouri as that the Harpes could have been present at the birth of Jefferson, given its time and place.

Faulkner's knowledge of Murrell may derive to a smaller degree from this and other brief references in the works of Mark Twain and Herman Melville. In *Life on the Mississippi* (1883), Twain mentions the tradition that Island 37 in the Mississippi "was one of the principal abiding places of the once celebrated 'Murel's Gang'"; and comparing Murrell to the more contemporary outlaw Jesse James, Twain concludes: "Murel was his equal in boldness; in pluck; in rapacity; in cruelty, brutality, heartlessness, treachery, and in general and comprehensive vileness and shamelessness; and very much his superior in some larger aspects" (404–5). Twain then offers passages from "a now forgotten book which was published half a century ago," which proves to be the Howard account of Stewart's adventures. (Twain paraphrases and quotes passages from pages 30, 52, 25, 54, 105–6, 64–66, and 40–41, in this order; *Life* 405–9). Unlike Simms, Twain stresses Murrell's slave-stealing and his plot for slave insurrections. The opening of Melville's Mississippi River novel, *The Confidence Man* (1857), also makes brief reference to "Murrel, the pirate of the Mississippi," linking him, as Faulkner so frequently does, with "Meason [*sic*], the bandit of Ohio" and "the brothers Harpe, the Thugs of the Green River country, in Kentucky" (841).

12. Ringo's given name is Marengo, the name of the Alabama community that is Richard Hurdis's home.

WORKS CITED

Blotner, Joseph. *Faulkner: A Biography.* New York: Random, 1974.
———. *William Faulkner's Library: A Catalogue.* Charlottesville: University Press of Virginia, 1964.
Coates, Robert M. *The Outlaw Years: The History of the Land Pirates of the Natchez Trace.* New York: Literary Guild of America, 1930.
Deen, Floyd. "A Comparison of Simms's *Richard Hurdis* with Its Sources." *Modern Language Notes* 60 (June 1945): 406–8.
Faulkner, William. *A Fable.* New York: Random, 1954.
———. "Mississippi." *Essays, Speeches, and Public Letters.* Ed. James B. Meriwether. New York: Random, 1965. 11–43.
———. *Requiem for a Nun.* New York: Random, 1951.
———. *The Unvanquished.* New York: Random, 1938.
Guilds, John Caldwell. *Simms: A Literary Life.* Fayetteville: University of Arkansas Press, 1992.

Howard, H. R. *The History of Virgil A. Stewart, and His Adventure in Capturing and Exposing the Great "Western Land Pirate."* New York: Harper and Brothers, 1836.

Melville, Herman. "The Confidence Man." *Pierre or, The Ambiguities; Israel Potter: His Fifty Years of Exile; The Piazza Tales; The Confidence Man: His Masquerade; Uncollected Prose; Billy Budd, Sailor (An Inside Narrative).* New York: Library of America, 1984. 835–1112.

Mississippi: A Guide to the Magnolia State. Federal Writers' Project of the Works Progress Administration. New York: Viking, 1938.

Penick, James Lal. *The Great Western Land Pirate: John A. Murrell in Legend and History.* Columbia: University of Missouri Press, 1981.

Polk, Noel. *Faulkner's "Requiem for a Nun": A Critical Study.* Bloomington: Indiana University Press, 1981.

Seelye, John. "Introduction." *The Adventures of Huckleberry Finn.* New York: Penguin, 1986. vii–xxviii.

Simms, William Gilmore. *Border Beagles; A Tale of Mississippi.* 2 vols. Philadelphia: Carey and Hart, 1840.

———. *Border Beagles: A Tale of Mississippi.* New and rev. ed. New York: Redfield, 1855.

———. *Richard Hurdis; or, The Avenger of Blood. A Tale of Alabama.* 2 vols. Philadelphia: Carey and Hart, 1838.

———. *Richard Hurdis: A Tale of Alabama.* New and rev. ed. New York: Redfield, 1855.

Twain, Mark. "The Adventures of Tom Sawyer." *Mississippi Writings.* New York: Library of America, 1982. 1–215.

———. "Life on the Mississippi." *Mississippi Writings.* New York: Library of America, 1982. 217–616.

Walton, Augustus Q. *A History of the Detection, Conviction, Life and Designs of John A. Murel, The Great Western Land Pirate.* Cincinnati: U. P. James, 1835.

Wimsatt, Mary Ann. *The Major Fiction of William Gilmore Simms: Cultural Traditions and Literary Form.* Baton Rouge: Louisiana State University Press, 1989.

William Gilmore Simms and Friedrich Gerstäcker: American and German Literary Perspectives and Parallels

The nineteenth-century authors W. G. Simms and Friedrich Gerstäcker not only share several biographical parallels[1] but also a similar literary fate: after being extremely popular in their century, interest in their books trailed off in the twentieth century until they all but disappeared from bookstores and the canon. Today, scholars in both authors' home countries are working on reestablishing their importance. Simms's and Gerstäcker's literary topics are in many cases similar and invite comparison and contrast, especially with regard to their narrative styles and their views of the American frontier; one difference is that, in his writings on America, Friedrich Gerstäcker represents a foreigner's perspective on what was to him an exotic country, while Simms as a native Southerner had an insider's perspective. Despite their different backgrounds, their works reveal a sufficient number of similarities—particularly in the areas of humor, hunting, Native American culture, and religion—and influences to justify a closer look.

A direct link exists between the two authors: Gerstäcker translated a work by Simms into German at a time when he was just beginning his own writing career. In 1846, Gerstäcker published both his first novel, *Die Regulatoren in Arkansas*, and his translation of Simms's *The Wigwam and the Cabin*. It is safe to assume that Gerstäcker, whose main interest at the time was the American frontier, was at least inspired and perhaps influenced by Simms's frontier stories collected in *The Wigwam and the Cabin*. The German publisher used only stories from the first series of the American original and omitted "Jocassee" from that volume.[2]

Friedrich Gerstäcker translated many American and English books into German, especially in the early years of his career. Among them were works by Seba Smith, Charles Fenno Hoffman, Bulwer-Lytton, and Melville (Ostwald 182–83). Jeffrey Sammons suspects that Gerstäcker was not proud of his translation of the Simms work because he left it out of the personal bibliographical catalogue he compiled toward the end of his life. Sammons describes Simms as "a staunch supporter of slavery and the Southern aristocracy" (87) and suggests that Gerstäcker's liberalism and antislavery stance caused him to ignore this translation later. However, there is no evidence to back up Sammons's contention. It is further weakened by the fact that he appears to be not entirely familiar with the work in question: he calls *The Wigwam and the Cabin* "a novel" (87).

While Gerstäcker's knowledge of Simms's work is easily traced, there is no proof that Simms was familiar with Gerstäcker's writing. He did know some German and read German authors both in the original and in translation (Thomas, "German Sources" 150). Many references to German literary works can be found in his writing, a subject that J. Wesley Thomas has explored in some detail.

Both Simms and Gerstäcker were prolific writers. Although the literary quality of their writing is not always up to par, in their books they created accounts of life on the frontier accurate enough to serve as sociohistorical sources—which is actually how Gerstäcker's writing is received in the United States. Gerstäcker scholars Clarence Evans and Liselotte Albrecht have noted that "we are beginning to see in it a record of a social *milieu* characteristic of the frontier process" (40). Waddy William Moore remarks that "Gerstäcker's realism, clarity of description, and straightforward prose is wonderfully enlightening about the way Arkansans of the last century lived, played, and worked" (188).

Gerstäcker's initial intention had been to inform his mother about his travels. He had never considered a career as a writer, but his mother arranged for the publication of the journals he sent her from his travels in America (1837–1842). They were so successful, and Gerstäcker was so poor after his return to Germany, that he began to write fiction and nonfiction about his adventures in order to support himself. Economic necessity proved a stronger motive than the urge to create (Ostwald 55); but Gerstäcker also wanted to inform Germans about the conditions of life in America.

In the mid–nineteenth century, an increasing number of Germans emigrated to the United States for political as well as economic reasons, looking for a paradise at the end of their sea passage. As Peter Brenner points out, "Paradies" was in fact the most common metaphor to describe America throughout the nineteenth century (93–98). Gerstäcker, who had lived the emigrant's life, tried to provide prospective emigrants with a more realistic description of the conditions in America than they would get elsewhere.[3] As Sammons notes, "At the center of his purpose was a concern with the expectations of the German immigrant. He worked hard to combat illusions of a land of ease and plenty" (84).

Friedrich Gerstäcker was not the first German to explore the New World. It had become increasingly fascinating to German artists, peasants, middle-class citizens, and the nobility since the sixteenth century.[4] The German interest reached a peak at the end of the eighteenth century and emigration became a realistic option for many lower-class Germans in the first half of the nineteenth century.[5] Gerstäcker's reports differed from those of most other German authors visiting America: G. T. Hollyday calls him "the author most concerned with presenting a true picture about life in America" (129). With the exception of Charles Sealsfield, these writers are forgotten today.[6] Ironically, Karl May (1842–1912), the German novelist whose books about America are still immensely popular and who shaped the image of America for generations of Germans, never went to the United States himself. As Gerstäcker editor Wolfgang Bittner points out, May seems to have copied whole passages of text from Gerstäcker (Afterword, *Regulatoren* 585–89).

Friedrich Gerstäcker thus was part of a fairly large literary movement of travel and adventure literature that began in the Enlightenment period, became stronger with Romanticism, lasted throughout the nineteenth century, and is echoed by a number of twentieth-century authors.[7] Remarkably, Gerstäcker traveled with few prejudices and an open mind—a fact that distinguishes him from many of his contemporaries.

Books by Gerstäcker that offer an abundance of material for comparison include the novels *Die Regulatoren in Arkansas* (1846; *The Regulators in Arkansas*) and *Die Flußpiraten des Mississippi* (1848; *The Pirates of the Mississippi*, translated into English in 1856), as well as some of his sketches and tales, among them *Germelshausen* (1871), a story that American teachers once used in German language classes as a prime example of German storytelling. Works by Simms that correspond best are *Richard Hurdis* (1838), *Helen Halsey* (1845), and several of the stories from the collection *The Wigwam and the Cabin* (1845). None of Simms's works is currently available in German translations, and only parts of Gerstäcker's writing have been translated into English.

Gerstäcker's fascination with the American frontier was based on the vastness of the country, the lack of restrictive class distinctions, and the unregulated life removed from the restraints of urban civilization. All this contrasted sharply with the life he had been accustomed to in Germany. Many critics have remarked on his love for individual freedom (Bittner, Afterword, *Regulatoren* 579–80), on his "liberal, democratic, and humane cast of mind" (Sammons 86), and on his active efforts to change the economic and political conditions in Germany (in the 1848 revolution, he played a leading role in Leipzig).

Gerstäcker's curiosity about and willingness to immerse himself in frontier life contradict Simms's general statement about Europeans in the "Advertisement" to the second edition of *Richard Hurdis:* "Our hardihood comes from our necessities, and prompts our enterprise; and the American is bold in adventure to a proverb. Where the silk-shodden and sleek citizen of the European world would pause and deliberate to explore our wilds, we plunge incontinently forward" (13–14).

Gerstäcker was less interested in writing about what he saw than in experiencing it; much of his writing is unpretentious, sometimes clumsy, but full of humor and keen observations of customs and language. His style being more that of a journalist than a novelist, he wrote quickly and gave more weight to descriptions and anecdotes than to analyses (Miller 15). "In the Backwoods" (1871), translated into English by James William Miller in 1991, is a realistic, funny, and straightforward story based on real events. Gerstäcker appears in it himself. A young farmer's family receives a visit from the girl he wants to marry. He has been out working in the field and is unaware of her arrival. "Ellen, by the way, made a show of pretending she wasn't at all interested in where Bill was. I felt sorry for the poor boy. He was working out there in the sweat of his brow, and here in his own house sat the treasure for whom he had pined so long. And all pretenses notwithstanding, she did seem unhappy not to find him there. I decided without further ado to go back and give him the good word. Bill threw down his ax at once" (240–41).

They run home, but Bill doesn't want to face Ellen as sweaty and dirty as he is. Frederick, the narrator, offers to go inside and get Bill's clothes for him. As it turns out, Ellen is sitting on the chest that contains Bill's new clothes, but the narrator manages to sneak them out of the house.

Bill was ecstatic, and hardly ten minutes later he strutted into the house in his new suit. Whether the suit had such an effect on her, or

whether she had already been soft on him, I don't know, but four
months later the justice of the peace united the still very young pair.
And there on the Mulberry in a delightful little valley, two happy
people began a new life together. The reader who is so inclined can
draw the lesson from this unassuming sketch that not only in European cities do young suitors carefully preen themselves before going courting. Even backwoods beaus worry a great deal about their
looks. (242)

While Friedrich Gerstäcker concentrated on topics that had to do with
his travels, W. G. Simms showed more ambition in exploring many different genres and topics. His vision was so broad that his books dealing with
American history alone, including the frontier novels, form "a sustained,
interconnected literary saga covering more than four hundred years. He
traced the American national consciousness through four centuries in two
dozen books which, taken together, form a powerful, intense, highly readable epic and constitute a unique national literary treasure" (Guilds 338).

Both authors showed a deep interest in the reality of frontier life. They
vividly described even violent and repulsive events. Simms justifies his realistic descriptions of violence with the necessity to preserve actual facts.
In the "Advertisement" to *Richard Hurdis*, he writes: "It was objected, to
the story, that it was of too gloomy and savage a character. . . . It is quite
enough, in answer to the objection, to say that the general portraiture is
not only a truthful one, in the present case, but that the materials are really
of historical character" (10).

Gerstäcker and Simms faithfully recorded the customs and dialects of
the frontierspeople and often used humor and irony to describe them (especially visible in Simms's "Sharp Snaffles" and "Bald-Head Bill Bauldy"
stories). The following brief dialogue is from Gerstäcker's *Die Regulatoren
in Arkansas*, but it displays a style very similar to Simms's. One of the novel's main characters is the Methodist preacher Rowson, whom the women
in his settlement admire because of his strong faith and pure soul, but who
is a member of a band of horse thieves. He brags to his friends that he is
well-known even in Missouri, from where he moved to Arkansas:

" . . . and because of my godfearing demeanor, all the people up
there have come to love me."

"And so did the horses," laughed Weston, "when he left there, three
of those sweet animals followed him out of sheer attachment." (21; this
and subsequent translations mine)

Gerstäcker also treats violence with realism and irony. In *Die Flußpiraten des Mississippi*, a quack goes on and on about the gruesome injuries he has treated. His listeners are horrified, but they also laugh about his lack of qualification:

> "I guess nobody goes to see him more than once," the farmer said.
> The man in blue laughed out loud and called:
> "By God, no—no living person can boast of having been treated by Doctor Monrove. The five that he *has* treated—all strangers, immigrants, of course—died speedily and are now stored in alcohol and God knows what else in his study, some whole, some by the piece." (47; this and subsequent translations mine)

The numerous apparent similarities, such as the choice of frontier settings and topics, have led critics to compare both Simms and Gerstäcker with Cooper, but his earlier Northern frontier is not the same as Gerstäcker's and Simms's Old Southwest frontier. Their frontier writings belong in the down-to-earth storytelling tradition that could actually be heard on the frontier. Even though there is a difference in location—Simms's frontier stretches from Georgia to the Mississippi, Gerstäcker's frontier lies beyond the river, in Arkansas and Texas—John C. Guilds's statement that "Simms's robustness precludes no form of boldness that exists in life" (341) certainly also applies to Gerstäcker. As an American, Simms naturally had a perspective on the frontier that differed from Gerstäcker's point of view. Gerstäcker realized a childhood dream by coming to America, and the frontier was certainly a new, exotic world to him. For Simms, having grown up in South Carolina and having traveled in the South, the frontier was closer, and a common part of his experiences.

Sharing an interest in hunting, both authors wrote numerous stories in which fights with bears or wolves and deer and turkey hunts constitute an important element and are often the main subject. Gerstäcker and Simms both described, for instance, a hunt that involved chasing an animal into a river before the hunter killed it there with a knife (*Regulatoren* 89; "Arm-Chair" in *Wigwam* 133). There are stories of men going out on hunting trips for days, spending the nights telling each other tales.[8] Gerstäcker, like Simms, had a great knowledge of hunting customs, down to the details of the uses of deer meat, skin, and brains (useful for tanning leather).

Gerstäcker was obviously fascinated with the tall tales he heard in America and quoted many of them in his works; most of them are in fact original to the New World and not just variations of German tales with which he might have been familiar. German oral tradition actually does not have very many examples of this genre. There are the Baron Münchhausen or Till Eulenspiegel stories, but the sort of tales found in Simms's "Bald-Head Bill Bauldy" and "How Sharp Snaffles Got His Capital and Wife," for example, are an American rather than a German tradition. Unlike Simms in these two connected stories, Gerstäcker does not set up frame stories within which the tales are told but instead creates narratives with impromptu tall tales. In the novel *Die Regulatoren in Arkansas*, for example, Gerstäcker portrays two masters of the tall tale, Bahrens and Harper, who have heard about each other but have never met; when mutual friends finally bring Harper to Bahrens's house, a storytelling competition ensues. Harper has just found the body of a murdered villager and cannot get the ghastly image out of his mind. His rival, "Lying Bahrens" (97), comments:

> "Ghastly, Mr. Harper? You should have lived on the Cashriver last year—I'll be damned if I didn't see two or three corpses float by every day—and great corpses they were! Some had no heads."
>
> "But where did all those people come from?" Harper asked, part horrified, part incredulous, "I thought you said it was a deserted region?"
>
> "The people? Now why should I care about that? Why should that be my business?" (103)

Simms uses the same dialogue technique of disbelieving listeners and impatient storytellers:

> "When I looked thar was the leetle wretch snatched up by an alligator, more than two hundred feet long!"
>
> "Two hundred feet!" was the exclamation of one of the group of listeners—Bauldy answered impatiently:
>
> "I don't mean edzackly! I never measured the beast! He mout have been only fifty five feet and a few inches. Don't you stop me *now!*" (*Tales of the South* 489).

While Simms could be very good at using vernacular and dialect, especially in the tall tale stories, Gerstäcker, writing in German, faced the obvious problem of conveying local color in a different language. He solved it by using many German immigrant characters, and when he has Americans speak, he uses a colloquial German but without adjusting the spelling.

Native American characters and the problem of relations between whites and Indians are featured in many of Gerstäcker's and Simms's works with frontier settings. Some of their white characters refer to Indians as savages and wild, violent people; there is, for instance, the narrator of Simms's "Oakatibbe," who thinks that "savages are children in all but physical respects" (*Wigwam* 196). Others show respect and even admiration for Native Americans. In "The Two Camps," Simms discusses the possibility of harmonious coexistence between white settlers and the Indians. Daniel Nelson, the narrator, describes his Indian counterpart, Lenatewà: "I must tell you that an Indian of good family always has a nateral [*sic*] sort of grace and dignity that I never saw in a white man" (*Wigwam* 62). There is even the beginning of a romantic relationship between the Indian and Nelson's daughter Lucy, but Simms resolves the difficult problem of a possible interracial marriage by having Lenatewà killed by an Indian enemy. Both Simms and Gerstäcker have created memorable Native American heroes and heroines (Oakatibbe, Nagoochie in "Jocassee," Sanutee and Matiwan in *The Yemassee*, Arapaha in *Die Regulatoren in Arkansas*). Chief Assowaum of *Die Regulatoren in Arkansas* is one of the main characters of Gerstäcker's novel and symbolic of the suffering of Native Americans pushed farther and farther west by white settlers. His wife is murdered by a white criminal, and even though he has many white friends, he cannot settle down among them: "The herds of the whites have thinned the reed thickets in the swamps, and the bear looks in vain for a bed there. Assowaum is sick; the meat of the buffalo will cure him. He is moving west" (496).

On the subject of slavery, Gerstäcker remains curiously quiet. It seems that he moved from a proslavery position in his youth to opposing it in later years; however, in his writings about America, black slaves are mentioned matter-of-factly without commentaries like the ones he gives to the situation of Native Americans. His characters often use derogatory terms in reference to blacks, and some blacks are shown as criminals. Even modest farmers have at least one slave. The character of the white owner is often transferred onto the slave, especially in the mulatto Dan, who appears in both Arkansas novels. Like his first two owners, he is a criminal, but the "good" people he later lives with turn him into a good man: "'It seems he has learned his lesson well,' replied James, 'Dan is now quite an honest fellow'" (*Flußpiraten* 519). The character of Bolivar in the same novel is an exception: he is an independent black man who has turned to evil because of white prejudice. He is confronted with the same prejudice even within the group of outlaws of which he is a member. Gerstäcker describes the complicated racial problems in the frontier society with insight:

"The young Olyo was a mestizo—of white and Indian origin. According to North American views, this fact placed him far above the black. . . . In Bolivar, however, who was the only black and thus stood below the boy (whose tyranny he had suffered many times), pure hatred festered" (199).

There is an interesting linguistic coincidence regarding the black characters in Simms and Gerstäcker. The black flatboatman in Simms's "Bald-Head Bill Bauldy" addresses his white passengers as "you buckrah people" (*Tales of the South* 470). In Gerstäcker's *Die Flußpiraten des Mississippi*, the black character Bolivar calls his white fellow-criminals "Bruckramann" (109) and "ihr Buckras" (208). The term comes from the Niger-Congo word *mbakara*, meaning someone who governs, and is used in the Southeastern United States by blacks in the sense of "white man" or "boss." Its presence in the writings of both authors suggests a familiarity with black culture, which is especially interesting in the case of Gerstäcker, who had, never seen a black person before he came to America.

The various aspects of religion on the frontier interested both Gerstäcker and Simms. Jeffrey Sammons believes that Friedrich Gerstäcker "had his prejudices, to be sure, some of a familiar German or German-American sort: . . . toward the ineffable variety of religious experience in America, so incomprehensible to the rational and orderly sensibility of the German Protestant" (86).

Gerstäcker was indeed quite suspicious of preachers. Many of his male characters complain about the susceptibility of their wives and daughters to unctuous preachers, but they see nothing wrong with religion itself. His was hardly a prejudice of "a familiar German sort." Two-faced preachers can also be found in Simms's writings. There is the Reverend Mowbray in *Helen Halsey*, a well-educated young man who lives with a band of criminals. In *Richard Hurdis*, Clement Foster, a criminal gang leader modeled on John A. Murrell, convincingly disguises himself as a parson who chides Hurdis for gambling: "You have lost money, my son, money—a goodly sum, which might have blessed the poor widow, and the portionless orphan—which might have sent the blessings of the word into strange lands among the benighted heathens—which might have helped on in his labors some wayfaring teacher of the word" (306).

This "excellent hypocrite" (306) has a counterpart in Gerstäcker's *Die Regulatoren in Arkansas*. The Methodist preacher, horse thief, and murderer Rowson has a large following among the farmers.

Simms and Gerstäcker use both two-faced characters (doubles in themselves) and *Doppelgänger* characters (doubles). The list of false preachers includes characters from *Richard Hurdis* and *Helen Halsey* to *Die Regulatoren in Arkansas*, but there are also reputable men with a secret life of crime in Simms's *Richard Hurdis*, *Voltmeier*, and *Guy Rivers* and in Gerstäcker's *Die Regulatoren in Arkansas* and *Die Flußpiraten des Mississippi*.[9] The *Doppelgänger* characters include Nelson and Lenatewà, Richard Hurdis and Edward Eberly, Henry Meadows and Mowbray in Simms's writings, and Brown and Assowaum in Gerstäcker's. This further parallel in their work needs to be explored in a future essay.

Gerstäcker understood the importance of faith for the individual but attacked those who represent organized religion. The preacher thus has no redeeming qualities. He frequently tries to convert Assowaum but employs insensitive missionary methods that are in stark contrast to Assowaum's tolerance of other religious beliefs. In this scene, Assowaum criticizes Rowson, and Gerstäcker presents biblical stories in an imaginative way through the eyes of the Indian:

> I have listened to your words. You have told me about the chief who turned sticks into snakes and squeezed water out of rocks; about the fish that stored a man in his stomach for several days and then spit him out again; about the prophet who drove up to the sky in a fiery chariot, and about the One who was sacrificed and died, and still returned to Earth alive. Assowaum believed everything. But now that I am telling you how the Great Spirit created His children in *this* part of the world, you call me a liar. Go! . . . the eye of the pale man only sees to the side of his own wigwam—everything else is black. (*Regulatoren* 49)

In conclusion, some attention must be given to two instances of a possible direct German influence on Simms and an American influence on Gerstäcker. J. Wesley Thomas has suggested that Simms frequently used German sources, especially in his stories: "Since by the eighteen-twenties the German tale was already exerting a definite influence upon the American short story, it is quite to be expected that Simms's German studies should be reflected especially in his shorter narratives. These works are characterized in general by an accentuation of the bizarre and irrational— elements which, in Simms's mind, were definitely associated with Germany" ("German Sources" 129).

There is evidence, however, of another influence that concerns form rather than topic: in *The Wigwam and the Cabin*, Simms experimented with the *Novelle*, a literary genre practically unknown in America at the time but very popular in the literature of German Romanticism with which Simms was familiar.

John Caldwell Guilds has expressed the opinion that among the stories in *The Wigwam and the Cabin*, the gambling story "The Last Wager" is one of the less successful (178). He criticizes the fact that the story "hangs" upon the "pack of ordinary playing cards" that are nailed above the fireplace at the Rayner house (*Literary Life* 178; *Wigwam* 86). This statement actually invites a closer examination of the story, because the presence of a strong central symbol is one of the characteristics of the German *Novelle*. The novella, an extended form of short story, originated in Italian literature, Boccaccio's *Decamerone* being the prime example of a collection of novellas. The German form became very popular in the literature of the nineteenth century. Goethe, whom Simms read and admired, wrote one of the most famous German novellas and provided an often quoted definition of the genre: "denn was ist eine Novelle anders als eine Sich ereignete unerhörte Begebenheit" (225). Although there is no single definition of what constitutes a perfect *Novelle*, most descriptions share at least a few characteristics. Most importantly, since it is not just a longer short story or a short novel, it differs from the novelette. It is remarkable that all the main elements of this literary form are present in "The Last Wager," which leads to the speculation that Simms consciously experimented with the genre.

The *Novelle* always has a striking symbol that holds the story together— here, the pack of cards. There is also usually a frame story, which is provided by the traveler spending the night at the Rayners', and a limited cast of characters. Goethe stated that the *Novelle* should feature an extraordinary, possibly supernatural event, which is certainly present in "The Last Wager." The *Novelle* is often a psychological study, dealing with issues of morals and guilt. All these aspects can be found in Simms's story. A small clue further indicates the German influence: the devil-like figure of the strange gambler is called Eckhardt, and Rachel's maiden name was Herder—the names of two German philosophers.

J. Wesley Thomas suggests E. T. A. Hoffmann's story "Spielerglück" as the source for "The Last Wager," but the similarities are quite superficial and—if Simms knew the story—could not have provided more than an idea for a topic. The differences are far greater than the parallels. For instance, the setting in Hoffmann's story is urban and upper class, and it ends tragically, whereas "The Last Wager" has a rural frontier setting, and the ending is at least ambiguous. Besides, Hoffmann's story is not a *Novelle* but rather a biographical sketch.

The second example concerns Simms's direct influence on Gerstäcker. In a 1953 article, J. Wesley Thomas suggested that Gerstäcker had read Simms's short novel *Helen Halsey* and modeled his story (which could actually be classified as a *Novelle*) *Germelshausen* after it. According to Thomas, "that Gerstäcker should have become interested in the American novelist seems almost inevitable, for Simms was at that time the foremost literary exploiter of the colorful border life of the Southwest, which Gerstäcker had experienced for six years" (141).

However, his examples and proofs are not conclusive. With the abundance of material available in German folklore, fairy tales, and romances, it simply seems implausible for Gerstäcker to use a fairly realistic American novel such as *Helen Halsey*, featuring criminals and a plot of doomed love, and turn it into a story about a German city from the past with clear supernatural elements that are completely absent from Simms's short novel. Thomas's contention that "there is a striking similarity between the respective plots and characters of the two works, [and] the definite indebtedness of Gerstäcker to the American writer is most clearly demonstrated by a comparison of specific scenes and incidents" (142) is exaggerated. There are many important differences between the two works. Gerstäcker's *Novelle*, for instance, covers a single event that takes place in less than a day, whereas Simms's novel covers several months. There is indeed a similarity regarding the protagonist's falling in love with a mysterious and elusive young girl, but whereas Simms's Henry Meadows actively pursues her, Gerstäcker's Arnold practically stumbles into his adventure. The complex relationships between Meadows and Mowbray and especially between Bud and Bush Halsey in Simms's novel have no counterpart in *Germelshausen*.

Clarence Evans showed that the setting of *Germelshausen*, a story that appears to be typically German, might actually be an area in the White River Valley in northwest Arkansas where Gerstäcker spent some time in the winter of 1842. As his suggestion only concerns location and not contents, it appears more conclusive than Thomas's theory (Evans 523–30).

From the materials available, it is impossible to prove that Simms had a direct influence on Gerstäcker; however, reading and translating Simms certainly inspired Gerstäcker in an indirect way. "Alone among American novelists of the nineteenth century William Gilmore Simms perceived a national literary need and opportunity, sensed his capability to fulfill it, developed a plan to attain it, and lived to complete it. Simms had vision, commitment, intensity, and perseverance—ingredients without which sustained literary accomplishment of first magnitude is impossible" (Guilds 333).

No such statement can be made about Gerstäcker's position in German literature. He enjoyed writing and considered it a pleasant way to earn a living, but he never developed a vision comparable to Simms's. Simms and Gerstäcker do present similar views of the American frontier and of common people as the backbone of the country's future. Although Gerstäcker was probably less ambitious as an author than Simms, they are equal in the "extraordinary gusto" (Guilds 343) with which they threw themselves into their professions.

NOTES

1. William Gilmore Simms, 1806–1870; Friedrich Gerstäcker, 1816–1872. Both authors lost a parent early in life, both lived with relatives, and both remarried after the deaths of their first wives. Their training was practical rather than academic, and for both, money was a concern throughout their lives.

2. The publishing company was Arnold in Dresden. Gerstäcker began working on the translation only a few months after the original appeared in the United States.

3. In 1849 he published *Wie ist es denn nun eigentlich in Amerika?* (What is it really like in America?), and for popular magazines he wrote articles with titles like "Wohlgemeinte Warnung für Auswanderer" (Wellmeaning warning for emigrants; *Gartenlaube*, 1862). On the expectations and the situation of German emigrants, see Brenner 68–77; Durzak 172–74; Hollyday passim; Ostwald 10–11, 28–29, 158; Sammons 81–84.

4. Sebastian Brant's *Das Narrenschiff* (1494) is considered the first book on America in German.

5. See Durzak 8–10.

6. Among those who preceded him were Gottfried Duden, whose enthusiastic report on his stay in Missouri, *Bericht über eine Reise nach den westlichen Staaten Nordamerikas* (1829), was responsible for much of the German euphoria regarding America; Duke Bernhard zu Sachsen-Weimar-Eisenach; the former Austrian monk Charles Sealsfield (aka Karl Postl); and Friedrich Strubberg. Several German writers were in America around the same time as Gerstäcker, for instance Balduin Möllhausen and Otto Ruppius.

7. See Durzak: "Perplexed and gnashing their teeth, Germans withdrew from the political misery to the poet's chamber. Escape was provided by the elation of a New World evoked through literature. It was seen both as the paradisiacally original past of a history-fatigued Europe in a configuration of historicized nature and as one's own future, starting out into a Cockaigne of political and economic progress, surrounded by the gloriole of democracy."

8. *Regulatoren* 97 and passim; "Bald-Head Bill Bauldy" and "Sharp Snaffles."

9. Bittner, Afterword, *Flußpiraten:* "such double identities form a recurring theme in the body of his literary work."

WORKS CITED

Bittner, Wolfgang. "Friedrich Gerstäcker—Moralist und Anarchist." Afterword. *Die Flußpiraten des Mississippi.* By Friedrich Gerstäcker. Stuttgart: Union; Berlin: Neues Leben, 1989. 585–94.

———. "Friedrich Gerstäcker—Spannend, widerborstig und wider-sprüchlich." Afterword. *Die Regulatoren in Arkansas.* By Friedrich Gerstäcker. Stuttgart: Union; Berlin: Neues Leben, 1988. 577–90.

Brant, Sebastian. *Das Narrenschiff.* Basel: Jo. Bergmann von Olpe, 1494.

Brenner, Peter. *Reisen in die Neue Welt.* Tübingen: Niemeyer, 1991.

Duden, Gottfried. *Bericht über eine Reise nach den westlichen Staaten Nordamerikas.* Elberfeld, 1829.

Durzak, Manfred. *Das Amerika-Bild in der deutschen Gegenwarts-literatur.* Stuttgart: Kohlhammer, 1979.

Evans, Clarence. "A Cultural Link Between Nineteenth Century Germany and the Arkansas Ozarks." *Modern Language Journal* 35 (1951): 523–30.

Evans, Clarence, and Liselotte Albrecht. "Friedrich Gerstäcker in Arkansas." *Arkansas Historical Quarterly* 5 (1946): 40–57.

Gerstäcker, Friedrich. *Die Flußpiraten des Mississippi.* 1848. Jena: Costenoble, 1889.

———. *Germelshausen.* 1871. Ed. Griffin W. Lovelace. Boston: Ginn, 1904.

———. *In the Arkansas Backwoods: Tales and Sketches.* Ed. and trans. James William Miller. Columbia: University of Missouri Press, 1991.

———. *Die Regulatoren in Arkansas.* 1846. Jena: Costenoble, 1889.

———. *The Regulators of Arkansas.* New York: Dick and Fitzgerald, 1857.

Goethe, Johann Wolfgang von. *Wisdom and Experience.* Ed. and trans. Hermann J. Weigand. New York: Pantheon, 1949.

Guilds, John C. *Simms: A Literary Life.* Fayetteville: University of Arkansas Press, 1992.

Hollyday, G. T. *Anti-Americanism in the German Novel 1841–1862.* Berne: Lang, 1977.

McCormick, E. Allen, ed. *Germans in America: Aspects of German-American Relations in the Nineteenth Century*. New York: Brooklyn College Press, 1983.

Moore, Waddy William. "*In the Arkansas Backwoods*." Rev. of *In the Arkansas Backwoods*, by Friedrich Gerstäcker. *Arkansas Historical Quarterly* 51 (1992): 186–89.

Ostwald, Thomas. *Friedrich Gerstäcker. Leben und Werk*. Braunschweig: Graff, 1976.

Sammons, Jeffrey L. "Friedrich Gerstäcker: American Realities Through German Eyes." *Germans in America: Aspects of German-American Relations in the Nineteenth Century*. Ed. E. Allen McCormick. New York: Brooklyn College Press, 1983. 79–90.

Shelley, Philip Allison, Arthur O. Lewis, Jr., and William W. Betts, eds. *Anglo-German and American-German Crosscurrents*. Vol. 1. Chapel Hill: University of North Carolina Press, 1957.

Simms, William Gilmore. *Helen Halsey*. New York: Burgess, Stringer and Co., 1845.

———. *Richard Hurdis*. Philadelphia: Carey and Hart, 1838.

———. *Tales of the South*. Ed. Mary Ann Wimsatt. Columbia: University of South Carolina Press, 1996.

———. *The Wigwam and the Cabin*. New York: Wiley and Putnam, 1845.

———. *The Yemassee*. New York: Harper and Brothers, 1835.

Thomas, J. Wesley. "The German Sources of William Gilmore Simms." *Anglo-German and American-German Crosscurrents*. Ed. Philip Allison Shelley, Arthur O. Lewis, Jr., and William W. Betts. Vol. 1. Chapel Hill: University of North Carolina Press, 1957. 127–53.

———. "William Gilmore Simms' *Helen Halsey* as the Source for Friedrich Gerstäcker's *Germelshausen*." *Monatshefte für deutschen Unterricht, deutsche Sprache und Literatur* 45 (1953): 141–44.

Contributors

EDWIN T. ARNOLD is professor of English and assistant dean of arts and sciences at Appalachian State University. He annotated Simms's Revolutionary War novel *The Scout* and has published books on Erskine Caldwell, William Faulkner, film director Robert Aldrich (with Eugene L. Miller), and Cormac McCarthy (with Dianne Luce). He is also coeditor (with J. W. Williamson) of *Interviewing Appalachia: The Appalachian Journal Interviews* (forthcoming).

JAN BAKKER is professor of English at Utah State University. He is the author of *Pastoral in Antebellum Southern Romance*, and various articles and papers on such antebellum Southern authors as William Gilmore Simms, Caroline Gilman, Augusta Jane Evans Wilson—and most recently, Caroline Lee Hentz and Eden Southworth. At Utah State, and abroad on Fulbrights, he teaches the literature of the American South, introducing Simms to both undergraduate and graduate students.

MOLLY BOYD is currently serving as a graduate teaching assistant at the University of South Carolina, where she is pursuing a Ph.D. in nineteenth-century American literature with a minor in Southern literature. Her special interests include exploring the persistent and underlying elements of social criticism in Gothic fictions, especially as these criticisms pertain to gender, race, religion, social norms, and codes of behavior.

CAROLINE COLLINS is a Ph.D. candidate in nineteenth-century American literature at the University of Arkansas. She received an M.F.A. in creative writing from the University of Arkansas in 1989. Her poems have appeared in *Texas Review, Mississippi Valley Review,* and *Southern Poetry Review.* She received the Felix Christopher McKean Award for Poetry in 1987 and the C. Vann Woodward Award for Nonfiction from the University of Arkansas Press in 1989. Her special interests include Southern literature and contemporary poetry.

GERARD DONOVAN was born in Ireland. He is currently assistant professor of English at Suffolk County Community College in New York. He holds an M.A. degree from Johns Hopkins University and an M.F.A. in creative writing from the University of Arkansas. In 1992 he was the Bread Loaf Scholar in Poetry at Middlebury College. He is the author of two collections of poetry. Every summer he teaches at the Johns Hopkins Center for Talented Youth.

NANCY GRANTHAM is a Ph.D. candidate in nineteenth-century literature at the University of Arkansas. She received her M.A. in English literature from Pittsburg State University in 1989. At Pittsburg State University, she received the English Department's award for graduate research and the Emily Dickinson Research Scholarship. She has published a paper on Virginia Woolf's *To the Lighthouse*. Her special interests include the American novel, Southern literature (especially Simms), and the Victorian novel.

JOHN CALDWELL GUILDS now holds the Distinguished Professorship of Humanities at the University of Arkansas. As editor and author, he has devoted much of his scholarly career to Simms. His *Simms: A Literary Life* appeared in 1992; he is now editing *Selected Fiction of William Gilmore Simms: Arkansas Edition*.

JAMES E. KIBLER, professor of English at the University of Georgia and founding editor of *The Simms Review*, has written on a wide range of Southern writers and subjects. The most recent of his four books on Simms is *Selected Poems of William Gilmore Simms*. His just completed narrative, *A Life on the Land*, has as its central character the land itself in its three-centuries-long relationship to a particular Southern family living on it.

DIANNE C. LUCE chairs the English Department at Midlands Technical College in Columbia, South Carolina, where she has been named Distinguished Lecturer in Arts and Sciences. As a graduate student at the University of South Carolina, she did several conference presentations and research projects on Simms. She has published two books on Faulkner's *As I Lay Dying* and edited his unfinished novel *Elmer*. Together with Edwin T. Arnold, she is coeditor of *Perspectives on Cormac McCarthy*.

THOMAS L. MCHANEY is Kenneth Murchison England Professor in Southern American Literature at Georgia State University. He wrote the Simms chapter in *The Chief Glory of Every People*. He is a frequent writer on the works of William Faulkner, one of the editors of the forty-four-volume *William Faulkner Manuscripts*, a sometime dramatist, and the author of a number of short stories that have appeared in literary journals.

DAVID MOLTKE-HANSEN is the director of the Southern Historical and Folklife Collections at the University of Chapel Hill. He also currently serves as associate editor of the quarterly *Southern Cultures*. He coedited *Intellectual Life in Antebellum Charleston* with Michael O'Brien. He is the author of numerous essays on aspects of South Carolina and Southern intellectual and cultural history. His work in progress is a study of the early development of Southern identity, tentatively titled *Southern Genesis*.

RAYBURN S. MOORE is professor emeritus of English at the University of Georgia. He is the author or editor of seven books, including two on Constance Fenimore Woolson, two on Paul Hamilton Hayne, and two on Henry James. He served as a senior editor of *The History of Southern Literature*. He is a past president of the Society for the Study of Southern Literature and a former member of the Executive Councils of SSL, SAMLA, and the South Atlantic Graduate English Group.

DAVID W. NEWTON is assistant professor of English at West Georgia College in Carrollton, Georgia, where he teaches courses in American literature and in linguistics. He received his undergraduate degree from the College of Charleston and his graduate degrees from Emory University.

SABINE SCHMIDT received a master's degree in American studies and German from the University of Hamburg in Germany and her M.F.A. degree in literary translation from the University of Arkansas. She was the recipient of the Lily Peter Fellowship in Translation in 1992–1993. She has worked as an editor and a freelance journalist and translator. Her translations and reviews have appeared in *Exchanges, Saison* (Germany), and *literatur konkret* (Germany). With H. Raykowski and M. Hannes, she collaborated on *Tobermory*, an English-German bilingual edition of short stories by Saki. She currently teaches German at Rhodes College in Memphis.

MIRIAM J. SHILLINGSBURG is dean of Arts and Sciences at Lamar University. She is the author of two books and more than sixty scholarly articles and refereed presentations, as well as book reviews. She holds degrees from Mars Hill College and the University of South Carolina. Her special interests include nineteenth-century American literature, Southern literature, and scholarly editing.

ELLIOTT WEST is professor of history at the University of Arkansas. A specialist in the social history of the frontier and the Far West, he is the author or editor of five books, including *Growing Up with the Country: Childhood on the Far-Western Frontier* and *Small Worlds: Children and Adolescents in America, 1850–1950*. He is currently researching the social history of the Great Plains in the nineteenth century.

MARY ANN WIMSATT, McClintock Professor of Southern Letters at the University of South Carolina, is the author of *The Major Fiction of William Gilmore Simms* and of many book chapters and articles on Southern literature. She is the associate editor of *The History of Southern Literature*, a volume she proposed while president of the Society for the Study of Southern Literature. She has served on the executive committees of SAMLA, SCMLA, and the Simms Society.